Voices
Revealed

Voices Revealed

Arab Women Novelists, 1898–2000

Bouthaina Shaaban

LYNNE RIENNER PUBLISHERS

BOULDER
LONDON

Published in the United States of America in 2009 by
Lynne Rienner Publishers, Inc.
1800 30th Street, Boulder, Colorado 80301
www.rienner.com

and in the United Kingdom by
Lynne Rienner Publishers, Inc.
3 Henrietta Street, Covent Garden, London WC2E 8LU

Library of Congress Cataloging-in-Publication Data
Shaaban, Bouthaina.
  Voices revealed : Arab women novelists, 1898–2000 / by Bouthaina Shaaban.
      p. cm.
  Includes bibliographical references and index.
  ISBN 978-0-89410-871-6 (hardcover : alk. paper)
  ISBN 978-0-89410-896-9 (pbk. : alk. paper)
  1. Arabic fiction—20th century—History and criticism. 2. Arabic
fiction—Women authors—History and criticism. I. Title.
  PJ7577.S448 2009
  892.7'360992870904—dc22

                                                          2008048404

British Cataloguing in Publication Data
A Cataloguing in Publication record for this book
is available from the British Library.

Printed and bound in the United States of America

The paper used in this publication meets the requirements
of the American National Standard for Permanence of
Paper for Printed Library Materials Z39.48-1992.

5   4   3   2   1

Contents

Preface

THIS BOOK was conceived as an attempt to discover and assess the contributions that women have made to the Arabic novel. The idea dawned on me when, during the 1980s, I attended dozens of conferences at universities across the Arab world and listened to one paper after another dealing with novels written by Arab men. Only occasionally was there even one paper about novels written by Arab women or about an Arab woman novelist. I became curious to know whether their absence was due to the lack of women's literary production or to the lack of interest in such production. My experience with the record of women's contributions in other areas encouraged me to think that the lack of representation of women's literary work did not necessarily represent reality. This idea occupied me for quite a while before I decided to pursue it, at which point I received a one-year research grant that enabled me to start systematic work on the issue.

My journey with this book started in 1990–1991, when I was awarded a Fulbright grant to spend a year as a research scholar at Duke University. I decided to trace women's writings as far back as I could, determined to find out when Arab women started to write novels and then to study the size and quality of their contribution. I had no idea that I was opening a Pandora's Box for myself. Sometimes I found names of novelists and titles of novels but no actual texts. There was no bibliography that I could rely on, nor any official history of the contribution that I was trying to assess. This consolidated my conviction that the undertaking was absolutely necessary, but it also foretold how difficult and challenging it was going to be.

I feel now that the most important decision I made at the early stages of this project was to act on the belief that I was on a journey of discovery and that I would be prepared to announce the results whatever they might be: negative or positive. I made the promise to myself that, even if I found that the results were not worth my endeavor, I would be candid with readers and tell them just that, so at least others would not waste their time trying to do what I did. But in fact, the more novels that I found and read, the more I appreciated women's contributions, and the more determined I became that the assessment of literature by Arab women depends on what those women have written, rather than on what men have written—or neglected to write—about it.

Thus, my approach over the last fifteen years of working on this book is something similar to the one I adopted for *Both Right- and Left-Handed*, in which I was essentially a microphone for women speaking to others through me. In *Voices Revealed*, I wanted to give the novels their own lives based on the merits that I saw in them. I was on a journey to discover Arab women's literary contribution to the genre of the novel and the importance of this contribution to Arabic literature. To accomplish the task, I had to look at the criticism that had been written on the subject without allowing it to influence my assessment of the texts under discussion, insofar as it is possible for one to avoid being influenced by one's reading.

Readers of the book will discover that women have written about war and peace, about society, family, human relationships, and dialogue between cultures. They were engaged with every aspect of life. How could we assume anything different? The range and level of their contribution in this genre is impressive indeed, and no study of the Arab novel in the twentieth century can be complete without taking their contribution into serious account. Arab women novelists are writers whose gender happens to be female but whose writings are deeply engaged and connected with men, women, children, home, country, and the universe.

Near the close of the twentieth century, the Arab novel in general and novels written by women in particular were entering a new stage in terms of both technique and theme. It is at the threshold of this new stage that my book stops. I am already eagerly anticipating work on a new book, a study of the new status that Arab women novelists are carving for themselves on the Arab literary scene. At the same time, I am hopeful that the present book contributes to the acknowledgment and understanding of what Arab women have expressed in their novels, and thus to a rethinking of the Arab novel overall.

*   *   *

I would like to thank my publisher, Lynne Rienner, who approached me about a different book but agreed to take on this one. Early on, Lynne asked me to address the issue of transliteration (among other points), and in this regard it was a most beautiful coincidence that I met with Kamal abu-Deeb soon afterward. Professor abu-Deeb immediately offered to help me with the excruciating task of transliterating hundreds of names and titles. Without the precious time that he spent on this book, it would not have seen the light of day. My thanks go to him and to Kamāl Abūdīb, Jr., who also helped so much with the transliteration. I would also like to express my gratitude to Lesli Brooks Athanasoulis at Lynne Rienner Publishers for her great effort during the publication process.

I am grateful to the Fulbright Program for giving me a research grant to start this project; to miriam cooke, with whom I spent hours during my Fulbright year at Duke University discussing the literary works of Arab women; and to all the women who helped me by sending their works to me or guiding me to where I could find them. Thanks go as well to the Library of Congress, which was most helpful and useful to me.

I would like also to thank the members of my staff, who helped me in many ways to complete this project. In particular, I thank Nizār Kabībū, Nuhā Zarāfa, Raghad Maḥrūs, Māzin ʿAjjān, and Maḥmūd Jadīd. Nizār, especially, followed up on every e-mail and every step with care and passion.

My children, Nāhid, Nāzik, and Riḍā, knew by heart the details of every step and encouraged me through moments of frustration and help-lessness to march on, never minding the hours I spent on the book that were sometimes at the expense of our togetherness. But the person I want to thank most is my husband, Khalīl Jawād, who considered this project his own and kept pushing me from day one to make it see the light. He looked after our daughters for a whole academic year, allowing me the time to launch the book, and then he urged me to complete it. I feel that the publication of this book is a fulfillment of his dream, and not just mine.

I am sure that there are other people who helped and supported me, but whose names do not come to mind now. I thank them, along with everyone else who has made it possible for the book to be completed.

—Bouthaina Shaaban

A Note on Transliteration

IN TRANSLATING the names, book titles, and other Arabic words that appear in this book, I have used the system familiar in British academic circles. However, in the case of writers who have chosen to present their names in English in a specific way, those names appear in the writers' preferred form.

CHAPTER 1

The Marginalization of Women's Writings

IT IS IN LITERATURE more than in any other domain that Arab women have an identity, a recognizable voice, and a long history, albeit intermittently recorded, of excellence. Yet, even though feminist movements, women's studies departments, and women's presses in the West have unearthed an impressive heritage of women's writings, such an undertaking has barely begun in the Arab world. Most Arab literary critics are men, and they have ignored, misinterpreted, or marginalized women authors. Like Western critics, they have for the most part dominated the "scholarly tradition that controls both the canon of . . . literature and the critical perspective that interprets the canon for society."[1] Thus, Arab women writers can either enter this field as "honorary men" or are criticized for writing "specifically for their own sex and within the tradition of their woman's culture rather than within the Great Tradition."[2]

The trivialization of Arab women's writings, therefore, has been undertaken largely under the pretext that their scope and imagination are limited. Arab literary critics often repeat and reinforce each other's judgments about Arab women's writings, which, they claim, fail to extend beyond the boundaries of home, children, marriage, and love and thus do not explore the social and political paradigms of their countries. The limited scope of that criticism reflects critics' misperception of the value of the topics that these women writers have addressed.

Alongside this argument, which informs the bulk of the criticism of Arab women's writings, the phrase *women's literature* remains a largely pejorative term. This negative, narrow view may serve to explain why many Arab women writers continue to resist classification of their literary work as women's literature. Laṭīfa al-Zayyāt, a pioneering Egyptian writer, critic, and educator, states that she has always rejected the term *women's literature*, because in both Arab and Western literary criticism the term suggests "a lack of creativity and a depreciation of women's perceived narrow concerns."[3] Al-Zayyāt stresses, however, that this popular understanding of the term cannot be based on a thorough examination of Arab women's writings; rather it is simply "a prejudgment made on the basis of the gender of the author and not of the written text."[4] Candid about her role as an innovator, al-Zayyāt reveals, "I have always refused to distinguish between men's and women's writings despite my deep sense that men and women write quite differently. My stance was dictated by my fear that such a terminology would only help to keep women in a second place in literature as they had been kept in a second place in life."[5] Until I learned about al-Zayyāt's position, I had constantly been surprised by Arab women writers who seemed to disparage their literary contributions, and perhaps even their own existence, by insisting that they were not "women writers" but simply "writers."

A second argument against the use of the term *women's literature* contends that a separate literary category would create a platform for women writers who, because of the inferior quality of their writing, would not otherwise be heard. I argue, however, on the contrary, that many excellent women writers have not been allowed a proper literary platform simply because they are women, literary quality aside. Studying women's literature as a separate literary genre allows not only the critique of women's writing through the application of recognized literary standards but also the discovery of many texts that have previously been ignored. The aim of such an undertaking is not to provide a venue for women writers who, based on the quality of their work, would not have gained much of an audience. Rather, it is to focus on the voices of prominent women writers who have been marginalized, underrated, or wholly silenced because they were women.

Male literary critics have long decided what constitutes quality writing. It may be argued that male literary criticism stems from critics' individual and collective experiences as men. The particular male experience, therefore, even with its nuances, inherently constricts any judgment of women's experiences and, in turn, women's writings. Projected further, it may be argued that women's and men's perceptions of quality writing may differ, as do their historical experiences and life concerns. Understanding that women's and men's experiences vary and that they may write differently about their experiences does not support the contention that one sex's *quality* of writing is superior to the other. As al-Zayyāt states, "With equality between men and women becoming a likelihood, we could acknowledge the different ways in which men and women had always written without signifying whatsoever that the one is superior and the other is inferior."[6]

This book attempts to integrate women's and men's writings into a whole rather than to separate them or to prove that women's writings are superior. To do otherwise would be to fall into the male literary mold—whether it exists consciously or merely as a result of practice and tradition—that has existed for centuries. This study of the works of Arab women novelists seeks to create awareness of both the quantity and quality of Arab women's contributions to the field of the Arabic novel.

Beyond the categorization of women writers' novels as "women's literature" or arguments as to the purported quality of women's writings, the issue of access to and knowledge of women's written works has also plagued the genre. Contrary to potential readers' contentions, women's creative writings have always been available or preserved. Dale Spender's assertion that "[w]omen have made just as much history as men"[7] can be substantiated across cultures, as may her argument that the reason for any perceived lack of women's creative literary initiatives is that

> it has not been codified and transmitted; women have probably done just as much writing as men but it has not been preserved; and women, no doubt, have generated as many meanings as men, but these have not survived. Where the meanings of women have been discontinuous with the male version of reality they have not been retained. Whereas we have inherited the accumulated meanings of male experience, the meanings of our female ancestors have frequently disappeared.[8]

To an inquiry as to why no continuous writing was undertaken by women before the eighteenth century, Virginia Woolf replies:

> The answer lies at present locked in old diaries, stuffed away in old drawers, half-obliterated in the memories of the ages. It is to be found in the lives of the obscure in those almost unlit corridors of history where the figures of generations of women are so dimly, so fitfully perceived. For very little is known about women.[9]

This explanation applies equally to the experiences of Arab women.[10]

One has to be both creative and determined to reconstruct Arab women's literary heritage, however, as there is a strong indication that Arab women's poetry was either not recorded or lost, even if it had been transcribed. In *Ādāb al-Nisā' fī al-Jāhiliyya wa al-Islām (Women's Literature in the Pre-Islamic and Islamic Periods)*, Muḥammad bin Badr al-Maʿbadī stresses that the women writers appearing in the book represent very few of the women who recited poetry and composed prose in pre-Islamic and Islamic times. He explains that there are two major reasons for the dearth of women's writings from these periods. First, he argues that when Arabs started to record their literature, they concentrated their efforts in preserving "men's poetry" because of its "literary value" and paid little attention to women's prose because it was deemed to be "soft and weak" (p. 190). Second, even the little that was recorded of women's literature was largely lost during the Tatar invasions in which "most of this literary heritage was destroyed" (p. 193).

Similarly, Sāmī al-'Ānī and Hilāl Nājī, editors of *Ash'ār al-Nisā' (The Poetry of Women)*, explain that their collection including thirty-eight women poets is only a small fragment of a 600-page manuscript edited by al-Marzubānī that they were unable to locate. In fact, they could only find the last fifty-nine pages of the third volume, entitled *Al-Kitāb al-Thālith min Ash'ār al-Nisā'* (vol. 3 of *Women's Poetry*). *Ash'ār al-Nisā'*, therefore, "records only one-tenth of eleventh-century writings; the rest is confirmed lost."[11]

During their search for earlier poetry by Arab women, al-'Ānī and Nājī located reliable references to four works of poetry by women, only one of which can be traced today. The works include *Ash'ār al-Jawārī (The Poetry of Maids)*, edited by the poet Muḥammad bin Aḥmad bin 'Abd Allah al-Mufjī in the first half of the tenth century, and *Al-Imā' al-Shawā'ir (Slave Women Poets)* in the tenth century, edited by Abī al-Faraj al-Aṣfahānī. The third and most important work is *Al-Shā'irāt al-Nisā' (Women Poets)*, edited by al-Ḥasan bin Muḥammad bin Ja'far bin Tāra, which must have appeared very early in the fourteenth century because its editor died in 1320. All sources agree that this work comprises five to seven volumes.

Al-Qiftī, a respected scholar of Arabic literature,[12] is reported to have seen volume 6 of the work and to have known that this volume was not the last, but the whole work is now lost.[13] *Nuzhat al-Julasā' fī Ash'ār al-Nisā' (A Journey of Companionship in Women's Poetry)*, edited by 'Abd al-Raḥmān bin Abī Bakr Jalāl al-Dīn al-Suyūṭi, seems to be the only book of poetry by women to have survived.

The editors of the aforementioned texts explain that other books by and about women existed, but those texts failed to be included in the collections because they did not relate directly to the editors' topics.[14] This scholarship emphasizes the fact that what we know about Arab women's literature today is only a fraction of that which once existed. Even the small fraction of women's poetry that is available, however, repudiates the notion that women's poetry only comprises elegies and the outpourings of bereaved mothers and sisters.

Although the quantity is limited, the existing Arab women's poetry clearly demonstrates that women poets engaged the issues of war and peace among tribes, justice, human rights, and the distribution of wealth. Moreover, the love poetry written by women in the eleventh and twelfth centuries is so frank and daring that no Arab woman poet would dare write its equivalent today. Laylā al-Akhyaliyya, a woman poet of the early Umayyad period, once recited a poem to al-Ḥajjāj (the governor of Iraq) and a group of men that she had composed to her lover, Tawba, in which she bestows upon him extremely desirable traits. One man in the audience says to Laylā: "I am sure he is not worthy of one-tenth of your endearing description." She asks the man if he has ever seen Tawba, and when he replies in the negative, she retorts that "you would have wanted all the virgins at your home to be made pregnant by him."[15]

Arab women seemed to have had an extraordinary amount of freedom to express their feelings toward their lovers between the seventh and ninth centuries. It is regrettable that despite this apparent freedom of expression and the abundance of love poetry written by men at that time, there remain only a few, scattered, and incomplete poems by women. In the second volume of Jamīl Buthayna's poetry, the editor (name unknown) comments that Buthayna never recited poetry, except on the occasion of Jamīl's death. Jamīl Buthayna is named after his beloved; when he died, Buthayna recited two lines of poetry (in Arabic) to him:

My separation from Jamīl, even for a moment
Is unwelcome and untimely.
After your departure, Jamīl, it's all the same
Whether life is hard or lovely.

Until the tenth century, poetry was the prevailing genre in Arabic literature. Women also wrote prose, however marginal that may have been. In fact, many women practiced the then-existing genres of prose, family letters, *maqāmāt*, stories, proverbs, descriptions, dialogues, and Islamic interpretations *(tafsīr)*.[16] Al-Ma'badī, the editor of *Ādāb al-Nisā' fī al-Jāhiliyya wa al-Islām (Women's Literature in the Pre-Islamic and Islamic Periods)*, regrets that his collection includes only fragments of women's prose writings that once must have existed. Nevertheless, even the few names of women prose writers he successfully traced, and the still fewer samples of their writings he collected, bear witness to women's deep involvement with the political, social, and religious issues of the time.

In many of these prose collections, women's writing is poignant and dignified and their reasoning logical, informed, and embedded in an understanding of the Qur'ān and literature that reflects a clear sense of culture. Because women had a reputation for loyalty and resilience, many tribal leaders would delegate women to negotiate with their adversaries. In fact, there is an underlying notion in Arab culture—one that is rarely highlighted, though often acknowledged in times of crisis—that women are courageous, strong, and patient, qualities that are often not shared by men. There is said to be a *ḥadīth* (a saying of the prophet Muḥammad) that describes a battle in which Muslims emerged victorious, after which the Prophet Muḥammad said, "Men had the hearts of women in bravery, and women had men's muscles in strength."

Female Literary Critics and Literary Salons

In addition to writing poetry and prose, Arab women have set a precedent as literary critics and hosts of literary salons since pre-Islamic and early Islamic days. Indeed, some of the earliest and most striking recorded critical comments on poetry in Arabic are attributed to women.

Tumaḍur bint 'Amru bin al-Ḥārith bin al-Sharīd, known as al-Khansā', is one of the earliest figures in Arabic literature to play the role of critic and judge of poetic talent and superiority. Although the exact date of her birth is unknown, she was born before Islam and lived well into the Islamic era, possibly dying in 646 CE (i.e., in the middle of the first century of Islam). The scattered pieces of information available about al-Khansā' suggest that she was a pretty, confident woman with strong personal views. She participated as a critic in Sūq 'Ukāẓ (the Ukāẓ market) in the Ḥijāz (now part of Saudi Arabia), where poets would converge at a set time of year from all parts of Arabia to recite their latest compositions and to share news of their respective tribes with the rest of Arabia. Al-Khansā' scrupulously examined the poetry recited, revealing a sensitivity to the language and a grasp of the poetic idiom. She herself was also a highly esteemed poet. The poet Jarīr, the most prominent poet of the Umayyad period, is said to have been asked who the best poet in Arabia was. "I am," he replied, "except for that wicked woman," referring to al-Khansā'.[17]

Um Jundub presents another example of an accomplished woman poet, a critic from the *Jāhiliyya* (pre-Islamic) period, who was better known for her critical observations than for her poetry. This recognition was never to be bestowed again on any other Arab woman poetry critic until Nāzik al-Malā'ika, the Iraqi woman poet and critic, began to publish her works and became one of the most influential twentieth-century poetry critics in the Arab world. Um Jundub's literary career was marked by a decisive juncture that had a lasting impact on her personal life. Her husband, the renowned *Jāhiliyya* poet Imru' al-Qays, had a poetry contest with the poet 'Alqama bin 'Abda al-Faḥl, which they failed to resolve. 'Alqama said to Imru' al-Qays, "I accept the judgment of your wife, Um Jundub." Both poets recited their poems to her, and she judged in favor of 'Alqama's poem, providing an elaborate analysis of the poems that eloquently justified her decision. Her husband was so vexed by his wife's decision, however, that he divorced her.[18]

During the early Islamic period, Arab women poetry critics started the tradition of hosting literary salons at their homes, where poets would meet, recite poetry, and await the judgment of their hostess.[19] The first literary salon of this kind was hosted by Sukayna bint al-Husayn, herself a poet and an acknowledged critic of poetry, who lived in the Ḥijāz and died in 735 CE. Her critical accounts of the best poets of the *Jāhiliyya* and early Islamic periods, such as Jarīr, al-Farazdaq, Kuthayyir, and Jamīl Buthayna, continue to provide contemporary students of literature with important insights.[20] She is also known for her originality, her candor, and the idea that poetry should reflect genuine feelings, experiences, and sentiments. Unlike most of her peers, al-Ḥusayn refused to write poetic eulogies, because she reckoned that particular genre of poetry was rampant with hypocrisy and opportunism.[21]

Wallāda bint al-Mustakfī, who died in 1087, is believed to have nurtured the talent of the Andalusian poet Ibn Zaydūn, who used to frequent her salon and later became her lover. Wallāda's poems to Ibn Zaydūn reveal that, contrary to prevailing assumptions, she was an active rather than a passive partner in their relationship. In one of her letters to him she writes:

Expect me when darkness falls,
I find darkness more discreet,
In order to be with you
I wish there were no sun, stars or moon.[22]

Literary salons continue to be held in different parts of the Arab world today, with certain time lapses that reflect more of the "law and customs of the times" than they do women's literary activity.[23] Occasionally, the name of a new and important woman surfaces, and at once a wealth of previously unknown literary outpourings are discovered.

In the 1990s, Claude Sāba published a few articles in *Al-Nahār*, a Beirut newspaper, about a Syrian woman named Maryāna Marrāsh (1848–1919), who ran a literary salon in Aleppo in the early twentieth century. Marrāsh's salon was a meeting place for intellectuals and politicians, including Qusṭākī al-Ḥimṣī, 'Abd al-Raḥmān al-Kawākibī, and Kāmil al-Ghazzī, who played an important role in modern Arabic history. There they discussed their latest literary productions and talked about literary, social, and political matters. Marrāsh participated and also read her poems and articles. She was published in important journals such as *Al-Jinān* and *Lisān al-Ḥal*.

Another literary salon, barely remembered today, belonged to Thurayya al-Ḥafiẓ in Damascus, Syria. From 1943 to 1953, it was called Muntadā al-Zahrā' al-Adabī (al-Zahrā' Literary Circle), named after the daughter of al-Ḥusayn and frequented by educated men and women from all parts of the Arab world. In 1953, the salon's name changed to Muntadā Sukayna al-Adabī (Sukayna's Literary Circle). The salons of Jūlyā Tūmā Dimashqiyya (1883–1954) in Lebanon and Mayy Ziyāda (1886–1941) in Egypt, particularly the latter, are better known and more frequently mentioned in literary references. Those that are mentioned here are only a few in a long and rich literary tradition that awaits careful study and documentation, so that it can become known not just to a few diligent scholars but to all students of Arabic literature.

Historical and Current Criticisms of Arab Women's Novels

In my endeavor to outline literary criticism of Arab women novelists, I eventually accepted Virginia Woolf's conclusions about her search for such criticism of women's fiction in the West. At first amazed by the number of books written by men about women writers, Woolf quickly determined that she "might as well leave their books unopened" because "whatever the reason, all these books . . . are worthless for my purposes."[24]

Existing literary criticism of women's novels in the Arab world in many ways reflects the social status of Arab women. Many male critics seem to consider the study of novels written by women as optional in their endeavors to assess the Arabic novel in general. Others consider women's novels to be merely biographical accounts of women's lives. In short, novels written by women are not yet considered part of mainstream Arabic literature.

With the exception of Ghāda al-Sammān, about whom seven books of criticism, many articles, and a number of comparative studies have been written, Arab women novelists have not been given much attention in studies of literary criticism. It is perhaps just as well, for it is easier to approach novels by Arab women about which no criticism is available than to disprove criticism that is diametrically opposed to one's own view of a text.

One Syrian critic, Samar Rūḥī al-Fayṣal, wrote *Tajribat al-Riwāya al-Sūriyya (The Experience of the Syrian Novel)* without managing to mention a single Syrian woman novelist. His conclusions, however, were meant to apply to Syrian novels written by both men and women. In his study, *Al-Riwāya al-'Arabiyya: Muqaddima*

Tārikhiyya wa Naqdiyya (The Arabic Novel: A Historical and Critical Introduction), Roger Allen devotes less than 4 out of 172 pages to novels written by women. Of all the Arab women novelists he could have mentioned, Allen in fact cites only Colette Khūrī, Laylā Ba'albakī, and Emily Naṣrallah. In *Silences*, Tillie Olsen makes a similar comment about critical studies of American fiction. "In Tony Tanner's *City of Words: American Fiction 1950–1970*, there are 445 pages. Plath is allowed two pages, and otherwise mentioned three times; Sontag is allowed four pages and three mentions. No other women are discussed" (p. 210).

In *Taṭawwur al-Riwāya al-Ḥadītha fī Bilād al-Shām, 1870–1967 (The Development of the Modern Novel in Greater Syria, 1870–1967)*, Ibrāhīm al-Saʿʿāfīn offers a more balanced account of women's novels, although the number of novels he includes remains limited relative to women's literary contributions during the period he covers. His study includes a thorough bibliography of novels written by Arab women, but he focuses on only four of them in the text. His second chapter, on historical and sociological novels, lacks any reference to works by women, though many novels written by Arab women during the first half of the twentieth century fall precisely within these two categories. Moreover, after an examination of only one work by Ba'albakī, al-Saʿʿāfīn arrives at a startling conclusion about women's novels in general: "female novels, in particular, are characterized by sexual frankness that is expressed in screams and hysteria" (p. 496). This statement is untrue, even of the work supposedly under discussion.

In *Al-Riwāya al-Sūriyya, 1967–1977 (The Syrian Novel: 1967–1977)*, Nabīl Sulaymān allows rather more space (34 out of 414 pages) to five novels written by women, and he focuses on two additional novels by women in *Waʿī al-Dhāt wa al-ʿĀlam: Dirāsāt fī al-Riwāya al-ʿArabiyya (Consciousness of the Self and the World: Studies in the Arabic Novel)*. Women's novels are also mentioned in a study entitled *Al-Riwāya al-Sūriyya: Dirāsa Nafsiyya (The Syrian Novel: A Psychological Study)*, by ʿAdnān bin Dhurayl. Dhurayl focuses on two novels each by Colette Khūrī and Georgette Ḥannūsh, and one each by Widād Sakākīnī, Inʿām Musālima, and Qamar Kaylānī.

The literary critic who has written more than anyone else about women novelists in the Arab world is George Ṭarābīshī, who studied the works of Nawāl al-Saʿdāwī. The culmination of his writings was the book *Unthā Ḍidda al-Unūtha (Woman Against Her Sex)*, which is full of accusations against al-Saʿdāwī for not writing about women in the way he thought she should. In one of his Arabic articles, "The Female of Nawāl al-Saʿdāwī and the Myth of Singularity," Ṭarābīshī argues that

> [i]t is not enough to say that women novelists were always a few in comparison with men novelists, but we have to add that even in the few cases in which women addressed the art of the novel their artistic treatment of it differed from that of the men. Man in the novel reconstructs the world, whereas as far as woman is concerned the novel is a concentration of feelings . . . Man writes the novel with his mind while woman writes the novel with her heart. The world is the center for what we might call the male novel, while in the female novel the center is the self.[25]

Ṭarābīshī's argument can easily be disputed. There is, of course, nothing wrong with women writing differently from men or with women approaching the art of the novel from a different frame of reference. Moreover, it is questionable how "man" can write the novel without including the self and how "woman" can isolate herself from the world. In this example it is easy, as Dale Spender suggests, "to substantiate the thesis that when women do not speak in terms that are acceptable to men, they do not get a proper hearing; in fact, it would sometimes be easy to substantiate that they get no hearing at all."[26]

There are studies that address one particular theme in the writings of Arab women novelists, such as 'Afīf Farrāj's *Al-Ḥurriyya fī Adab al-Mar'a (Freedom in Woman's Literature)*. Before even reading the work, a glance at its table of contents indicates its author's attitude toward the works discussed: "Fleeing Freedom After Fleeing to It" (Colette Khūrī's writing); "Loss of Aim Equals Loss of Freedom" (Umayya Ḥamdān's works); "A Topic Without a Shape" (Laylā 'Usayrān's fiction); "The Bird Migrating to and From the Village" (Emily Naṣrallah's writing); "The Phenomena of Narcissism" (Nūr Salmān's works); "The Search for Salvation in the Wrong Place" (Ghāda al-Sammān's writing); and "The Danger of Putting the Cart of Thoughts Before the Horse of Character and Event" (Nawāl al-Sa'dāwī's works). In the text, Farrāj argues that through their writings Arab women move in the world of men: man is their fate, the blessing and the curse, the adversary and the judge. Woman rebels against man only in order to return to him to fill her psychological emptiness. For her, a man represents the much-desired marital home.

Farrāj holds Arab women novelists responsible for wanting their heroines to achieve sexual freedom, regardless of social reality, which, he argues, should be taken into account. He also contends that every Arab woman novelist has written one good novel derived from her personal experience, but after doing so has had nothing else to say. This sexist argument has remained unchallenged by most critics of Arab women novelists, particularly as Farrāj's book has become one of the most widely circulated works of criticism of novels by women in the Arab world. In *Al-Ḥurriyya fī Adab al-Mar'a*, Farrāj prejudges future Arab women novelists, saying they will write about the "wrong" themes and the "wrong" concepts of freedom and, more importantly, that Arab women will be feminists at the "wrong" time.

Other critical works about Arab women's novels have concentrated on one particular author, such as Ghāda al-Sammān and Nawāl al-Sa'dāwī. Although Ghāda al-Sammān is a very important Arab writer, critiques that purport to favor her work on the whole do not do her justice. In fact, the elevation of writers such as Ghāda al-Sammān and Nawāl al-Sa'dāwī to celebrity status, to the exclusion of all other women writers, indicates a sexist attitude that aims to prioritize the few in order to exclude the many.

Many articles on Arab women novelists have acquired importance in the field and have played a part in formulating the opinions of generations of students. Among these are three articles by Ḥusām al-Khaṭīb, collectively entitled "Ḥawl al-Riwāya al-Nisā'iyya fī Sūriyya" (About Women's Novels in Syria). Like other critics, al-Khaṭīb assumes that "the heroine does not differ much from her author and that this biographical element is responsible for many of the intellectual as well as artistic defects of the work" (March 1976, p. 87). In one of his comments on Widād Sakākīnī's novel, *Arwā bint al-Khuṭūb (Arwā, the Daughter of Upheavals)*, al-Khaṭīb writes: "Widād Sakākīnī makes men kiss a woman's feet; is this a compensation for her heroine's sexual frustration or an escalation to it from below?" (1975, p. 94). He finds the heroine, Arwā, to be fierce, antimale, and Freudian, adding dismissively, "this Freudian bent should be pursued in the life of the author, in her childhood and her experience with men" (1975, p. 86). The problem with this kind of criticism, aside from how it encourages contempt for the work itself, is that it perpetuates a certain attitude among students who are prepared to trust whatever interpretation their professor offers.

Recent scholarship in the Arab world by women on women's writings includes a three-volume anthology by Laylā M. Ṣāliḥ entitled *Adab al-Mar'a fī al-Kuwait (Women's Literature in Kuwait)*, and a two-volume anthology, also by Ṣāliḥ, entitled *Adab al-Mar'a fī al-Khalīj (Women's Literature in Arabia and the Arabian Gulf)*. Although the latter is neither an evaluative nor a critical study of women's works in the Arabian Gulf and Saudi Arabia, it is an important work that documents the names of women authors and the titles of their works and provides extracts that give an impression of the works it mentions. This anthology paves the way for literary critics to study these works and assess them in the hope of integrating them into the literary mainstream of these countries. In her introduction of volume 1 of *Adab al-Mar'a fī al-Khalīj*, Ṣāliḥ supports the view I expressed earlier regarding the treatment of women's literature by male critics. She posits that

> the study of women's literature might well be considered new in modern literary experience in Arabia and the Arabian Gulf, which lack such studies. Many studies of poetry, story and the essay have been published in this area, some of which have scattered remarks of women's work and others have dropped the writings of women altogether as if they were unrelated to the literature of the area as a whole. (vol. 1, p. 9)

In *Al-Mar'a fī al-Mir'āt: Dirāsa Naqdiyya li al-Riwāya al-Nisā'iyya fī Miṣr, 1888–1985 (Woman in the Mirror: A Critical Study of Women's Novels in Egypt, 1888–1985)*, Suzān Nājī from Egypt begins her study of women's novels in Egypt with this very quotation from Ṣāliḥ's introduction, which suggests that Ṣāliḥ's statement applies as much to the writings of women in Egypt as it does to the writings of women in Arabia and the Arabian Gulf. Nājī offers a tentative explanation: "the reason for this neglect of women's writings perhaps lies in the fact that critics and specialists in the field still consider women's writings an immature art that has not taken its proper place in our literature, and therefore it is difficult to assess its development" (p. 5).

When Nājī herself decided to study women's novels in Egypt, she encountered strong objections to focusing on such "immature literature," and was accused of being biased in women's favor (p. 5). Unfortunately, Nājī's study does not fulfill its promise of being a critical assessment of women's novels in Egypt, although it may prove very useful because of the thorough bibliography she provides. Regarding her study of the novels themselves, she seems torn between challenging mainstream criticism, which, she says, does not take women's works seriously, and wanting to be considered part of it so that she may gain the respect every young scholar yearns for. On balance, Nājī does not break away from established modes of criticism; neither does she offer a new reading of women's works. Although her work remains a welcome introduction to beginners in the field and an appreciable effort in recording women's works, it can hardly be considered a perceptive critical study that induces the reader to reexamine the works.

Like Nājī's work, Īmān al-Qāḍī's book *Al-Riwāya al-Nisā'iyya fī Bilād al-Shām, 1885–1950 (Women's Novels in Greater Syria, 1885–1950)* attempts to cover all the works that have been published about women's novels at the expense of offering a fresh assessment of these works. She focuses on what other critics have said about the subject instead of her own opinion. Even so, after comparing al-Qāḍī's book with al-Sa''āfīn's, which deals with women's novels of the same period, I am grateful to al-Qāḍī for devoting such a large amount of space to novels that were largely ignored by al-Sa''āfīn.

Both Nājī and al-Qāḍī appear to be intimidated by accusations that the mere choice of their topic signifies they are feminists or biased in favor of women. Hence they seem to be trying to prove their objectivity to male critics, an attempt that undermines any possibility of a fresh perspective on the works under consideration. In their unannounced, yet diligent, effort to present male-sanctioned "objectivity," both Nājī and al-Qāḍī refrain from making any reference to studies by women critics in the Arab world. In so doing, they have measured the mainstream criticism as "male" and have tried their best to stay within its parameters. Nājī and al-Qāḍī thus prove Dale Spender's statement that "being evaluated by a woman is not of itself necessarily an advantage precisely because women have been required to take on male definitions of the world and themselves."[27] One can see how the trend of male criticism perpetuates itself in women's literary history, even when women are writing that history.

It has to be stressed that, apart from a few studies, literary criticism in the Arab world of both men's and women's works is sparse. Literary criticism in the Arab world presents itself mostly as journalistic criticism in daily newspapers for the consumption of unspecialized readers.

In 1978–1979, Evelyne Accad, Kamal Boullata, and Mona Mikhail each published a book in English on Arab women's writing. Accad's book, *Veil of Shame*, deals with novels written in French rather than Arabic. Boullata's work, *Women of the Fertile Crescent*, is an anthology of poetry by women, and Mikhail's *Images of Arab Women* offers monographs about Arab women writers. Fātima Mūsā Maḥmūd, in her study *Al-Riwāya al-'Arabiyya fī Miṣr, 1914–1970 (The Arabic Novel in Egypt, 1914–1970)*, devotes six pages to women novelists, and even in these pages she merely reproduces men's opinions of women's works. In his study *Modern Arabic Literature, 1800–1970*, John A. Haywood does not find it necessary to deal with Arab women authors; neither does Issa Balata, editor of *Critical Perspectives on Modern Arabic Literature*. Not a single essay in that collection considers works by women.

miriam cooke's *War's Other Voices: Women Writers on the Lebanese Civil War* was the first book on Arab women's literature to examine the writings of Arab women independently of men's paradigms. *Opening the Gates: A Century of Arab Feminist Writing*, edited by Margot Badran and miriam cooke, is an anthology of Arab feminist writings, the first anthology in any language that attempts to encompass the variety of Arab women's writings. In 1995, Joseph T. Zeidan published his book *Arab Women Novelists: The Formative Years and Beyond.* In this study, Zeidan offers interesting readings of a few novels written by women within the literary, social, and political contexts of Arab society and also presents an excellent bibliography and references to source material in both women's presses and novels. The problem, however, is that the book presents, perhaps inadvertently, the most common readings of Arab women's novels instead of focusing on new insights and unraveling new facts. Also, Zeidan's study is limited only to the best-known Arabic novels written by women. Despite these shortcomings, his book is a welcome addition to the sparse English scholarship on Arab women novelists.

It is time that novels written by women be read as texts rather than as biographies, and as literature rather than as social commentaries. It is also time to stop blaming women novelists for writing the "wrong" kind of novel or for addressing the "wrong" topic. Novels by women should be read and discovered for what they actually offer, rather than for what male literary critics think the novels should offer, and critical evaluations of texts should not be based on stereotypes.

Feminist Consciousness

Arab women's writings have been recorded for fourteen centuries, but these writings have not become a popular subject for literary criticism by either men or women. Zaynab Fawwāz (1846–1914), a woman writer and feminist of the nineteenth century from Greater Syria (see discussion in Chapter 2), made the first attempt to describe this female heritage in *Al-Durr al-Manthūr fī Ṭabaqāt Rabāt al-Khudūr (Scattered Pearls in Women's Quarters)*, which documents the literary achievements of 459 women from both the Middle East and the West. Fawwāz's second book, *Al-Rasā'il al-Zaynabiyya (Zaynab's Letters)*, focuses on the rights of women to both education and professional involvement. She also wrote a play entitled *Al-Hawā wa al-Wafā (Love and Loyalty)* and four novels, two of which have been published and two of which are in manuscript form.[28] Fawwāz was the first Arab to attempt the genre of the novel, yet schools across the Arab world still teach that Muḥammad Ḥusayn Haykal of Egypt wrote the first Arabic novel, *Zaynab*, in 1914. In fact, Fawwāz's novel, *Ḥusn al-'Awāqib: Ghāda al-Zahra (Good Consequences: Ghāda the Radiant)* was written fifteen years before Haykal's novel.

Fawwāz was also the first Arab woman who, both in her personal life and writings, expressed a feminism that accepts nothing less than full social and political equality between men and women. Significantly, she was also the first Arab woman to identify her struggle as that of a woman in a man's world, a subject relevant not only to Arab women but to women all over the world. She objected to male interpretations of Islam with regard to feminist issues, and in support of her claims she cited examples of many women who "ha[ve] ruled over men, conducted the business of state, determined status of law and behavior, recruited soldiers, gone forth into battle, and carried out wars."[29]

Because Fawwāz wanted to increase women's participation in the public sphere, she was alarmed to learn that the International Women's Union convention, held in Chicago in 1893, had called upon women members to limit their activities to "feminine" concerns, that is, home and family. She immediately dispatched a letter to the convention in which she strongly objected to such a call, stressing her conviction that both men's and women's lives were impoverished by women's confinement to the private sphere. She also sent Berta Onori Palmer, the head of the women's section in the Chicago World's Fair of 1893, a copy of her work *Al-Durr al-Manthūr fī Ṭabaqāt Rabāt al-Khudūr (Scattered Pearls in Women's Quarters)*, albeit in Arabic, and in her letter called upon women everywhere actively to resist the injustices inflicted upon them.[30]

Mayy Ziyāda's (1886–1941) biographies of her fellow writers Warda al-Yāzijī (1838–1924) and 'Ā'isha al-Taymūriyya (1840–1902), may be considered the next most important works in Arab women's literary heritage. They assessed Arab women's contributions and also contributed to a vision for future generations of women. In *Warda al-Yāzijī*, Ziyāda writes: "I have only time to indicate in passing my esteem for what women from earlier generations have done to open up the way for us" (p. 10). Like Virginia Woolf, Ziyāda situates herself within the literary heritage she attempts to construct:

> I, the daughter of two continents [referring to her Lebanese and Egyptian ancestry], consider myself happy to have been able to draw the portrait, however pale, of an Eastern woman for Eastern sisters whose nationalism I admire. Like them I cry out enthusiastically and, following their model, I call for progress, understanding and the good of nations. (p. 61)

Ziyāda was sent by family and friends to a rest house, where, like Woolf, she committed suicide in 1941. Like Woolf, too, Ziyāda became the martyr of Arab feminist consciousness, just as Woolf was considered by some Western feminists to be the martyr of Western feminist consciousness.

In addition to writing innumerable articles, Ziyāda is the subject of at least four biographical studies by Arab women writers. Ros Ghurayyib from Lebanon and Widād Sakākīnī from Syria wrote enlightening biographies of Ziyāda in 1978 and 1969, respectively. Syrian writer Salmā al-Ḥaffār al-Kuzbarī dedicated many years of her life to compiling and publishing *Al-A'māl al-Kāmila li Mayy Ziyāda (The Complete Works of Mayy Ziyāda)* in 1982. Lebanese novelist Emily Naṣrallah also devotes significant space to Mayy Ziyāda in her work *Nisā' Rā'idāt (Women Pioneers)*. In her work, Ziyāda made a significant contribution to the historical links between Arab women writers. Subsequent Arab women writers are drawn to her, paying respect to the first Arab woman who made a serious attempt to construct the literary heritage of Arab women that we continue to reclaim today.

Arab Women's Journals

An assessment of Arab women's literature is incomplete without evaluating Arab women's journals. For the first half of the twentieth century, they were a major platform for Arab women writers at a time when women usually published short pieces in journals and magazines rather than writing entire books.

The dividing line between journalists and writers that exists in the West has always been blurred in the Arab world. Many Arab journals and newspapers were launched by writers and educators who considered journalism an extension of other forms of writing. Between 1892 and 1940, the period that marked the rise of political consciousness, first against the Ottoman Empire and then against Western mandates, Arab women writers concentrated their efforts on publishing journals that featured poetry, fiction, and critical pieces, as well as essays relating to different academic disciplines, all written by women.

In 1892, a Syrian woman named Hind Nawfal started the first Arab women's journal, *Al-Fatāt (Young Girl)*, in Alexandria, Egypt, ushering in a flourishing phase of Arab women's journals that brought Arab women writings into the limelight. Before World War II there were over twenty-five journals in the Arab world that were owned, edited, and published by women.[31] The editors of these journals made clear that their most important concern was women: women's literature, women's rights, and women's future.

In her editorial in the first issue of *Al-Fatāt*, Nawfal wrote: "*Al-Fatāt* is the only journal for women in the East; it expresses their thoughts, discloses their inner minds, fights for their rights, searches for their literature and science, and takes pride in publishing the products of their pens."[32] Also in the same issue, editors of other journals published by women urged women "attentive to the future and betterment of their sex to write so that their works may be read and become in the meantime a part of the literary heritage."[33] These journals, which appeared in Cairo, Beirut, Damascus, and, to a lesser extent, Baghdad, published poetry, fiction, critical essays, feminist articles, and biographies of both Arab and Western women.

Although the journals as a whole regularly covered the experiences and particularly the achievements of Western women, and although they all stressed the need to learn from women's movements in the West, they also focused on positive elements in Arab culture. The journals made the point that women's emancipation should go hand in hand with national independence rather than be deferred to a later stage. This argument was based on the premise that no country can be truly free or independent as long as its women remain shackled.

To paraphrase Louise Bernikow, the problem remains that the importance—and even the survival—of women's literary heritage depends on who notices it and, then, whether such notice is actually recorded.[34]

CHAPTER 2

The Beginnings

WOMEN WERE AND ARE the first storytellers. It is through stories related to us by our mothers and grandmothers that we gain our first inkling of the elements of fiction, as well as our first notions of love, justice, and sacrifice. Since the publication of *A Thousand and One Nights*, this entertaining and educational activity has enjoyed a significant role in women's lives. Shahrazād demonstrated to both men and women the power of storytelling and the effect it might have on us. It was through her enchanting stories, full of tension, that Shahrazād was able to undermine her husband Shahrayar's decision to wed a virgin each day and then execute her that night. Shahrazād avoided this fate through her shrewd manipulation of the word. For the very first time, language saved women from physical violence, and the use of the word absolved them from the curse of their sexuality. Indirectly, though meaningfully, the word shields women's bodies from male violence.

Moreover, studies of oral history have shown that in most parts of the world, women have always been the major, perhaps the only, storytellers.[1] Their stories, transmitted by women from one generation to the next, are the summation of a given society's social experience, sorrow, happiness, and headline events throughout its history. Many studies of oral histories conclude that women are not only the mothers of civilizations but are also the mothers of popular culture. Through them, culture has been preserved and transmitted from one generation to the next.

Yet once the official recording of literary history began, as has often happened in other cultures, Arab women were barely mentioned, relegated to a secondary status before their record as writers was adequately assessed. Men recorded literary history, as they did all other histories, and women were therefore the last to feature in it. For example, the argument about the origin of the Arabic novel has considered various authors, eras, and qualities but has rarely taken into account works written by women—as if women had suddenly ceased to tell stories once Arab societies began to record their literary history. All literary sources agree that the novel was a new genre in Arabic literature in the early twentieth century, although Arabs were intimately familiar with different forms of prose, especially *maqāma, ḥikāya,* and *sīra.*[2]

In Arab literary circles today there is a dispute about who wrote the first novel in Arabic. In essence, the problem revolves around an unresolved issue regarding the technical elements of the novel, and whether there is an Arabic novel as such or whether this genre has entered our literature from the West. For those such as the Egyptian writer Jamāl al-Ghīṭānī, who believe that the element of story is the most important component of a novel, the Arabic novel is over sixteen centuries old, because the story element is found in Arabic poetry. For those who think of the novel more in Western terms, however, claiming that it should include elements of story, characterization, setting, a sense of development, artistic structure, and the efficiency and proficiency of language, the Arabic novel is not yet 100 years old.

In his book *Al Katib wal Mānfa* (Beirut, 1992) *(The Writer and Exile)*, 'Abd al-Raḥmān Munīf tentatively argues that a kind of novel made an appearance in the Arab world in 1867 with the following works: *Majma' al-Baḥrayn (The Collection of al-Baḥrayn)* by Ibrāhīm al-Yāzijī (1846–1906), *Al-Sāq 'alā al-Sāq (The Leg on the Leg)* by Aḥmad Fāris al-Shidyāq (1804–1887), and *Al-Hiyām fī Jinān al-Shām (Love in the Paradise of al-Shām)* by Buṭrus Salīm al-Bustānī (1846–1884). These works comprised a mixture of *maqāmāt* and aspects of modern Western novels as they appeared in translation, but they were not recognized as proper novels. Like many other critics, 'Abd al-Raḥmān Munīf claims that with the publication of Muhammad Ḥusayn Haykal's novel *Zaynab* in Cairo in 1914, the Arabic novel experienced a qualitative leap. For the first time, critics agreed that this particular book possessed the literary characteristics necessary to meet the classical definition of the novel. Munīf adds that men of letters who came after this date, such as Aḥmad Luṭfi al-Sayyid (1872–1963), 'Alī 'Abd al-Razzāq (1934–1991), Manṣūr Fahmi (1886–1959), Ṭāha Ḥusayn (1889–1973), and Tawfīq al-Ḥakīm (1898–1987), all acknowledged the significance of *Zaynab* (p. 38).

Because it has been generally accepted that Haykal's novel *Zaynab* was the first Arabic novel, studies of women's literature, such as those conducted by Īmān al-Qāḍī and Hiyām Duwayhī, began their search at a much later date for the first novel written by a woman. They both came to the same conclusion, claiming that Widād Sakākīnī's novel *Arwā Bint al-Khuṭūb (Arwā, the Daughter of Upheavals)*, published in Cairo in 1949, is the first novel written by an Arab woman.

According to the general tendency of expecting men to be the pioneers in every field, it seemed natural that the first novel written by a woman in the Arab world should come over thirty years after the first novel written by a man. In my attempts to retrace the chain of women writers, however, I came across more than one Arab woman who had written a novel before 1914. Most of the pioneering attempts seem to have come from Lebanon or to have been written by Lebanese women living outside the Arab world.

A Note on the Nationality of Early Female Arab Novelists

Around the turn of the twentieth century, Syria and Lebanon did not exist as independent states but as Bilād al-Shām, or Greater Syria. These geographical differences should be borne in mind when we study novelists writing in Arabic. During the late nineteenth and early twentieth centuries, the borders between Arab countries, as well as the identity of each country, were very different from what they are today. In addition, the movement of Arab writers, particularly among Damascus, Beirut, and Cairo, was much more fluid than it is today. Intermarriages between people from different Arab regions, particularly among writers and the educated, were the rule rather than the exception.

It is therefore difficult to establish the exact nationality of Arab writers who were born in the nineteenth or early twentieth centuries. For example, Widād Sakākīnī (1913–1991) was born of Lebanese parents. She married a Syrian and lived an important part of her life in Egypt, where she published many of her works, but she spent her last years in Syria, where she died and was buried. Mayy Ziyāda's identity and nationality is also complex: is she Palestinian, Lebanese, or Egyptian? In my view, it is unnecessary to classify these women writers according to their nationality; they saw themselves as Arab writers in an Arab world when borders did not exist. Syria, which then included present-day Syria, as well as Lebanon, Palestine, and Jordan, was experiencing one of the most tyrannical periods of the Ottoman occupation. In response, Syrian writers migrated to Egypt, at that time the Mecca of the Arab literary scene, where they were able to write in a more liberal atmosphere.

When I was studying the works of the Arab women writers of the late nineteenth and early twentieth centuries, I decided to recreate the climate they experienced, felt, and expressed in their works. Arab identity superseded any other narrower identity with which some Arabs identify today. That was a major reason why I decided that this work should be about *Arab* women novelists, because any other study with a limited geographical focus cannot and will not express either the spirit of the works or the atmosphere in which they were both written and published. Nevertheless, when borders between countries become important, and the importance is reflected in the works themselves, my study will reflect that.

In 1904 Labība Mikha'īl Ṣūyā, who was from Lebanon, serialized her novel *Ḥasnā' Sālūnīk (The Beauty of Salonika)* in *Al-Hudā* newspaper in New York. Another Lebanese woman named Labība Hāshim, who was living in Egypt at the time, published a novel in 1904 entitled *Qalb al-Rajul (Man's Heart)*, followed by *Shīrīn: Ibnat al-Sharq (Shīrīn: The Daughter of the East)* in 1907. I also found that Lebanese writer Farīda 'Aṭiyya published her interesting historical novel, *Bayn 'Arshayn (Between Two Thrones)* in 1912. After further research, I discovered that 'Afīfa Karam, a Lebanese writer who migrated to the United States, had published at least one novel before 1914.

But undoubtedly the pioneer of the modern Arabic novel is Zaynab Fawwāz (1846–1914), who published her first novel *Ḥusn al-'Awāqib: Ghāda al-Zahra (Good Consequences: Ghāda the Radiant*; Ghāda is used in Arabic to describe a beautiful young woman*)* in 1899 and another entitled *Al-Malik Qūrūsh (King Qūrūsh)*, a historical allegory, in 1906. Fawwāz is sometimes described as Lebanese and sometimes as Syrian. On the cover of her critical study of women writers, *Al-Durr al-Manthūr (Scattered Pearls in Women's Quarters)*, for instance, we read: "By the honorable writer and the singular talent Mrs. Zaynab Fawwāz Bint 'Alī bin Ḥusayn bin Obeid Allah bin Ibrāhīm bin Muḥammad bin Yūsuf Fawwāz al-'Āmilī, who was born in Syria and who lived and resided in Egypt."

In this chapter I discuss the novels written by Arab women before the publication of Haykal's *Zaynab* to establish women's contribution to this literary genre during its early stages. By the time *Zaynab* was published in 1914, Zaynab Fawwāz, along with 'Afīfa Karam and Farīda 'Aṭiyya, had already written and published eleven novels.

Zaynab Fawwāz

Whenever the name of a new woman novelist is recovered from the dark pages of history and whenever a new novel is found, the immediate question asked of the finder is: "Is the novel any good?" Fawwāz's novel met most of the requirements of the historical-realistic novel and dealt sufficiently with characterization, theme, setting, and artistic development to be considered the first novel according to Western standards. In her introduction to *Ḥusn al-ʿAwāqib*, the author showed a deep understanding of the novel's elements and its objective. She wrote: "As literary novels are the most important writings that mirror one's thought and entertain and benefit (others), and as they reproduce an image of reality and fantasy in its raw form, I decided to write this novel hoping that it will benefit (others) and entertain" (p. 37). At the time, important men of letters praised the literary merits of her work, recommending it to general readers. The chairman of *Al-Nile* newspaper, Ḥasan Ḥusnī Bāsha, wrote:

> I've read the novel *Ḥusn al-ʿAwāqib* by the renowned writer whose fame is unparalleled for her enlightened mind and creative pen, and found it very well-structured with far-reaching themes and beautiful literary features. We hope that our writer will continue to endow our modern times with such precious literary writings. (p. 37)

The poet ʿAbd Allah Furayj wrote a poem praising Fawwāz's novel, which was indicative of the literary reputation this novel had established, not only in Egypt but also in surrounding Arab countries. It is obvious from what is written about both the novel and novelist that Fawwāz was a very important writer of her time and that she was then at the center of the Arab literary movement. She was often described as a rare literary talent.

Ḥusn al-ʿAwāqib is a sociopolitical novel that explores the contemporary political atmosphere and its consequent social implications. There is a matrix of family relations, the interactions of which are defined by rivalries, hatred, and competition for power, that mirror the political system. Cousins are set against each other, each one aspiring to the throne. Shakīb, who is entitled to the throne and whose moral traits are appreciated by his society, falls in love with his cousin Fāriʿa, who returns his love. Their cousin Tāmir wants to usurp the throne and replace Shakīb. Tāmir plans to gain Fāriʿa's favor and arrange to marry her. Fāriʿa's parents have good reason to welcome Tāmir's proposal; he is her cousin, possesses wealth, and has excellent prospects for the future, whereas Shakīb is an orphan who has only his ethics and good reputation to speak for him. Tāmir resorts to all kinds of tricks, including kidnapping Fāriʿa twice and shooting and wounding Shakīb. Neither Fāriʿa nor Shakīb, however, are swayed by Tāmir's machinations. The novel pinpoints the selfish individuality of Tāmir, which represents the practices of ruling families and potential rulers in the Arab world of that period. The novel epitomizes modern Arab politics. Personal rivalry, competition, and selfish interests have been responsible for some of the most devastating political disasters in Arab history.

Interestingly, in this novel women appear as an important component of their society, who understand the political game, take firm stands, speak openly and with conviction, and enjoy a high degree of independence. Through the exchange of love letters between Shakīb and Fāri'a we discover that Fāri'a appreciates Shakīb's political stance and is neither shy nor reserved about expressing her feelings of love and devotion to him. Thus, when she receives a letter from Shakīb, she immediately writes back, expressing her feelings of love and longing to see him and enclosing a poem complaining about unsatisfied desire. Her family does not interfere in her choice of a husband, in spite of the fact that Tāmir is her cousin by blood and an individual with personal and political prospects (p. 80). The novel concludes with the triumph of the honest and decent hero Shakīb and the defeat of his conspiring cousin Tāmir.

The prominent links between social and political behavior distinguish this novel. We notice that Shakīb, who is morally correct and politically sound, is a faithful and dedicated companion. He is as serious and as committed in his social and emotional life as he is in his political life. When Shakīb is in a position to mete out retribution to Tāmir for his plotting, he shows mercy.

Ḥusn al-'Awāqib, as the title suggests, is a moral novel that explores sociopolitical relations and indirectly provides a lesson in the importance of good faith, good intentions, and good behavior. The characters are credible and consistent in their actions and are able to elaborate at length on their feelings, which are often reflected in the novel's descriptions of nature. Their future destiny is sometimes revealed through their dreams, which they take seriously and which sometimes serve as omens of things to come or of news yet unheard. Although the novel has a clear moral objective, the morality is neither imposed on the events of the novel nor presented abruptly or unnaturally. Rather, the action develops slowly and naturally, and the setting is appropriate to the characters' behavior. The novel takes place in both town and country, but there is no significant difference between the two. Both urban and rural dwellers are shown to share the same mentality, customs, and traditions; it is their moral behavior that distinguishes characters from each other. Position and power do not corrupt those that are upstanding, such as Shakīb, but essentially corrupt men, such as Tāmir, are not any purer because they live in the country. Good people are difficult to corrupt, either with money or power, whereas those who have ill intentions are difficult to redeem.

The author's writing both educates and enlightens new generations, and the message is neither vulgar nor direct. It emanates quite naturally from a succession of events that are both interesting and convincing. The novel's plot blends social, political, and historical events that are meant to educate and entertain. Women feature quite remarkably. They take correct political stands and are stubborn fighters in defense of their beliefs. Fāri'a, for example, is not persuaded by Tāmir's promises of the good life and refuses to marry him. She remains devoted to Shakīb, even when others test her faith in their relationship. Throughout the novel, women are most certainly not marginal human beings; rather, they are at the center of family, society, and politics.

If we wish to consider the element of storytelling as the most significant element in early attempts at the Arabic novel, that element is certainly provided for in Fawwāz's novel. As for other technical elements, the novel should be measured against what was available in Arabic literature at the time, rather than against the novels of Jane Austen and George Eliot. It should be measured against the novels of Ibrāhīm al-Yāzijī and Salīm al-Bustānī, whose works mixed *maqāmāt* and the modern Western story—an amalgamation of literature, medicine, and geography. It would also be unfair to expect Fawwāz's story to closely imitate the Western novel, which has a different history, atmosphere, culture, and audience. If we read this particular novel in the literary context of its time, we will concur with Fawwāz's contemporary critics that she is a rare talent and a pioneer in writing in the genre of the novel.

Fawwāz' s overall literary production shows that she was well aware of the differences between literary genres and that she wrote each of her works with the specific characteristics of that genre in mind. Along with *Ḥusn al-'Awāqib*, she published a play entitled *Al-Hawā wa al-Wafā (Love and Loyalty)*. Composed in four acts, it showcases her playwriting skills. The script targets a female audience, which she may have intended for her novel.

Fawwāz wrote poetry, novels, and plays that addressed many of the contemporary as well as the feminist issues of her time. Her works leave no room for doubt about her literary ability; she covered a wide range of social topics and had an unquestioning commitment to social reform. Regrettably, her writings, which should be placed among the works of the pioneering writers in Arabic literature, are extremely hard to find: only a few copies still exist in a handful of libraries in Syria, Lebanon, and Egypt. Her important work *Al-Durr al-Manthūr fī Ṭabaqāt Rabāt al-Khudūr (Scattered Pearls in Women's Quarters)* is a landmark anthology in the history of Arab women's literature in general and of Arab feminist literature in particular. In this valuable work, she introduces

459 women writers and professionals from both East and West, past and present. She provides a biography of each woman and then describes her contribution to her era, whether literary, social, or political. The two lines of poetry that serve as an epigraph for the book clearly indicate that Fawwāz shouldered this immense undertaking in the service of women and their cause. She was determined to establish a history for women and record their contributions in various fields. Her epigraph says: "My book appeared as Eden in their palaces and introduces the best women thinkers from both East and West. I did it as a service to my kind gender, and I believe it is the best present [I can give to] these most honored women" (p. 1). The anthology is the product of many years' work by a committed scholar and clear-sighted feminist. It is lamentable that so few copies of the book still exist; it should be made available to all students of Arabic literature, Arabic history, and comparative literature. Arguably, it is also appropriate reading for students of Islamic studies because it includes important details about pioneering Muslim women who provided examples of strength and independence to successive generations of women.

An important element in Fawwāz's thought and work was brought to light by her descendant Fawziyya Fawwāz only in the late twentieth century. She noted that Zaynab Fawwāz spoke of women's emancipation in the Arab world long before Qāsim Amīn, who has been acknowledged for almost a century as the father of Arab women's liberation.[3] In her introduction to the 1984 edition of *Ḥusn al-ʿAwāqib* published by the Southern Lebanese Cultural Council, Fawziyya Fawwāz writes:

> Zaynab Fawwāz called for legislation to organize women's lives and to guarantee them the right to education and work. Hence, she was the first woman to undertake the responsibility for her own cause and to discuss it in international courts. She pioneered a message in the whole of the East, considering that civilization, development and reform cannot be achieved without knowledge and work, and pointed out that the role of women is of paramount importance in establishing civil and civilized society. Qāsim Amīn (1863–1908) followed Fawwāz in his call for the emancipation of women. It is certain that her letters on the subject of women which appeared in Egyptian papers started prior to 1892 (most of her essays were published between 1891–1900) while Amīn's book on the emancipation of women did not appear until 1898. (pp. 20–21)

ʿAfīfa Karam

Another important Greater Syrian novelist, who wrote a few novels before the appearance of *Zaynab* by Muḥammad Ḥusayn Haykal, is

'Afīfa Karam (1883–1924), who worked as the acting executive editor of *Al-Hudā* newspaper in New York. Some of her works were published; others remain in manuscript form. Like Fawwāz, Karam showed a clear understanding of the novel as a literary genre and approached it fully aware of both its potential and its limitations. In the introduction to her first novel, *Badī'a wa Fu'ād (Badī'a and Fu'ād)* (1906), Karam discusses the novel as a literary genre and its most important characteristics and goals. First she explains her absence from the pages of *Al-Hudā* by mentioning that she has decided to write a novel. That genre, she says, permits the expression of a chain of thoughts that make a more lasting effect on a reader than short, disruptive essays and columns appearing in the pages of newspapers. She adds that women are her primary audience because they have more patience for reading novels than for any other literary genre. That, she argues, makes it easier for the author to influence their minds and hearts as well as entertain them.

Like Fawwāz, Karam strongly believed that the novel should both educate and entertain. She makes it clear that she is not writing under anyone's influence and that she is not in pursuit of either money or prestige. Instead she emphasizes that she is writing a novel for the benefit of humanity at large, one first and foremost dedicated to the mothers, wives, and daughters who built the past and present and will build the future of humanity. Her objective, as she emphasizes in her introduction, is to help to change the position of Syrian women both abroad and at home. Karam asks her readers to forget that the author is a Syrian woman, not to judge her novel on that basis, and not to criticize her for writing about love and marriage or for asking provocative questions about outdated practices that concern women. The introduction makes it abundantly clear that the author is acutely aware of the handicap that her gender imposes on her and of the fact that a novel written by a woman is approached differently by readers than a novel written by a man. She is asking for an objective judgment of her work.

The writings of Fawwāz and Karam resemble Samuel Richardson's works *Pamela* and *Clarissa,* which are considered to be two of the earliest novels written in English, in spite of the fact that they are epistolary and do not fulfill all the requirements of the modern novel. Like *Pamela* and *Clarissa*, Fawwāz's and Karam's novels have a clear moral objective. The significant difference is that *Pamela* and *Clarissa* provide examples of women who are morally correct, whereas Fawwāz's *Ḥusn al-'Awāqib* and Karam's *Badī'a wa Fu'ād* aim to reform both men and women. Although women are portrayed as the victims of men's conspiracies, they are not totally innocent, especially those appearing in *Badī'a wa Fu'ād*. In fact, that novel is not at all divided along gender lines; rather, it tends to focus on class and culture. Still, it is true that Badī'a, the major female character in the novel, is unworldly and adheres to her ideals more than to worldly benefits or advantages.

The events of the novel take place in both Lebanon and the United States. The novel opens during the summer in a Lebanese village, where the author carefully details women's lives and status in the community and dares to criticize everything negative in Lebanese society. One of the novel's significant concerns is national identity, which the author suggests should neither be insulated from new or external influences, nor dissolved in nor overwhelmed by such influences. The novel strives to balance the positive elements of Arab culture with the positive things Arabs might learn from other cultures.

That theme is conveyed by contrasting two female characters, Badī'a and Lucia. Badī'a is a simple, honest, solid girl who is not taken in with Western appearances and who appreciates the merits of her society without defending its ills. She works as a maid, and her employer's educated son, Fu'ād, falls in love with her. She tries to terminate the relationship with Fu'ād as soon as it starts, but he refuses to let it happen. When they become engaged to be married, Fu'ād's cousin, Nasīb, and his mother, Miriam, conspire to end the relationship. Badī'a leaves Lebanon and goes with Lucia to the United States in search of work and wealth. Badī'a views the United States from a very practical and realistic perspective, whereas Lucia exaggerates the glamour of the country and ends up lost on the streets of New York, unable to discriminate between what is civilized and what is ruinous.

In this novel, events and characters address an important dilemma that the Arab world has yet to resolve: the balance between cultural variations and modernity's tendency to make every culture the same. The fate of Arab women today is still very much governed by this dilemma. In her treatment of the relationship between East and West and the place of women in each of these world sectors, Karam demonstrates a deep knowledge of her culture, as well as an open mind about what can and should be learned from the West.

Karam's is the first Arabic novel to deal with this issue. It was published in 1906, over thirty years before Tawfīq al-Ḥakīm's novel '*Uṣfūr min al-Sharq (A Bird from the East)* (1938), which was acclaimed by George Ṭarābīshī as the first Arabic novel to establish what he called "the civilized anthropology," which he defined as the subject matter that concerned relations between East and West. Ṭarābīshī adds that this subsequent stream of novels rendered the best fruits on the Arabic novel family tree. There is no Arab who does not know al-Ṭayyib Ṣāliḥ's novel, *Mawsim al-Hijra ilā al-Shamāl (Season of Migration to the North)*, for example.[4] The important qualification of Ṭarābīshī's statement, however, is that this type of novel was first created by 'Afīfa Karam in her novel, *Badī'a wa Fu'ād*.

Class differences also play an important role in directing the events of the novel. Fu'ād's mother, Miriam, and her nephew, Nasīb, conspire against Badī'a because her working-class background makes her an unsuitable match for Fu'ād. Later in the novel, however, Miriam decides that Badī'a is worthy of her son, and she provides her son and Badī'a with an elaborate wedding party. Lucia, however, who falls blindly into the arms of the West, finds her life in shambles, mainly because she has shallow and distorted concepts of freedom and women's rights. Badī'a enjoys a more genuine sense of freedom: freedom for her is to travel, work, and be truly independent, which she believes is the only type of freedom that delivers fruitful and satisfying results.

The ship on which the Lebanese women leave to go to the United States becomes a kind of feminist salon, where women speak about their experiences and the problems they face, both within their families and in their society at large. They express deep sympathy for and understanding of each other and find each other's company very comforting. They introduce new meanings to long-established customs and inherited concepts, such as the concept of honor that was strictly linked to women's sexual behavior. In their discussions they broaden the concept to embrace various social behaviors and attitudes. What these women find most frustrating is that in almost every domain, women are stereotyped as having not only one gender but also one identity, one mind, and one type, without any allowance being made for the uniqueness of individual women. Men, however, are discussed as individuals worthy of blame for their own errors and praised for their own merits.

On the ship, one of their fellow passengers commits suicide by throwing herself overboard. In this instance, Karam has revisited the solution of last resort that is common to women in both Western and Arabic literature. When women feel misunderstood by husband, family, or society, they often feel that the only path to personal salvation is to end their own lives. That phenomenon in novels written by women is worthy of a literary-sociological study to highlight the fact that those female characters are choosing the worst possible alternative for themselves. Feminist studies have to stress that this personal "salvation" (if death can be called salvation) leaves women exactly where they are and where they have been for very many generations in the past. Instead of seeking personal salvation in other cities, on different continents, or in death, women should strive to create the space they need within their own culture to act as they would like and to be the people they truly want to be.

Badī'a wa Fu'ād offers a balanced view of characters, cultures, countries, and genders, with few biases or preconceptions. Issues are fairly addressed. For example, Nasīb claims to be in love with Badī'a, yet he inflicts suffering on her, on his cousin Fu'ād, and on his aunt Miriam. Fu'ād is a decent man, however, open-minded about women and prepared to change his mind in the light of genuine new findings. Miriam is initially unable to accept the thought of her servant becoming her daughter-in-law, but her son questions her viewpoint and discards class differences as artificial and therefore insignificant.

The novel strikes a similar balance concerning women's duties. At a time when women's duties to their children and husbands were expected to supersede any personal need or concern, the novel clearly suggests that women's first duty is to themselves, followed by duties to parents, siblings, husband, and children. There are two important elements here: the self and gender. The novel does not deny women's duties to their families; rather, it lays the foundation for those duties by emphasizing a woman's duty to herself, for how can she serve others except by first preserving herself? Thus arguments in the novel try to establish new feminist and social concepts and to undermine concepts that have been passed perfunctorily from one generation to another. One such concept is that women are assumed to be potential traitors to their lovers and husbands. The story of Desdemona resurfaces in different versions in both Western and Arabic works. Indeed, considering this particular accusation, distinctions are hardly, if ever, made between one woman and another. Treachery is considered an intrinsic part of the female character, which men must temper.

Instead of these outdated notions, new and more realistic concepts of women, cultures, and countries are introduced. One such important concept is that equality is an important prerequisite of love, that no true love can exist without true equality. This maxim undermines the traditional bases on which male-female relations have been built—that of servitude and inequality. Another important alteration to accepted modes of thinking is the change that Badī'a tries to introduce, once she has returned to Lebanon, to Lebanese people's concept of the United States. She stresses that it is a fallacy that all women in the US are loose and immoral or that sexual promiscuity is as prevalent as many suggest, because decent people carry their values with them wherever they are, whether in the East or West.

This novel, therefore, strives to bring about a better understanding not just between sexes and classes but also between East and West, an understanding that nearly a century later both cultures are still striving to achieve. The secret of Fu'ād's happiness at the end of the novel is that he no longer believes in commonly held generalizations and misconceptions about women. He reexamines all the unexamined maxims that he has inherited about women, and Badī‘a similarly reassesses her beliefs about Western culture. All gender, class, and cultural barriers collapse, and individuals are assessed according to their merits, regardless of sex, class, or nationality.

Events in the novel are both logical and convincing, with the theme embracing gender, class, and cross-national concerns. The attitude toward women appears to be part and parcel of the more general attitude toward other issues. The novel shows that those who treat women badly or think ill of them also have very little national pride. The personal, the social, and the political are inextricably linked. The author shows that the personal is most certainly political, a notion that even today, almost ninety years later, is not easily accepted within the Arab world.

The novel takes place in both Lebanon and the United States, with the ocean in between acting as a neutral territory where women can exchange stories and experiences. It is as if the neutrality of the water has granted them a freedom to which they have always aspired, so that they can unloose their accumulated ordeals and agonies. The author is able to show that there are few differences between the United States and Lebanon. Life is pleasant, civilized, or complicated because of the people and the nature of their attitudes, not because of where they live. Although women seem to have harder times than men, they depend on each other, finding support and empathy within their female circles. Social reality as conveyed in both Lebanon and the United States (as far as Syrian immigrants are concerned) seems to be difficult to change or even to challenge. The way in which the sociopolitical subject of immigration is addressed stresses the importance of fostering a national identity that has the courage to criticize what is negative in one's own culture, build on what is positive, and benefit from the experiences and knowledge of other cultures.

The language of *Badī‘a wa Fu’ād* flows pleasantly, although superfluous details sometimes impede the flow and distract the reader. As one of the pioneering novels in Arabic literature, it may well be appreciated within the historical-realistic genre, the themes and concerns of which still occupy both male and female Arab novelists today in the East and West. It is more ambitious than Fawwāz's *Ḥusn al-‘Awāqib* and prioritizes themes more than technique and structure, which was natural for the writings of that early stage of the novel since the express purpose of such writing was to educate and entertain.

Before writing this novel, ‘Afīfa Karam was an acting executive editor of *Al-Hudā* newspaper in New York. In 1911 she issued a weekly supplement called *Syrian Woman in New York*. Later she started a monthly called the *New Year*.

Following *Badī'a wa Fu'ād,* Karam wrote seven more novels, completing a total of eight before she reached the age of thirty.[5] This was before 1914, the year in which Haykal's *Zaynab* first appeared in Egypt.

Farīda 'Aṭiyya

Farīda 'Aṭiyya's historical novel *Bayn 'Arshayn (Between Two Thrones)* contains a wealth of historical information about the Ottoman Empire and the status of the Arab provinces within, interwoven with the sociopolitical and socioeconomic facts that led to the catastrophe of the Armenians in Turkey. On the title page the novelist describes the novel as a "historical, literary novel that probes the secrets of the Ottoman coup d'état, the fall of 'Abd al-Ḥamīd and the inauguration of the present Sultan along with the spiritual state of the times and other things." In the introduction, 'Aṭiyya describes the bloody battles and clashes in different quarters of the Ottoman Empire before the inauguration of Sultan 'Abd al-Ḥamīd. The writer continues: "I saw fit to write a historical novel that personifies facts in their places and positions and is a pleasure for the reader to read" (p. 1).

But it is not purely a historical or a realistic novel. Although it carries a considerable amount of historical information, it nevertheless reveals a very active imagination on the part of the writer that embraces detailed accounts of the lives of Jewish women, romantic love affairs, adventures, and a fascinating revelation of the socioeconomic roots of the Armenian tragedy. The latter is shown through the story of an Armenian family and its intricate entanglement in what was happening within the Ottoman Empire during that time. The novel travels backward and forward through time with ease, treating the themes separately that it carefully establishes at the outset.

The novel alternates between two very different themes, which enhances the state of suspense. There is the story of Olga, an innocent, attractive Armenian girl whose life, love affair, and family blessing are disturbed by the power of evil to affect herself and her family, as well as the entire Armenian community. There is also the story of the extravagance of Sultan 'Abd al-Ḥamīd, with his mistresses and *jawārī*.[6] The personal is linked smoothly and tacitly to the political.

This novel is remarkable for the ease of its flow. It moves from one subject to another without disruption, showing how the Armenian tragedy started and how quickly it got out of hand. Of the novels published before *Zaynab*, I found *Bayn 'Arshayn* the most interesting and most artistically mature.

With the same ease, the stream of events follows the repercussions of the Armenian genocide on both Turkey and the Arab world. The letter that was sent by Shaikh al-Azhar Salīm al-Bishrī to the Muslims of Anadol denouncing the massacres of the Armenians is a poignant demonstration of the interreligious harmony that existed between Christians and Muslims in this part of the world at that time. It also shows how tyrants use religion as a pretext for violence that furthers their political objectives. The shaikh writes:

> We have read in local newspapers disturbing rumors and very sad news suggesting that some Muslims in some Ottoman states are attacking Christians. We found this hard to believe, because Islam opposes aggression . . . and prohibits harming or shedding of the blood of any person, be they Christian or Jewish.[7]

Although the novel is based on historical facts, the author reimagines events and derives wisdom from them. The historical, the realistic, and the sensitively humanist are so well intertwined that reading the novel is both pleasurable and enriching. In many ways the novel is also didactic, but in an indirect way; it uses parallels, analogies, and comparisons to drive its messages home to the reader. The author probes the inner lives of her characters in depth to lay bare the fact that individuals, even the most powerful, are the product of circumstance. It also shows the strong and weak aspects of three ethnic groups—Turks, Arabs, and Armenians—to guide the reader toward the conclusion that all human beings are fundamentally the same.

In spite of their innovative techniques, the novels written by these three Arab women conform to the strict classical rule adhered to by Jurjī Zaydān and Salīm al-Bustānī (considered to be the founders of Arabic fiction), which is that morality and traditional ethics and customs must be paramount concerns. For that reason, social reformers such as Muḥammad 'Abdo called upon people to read the early novels written by al-Bustānī and Zaydān, as well as those by Labība Hāshim and Zaynab Fawwāz. In general, characters in the early Arabic novel have clear-cut standards of behavior. In the novels of both Fawwāz and Karam, in particular, and also to a great extent in 'Aṭiyya's novel, the characters of both the men and women are either entirely good or absolutely evil. These novels also started a trend that still prevails in the novels of Arab women today, in which most characters belong to the upper classes (though it is less true of Karam's *Badī'a wa Fu'ād*).

It is important to stress that by publishing more than ten novels before *Zaynab* came out, Arab women made a major contribution to the birth of the Arabic novel. Oddly, however, all the literary studies I have encountered discuss the origin of the Arabic novel with total disregard for the novels written by women. It is impossible to accuse writers such as Jamāl al-Ghīṭānī, 'Abd al-Raḥmān Munīf, and Muḥammad Dakrūb of taking a deliberate stand against women, yet their important studies of the origin of the Arabic novel fail to mention a single woman novelist. As I have shown, however, Arab women started writing novels before Arab men. When I asked Dakrūb why all these male studies, including his, never mentioned a single woman novelist, he answered totally frankly: "The only reason I can think of is that male writers (myself included) must unconsciously believe that the literature written by women is insignificant."[8] It was a candid confirmation of what I had always believed to be the case. Otherwise, how could one possibly explain the appearance of a special issue of the Arabic journal *Mawāqif* on the Arabic novel that did not include a single article on Arab women novelists?[9] Indeed, the title of this issue was, "Toward a Comprehensive View of the Arabic Novel." Ironically, it does not include a single critical essay on Arab women novelists. Additionally, of the eight novelists who provided testimony about the writing of the novel, only one was a woman. This neglect may have been inadvertent and unconscious, but perhaps the most dangerous discrimination is that which originates from within the unconscious mind.

To answer the arguments raised by Ghīṭānī, Munīf, and others, 'Alī Shalash published an article in *Al-Sharq al-Awsaṭ* entitled, "Correcting a Literary Mistake That Is a Half-Century Old."[10] In this article, Shalash argues that the first Arabic novel was written by Francis Marrāsh (1836–1873). The novel was entitled *Ghāyat al-Ḥaq (The Objective of Justice)* and was published in 1865. The writer of the article tries to prove that this novel predates novels by Salīm al-Bustānī and Jurjī Zaydān and that therefore the record should be corrected to show that the Arabic novel originated in Aleppo. But rather than concentrating on a single name, we should study *all* the writings that contributed to the birth of the Arabic novel and to its development throughout the twentieth century. Instead of scoring points against each of the early contributors, it would be better to try to see them as elements forming the first step in the direction of a new genre. There is no doubt that the writings of al-Bustānī, Zaydān, Marrāsh, and Haykal all contributed to the eventual artistic development of the novel and to making the Arabic novel what it is today. It is impossible to attribute the birth of the Arabic novel to one name. Unlike the birth of a baby, a novel does not have to be born at a certain place and time. Hence, although I refrain from supporting any particular argument against another, I would like to emphasize that everything written about the origin of the Arabic novel is only partly true. Each article can only become truly valuable if it is placed in the context of what others have found about the same topic. Thus, neither al-Bustānī nor Zaydān nor Marrāsh wrote the first novel in Arabic literature, but all contributed to the establishment and development of the Arabic novel.

What has been consistently lacking, however, in all that has been written about the origin of the Arabic novel is mention of any Arab woman novelist who contributed to the emergence of the novel as a literary genre in the Arab world. Accepting all the arguments put by my male colleagues as arguments that complement rather than negate each other, I would like to add Zaynab Fawwāz, 'Afīfa Karam, and Farīda 'Aṭiyya to the list of Arab literary pioneers. Their contributions to the birth of the Arabic novel are undeniable and are on a par with those of al-Bustānī, Zaydān, Marrāsh, and Haykal. Their works have not been mentioned before by critics, not because of any artistic or other failure, but simply because they were written by women. The record must be set straight. Any talk about the origin of the Arabic novel that does not take into account these three important women novelists is deficient and incomplete.

The novels written by these three women depart much farther from *maqāmāt* than the works of al-Bustānī and Zaydān and are much closer in both form and content to the modern Western novel. They are, of course, the products of their time. They are didactic and historical, but they have definite artistic value, and their writers were fully aware that they were writing novels and were conscious of the audience they were addressing. All three novelists agreed that novels should have three main functions: to educate, entertain, and set an example of moral behavior.

What needs to be done, perhaps, with the novels published before 1914 in the Arab world is to study them, taking into account their social and historical contexts, and to evaluate them accordingly. Such a study might be able to discover the characteristics of the Arabic novel in its very early stages without placing too much emphasis on who said what first. Perhaps no one said anything first, but there were certainly men and women who wrote novels documenting the literary, social, and political conditions of their time. It is about time that we study these novels in this light and keep accurate records, instead of trying to evaluate the relative importance of Beirut, Cairo, or Aleppo in the creation of this particular genre. Such a study will not be complete without including all the Arabic novels written at the end of the nineteenth and the beginning of the twentieth centures.

CHAPTER 3

The Quest for Parity

DURING THE FIRST HALF of the twentieth century, when Arab countries were heavily involved in national resistance against European colonial powers, Arab women novelists were endeavoring to reshape their world. Novels by women examined the social and political dogma relating to women, and tried to prepare the ground for greater equality between the sexes. The novels were aimed at both men and women, and the ultimate objective was to participate in creating a better world for both. The novelty and seriousness of such an endeavor might well have been too threatening at that time. Thus, the stifling of women's writings might well have been intentional. Indeed, the seemingly "pure" controversy relating to "women's literature" discussed in Chapter 1 that sought to marginalize Arab women's literary works mirrors blatant efforts to keep women at the periphery of social and political life.

The first half of the twentieth century evinced a serious setback to women's status everywhere in the world. In Germany, National Socialism saw "the sexual revolution and feminism as forces to be dealt with seriously."[1] Hitler's political apparatus was directed toward implementing the ideas articulated in *Mein Kampf*, where he claimed "the German girl is a State Subject and only becomes a State Citizen when she marries."[2] In the Soviet Union, aspirations to overthrow a patriarchal system were raised in the 1920s but dashed in the 1930s and 1940s, and Soviet society found itself "in the same boat with other patriarchal systems in Western countries."[3] Kate Millet argues in *Sexual Politics* that although laws liberalizing marriage and divorce were passed, the real test remained to change attitudes (p. 240). In the United States, feminist movements suffered from the impact of Freudian philosophy, which fostered a "counterrevolutionary attitude" (p. 252). Freud's psychoanalytic theory had a greater adverse effect on the women's movement than any other single theory. It permeated all spheres of thought in the United States during the 1950s and 1960s, when the feminist movement was just beginning to provide a leading example to women in different parts of the world. The detrimental consequences could be shown through restating a simple fact: that Freud's entire psychology of women, "from which all modern psychology and psychoanalysis derives heavily, is built upon an original tragic experience of being 'born female'" (p. 254).

From the 1920s to the 1940s, national independence movements against French and British rule fermented in Arab countries, and women, as is usually the case during times of crises, were called upon to play a role in the liberation of their countries. They joined demonstrations, demanding freedom for nationalist leaders and voicing opposition to colonial schemes to divide and weaken the Arab nation. They founded the Pan-Arab Women's Union in 1928, nearly two decades before the formation of the Arab League in 1947. Arab women constantly warned against Arab leaders signing treaties such as the British-Egyptian treaty of 1936. They also convened the Conference on Palestine in 1938 in Cairo to discuss the Palestinian problem, demonstrated against Arthur Balfour's visit to Syria and Lebanon in 1924, and opposed the Balfour Declaration of 1917, in which the British promised the Jews a home in Palestine.

During this period, political and feminist ideologies in the Arab world were interwoven. Arab women demonstrated against the veil and held conferences calling for women's equal social, political, and economic rights with men. A flourishing list of Arab women's journals and magazines kept Arab women informed about international feminist movements. Women editors of feminist journals had correspondents in different parts of the world and sent representatives to attend women's conferences. In 1932 Arab women joined the international peace movement in its call for disarmament, collected signatures, and sent them to the Committee for Disarmament in Geneva. In brief, the voice of Arab women was very much heard in relation to regional, political, and international issues.

In 1947, however, Palestine was partitioned and the newly independent Arab states, Syria (1946), Lebanon (1946), and Egypt (1952), were ruled largely by military and secret police who considered any voice that did not echo theirs to be dissident. Thus by the late 1940s and early 1950s, Arab hopes of living in free, democratic states once national independence was achieved had been dashed, giving rise to frustration and resentment. As is often the case, "the less freedom there is in any society, the deeper the crisis, the more oppressive the feeling of frustration, the more desperate the need becomes for finding a prey, a victim, [and] the worse women's position becomes."[4]

Arab women novelists in the 1940s and 1950s were deeply aware of their societies' ills, epitomized in their societies' attitudes regarding women. Their endeavors aimed to undermine dogma and misconceptions and to change men's attitudes about women. They acted on the premise that changing social attitudes is the first prerequisite for any social or political change. Men were not seen as the adversaries; rather, they were portrayed as the victims of wrongly conceived and deeply erroneous images of women. The novels were therefore directed at a male, rather than a female, audience. An explicit effort was made to explain to men that the relationship between the two sexes should not be seen in terms of "gain and loss," "superior and inferior," or "strong and weak." In their literary works these women constructed a vision of a world where parity between the sexes reflected positively on both. What women strove to achieve was neither superiority nor authority over men but a place for all women to function as rational individuals who might positively contribute to human advancement. Thus, Arab women novelists' first pressing agenda was to liberate women from the aberrant concept of woman as "sex" or woman as "body" and to educate men about the rich dimensions of women's lives. In their efforts to change women's position within the family, they were trying to undermine the most hierarchical unit within an oppressive, patriarchal system: "the family structure that involved the subordination of women."[5] Interestingly, in no work did Arab women novelists ever advocate either separatism or the dissolution of the family; rather, they sought to change attitudes so that women might have the freedom to function on an equal footing with men within existing social structures.

In 1927 Zaynab Muḥammad published her epistolary novel *Asrār Waṣīfa Miṣriyya (The Secrets of an Egyptian Mistress)* in Cairo. This work is a novel of manners, like Samuel Richardson's *Pamela* and *Clarissa*, but it reverses the gender roles in the latter. *Clarissa* was written by a man to prescribe moral behavior for young women, whereas *Asrār Waṣīfa Miṣriyya* was written by a woman to provide moral lessons for young men. The correspondence in *Clarissa* is between Clarissa Harlowe and her friend, Anna Howe, and Lovelace is seen through their letters. The correspondence in *Asrār Waṣīfa Miṣriyya* is between Khayrī (the lover) and his friend, Fawzī; the woman is introduced only through their descriptions of her. Yet the woman, Fikriyya, still has something essentially in common with Clarissa. Despite the endeavors of the two men to portray her as a loose, immoral woman, and despite the fact that she is given neither voice nor opportunity to write or speak in her own defense, Fikriyya emerges as a strong, confident woman who commands the reader's respect. The two men, however, fall victim to their own naive behavior and misconceptions.

Fawzī considers Fikriyya to be a fallen woman and warns Khayrī against getting involved with her. But she agrees to see her lover and allows him to hold her hand. In brief, she responds to his love in kind, which Fawzī considers immoral. Fawzī tells Khayrī about an incident with his wife, in which she slapped him when he tried to kiss her before marriage: "Every time I remember how she slapped me I find myself to be the happiest man with a woman who rejected the temptation of a kiss. How could you want to marry a woman who gives up her dearest possession, her honor?" In another letter he tells his friend that a woman's premarital chastity is the foundation of a happy marriage (p. 13).

The only proof the two men have of Fikriyya's unchaste behavior is that she agrees to meet her lover in a public place. When Khayrī slights her by failing to show up at an agreed meeting, she leaves him and marries her cousin, but subsequently divorces him when he stays out late one night without explanation. Khayrī tries to win her over once more, but she pays him no attention. He writes to his friend Fawzī,

> It is amazing that Fikriyya has forgotten me completely. During the school holidays I went with her brother to their home, but she would pass us in the garden and look the other way. Her brother asked her many times to come and join us, but she paid him no attention either. I have no doubt that she has forgotten me completely. (p. 36)

The moral of the story, according to Fawzī, who overwhelms his friend Khayrī with an influx of letters about women's honor and chastity to the extent that he drives him to commit suicide, is to warn young men against "fallen" women. In their advance publicity for the third part of the serialized story, the publishers promise readers they will learn about "the secrets of prostitution, the reasons men become sinners, and valuable advice provided to young men and women" (p. 39). Yet even as the narrative betrays the correspondents' intentions to ruin Fikriyya, the two men emerge as the victims of their own misconceptions and misreading of Fikriyya's character. Just as Clarissa's resilience triumphs over the artifice of Lovelace's strength, Fikriyya's confidence and self-assurance make the two men and their moral concerns appear quite ludicrous. Zaynab Muḥammad's implicit message matters more than her explicit one. That is not surprising, as women writers often find themselves in a position in which they have to negotiate the activity of writing with a conditioned social reality by incorporating a surface story that masks a more profound point. In *The Madwoman in the Attic,* Sandra Gilbert and Susan Gubar observe that "women from Jane Austen and Mary Shelley to Emily Brontë and Emily Dickinson produced works that are in some sense palimpsestic, works whose surface designs conceal or obscure deeper, less accessible (and less socially acceptable) levels of meaning" (p. 73). Yet it is only when we explore this deeper level of meaning that the works start to make sense.

In the late 1940s when Widād Sakākīnī was living in Cairo, at that time the center of Arab enlightenment, many Arab writers were belittling women's writings and publicly suppressing them. Tawfīq al-Ḥakīm (1898–1987), one of the most highly regarded Arab writers of the twentieth century, portrays women in his novel *Al-Ribāṭ al-Muqaddas (The Holy Bond)* as men's possessions, devoid of social, economic, and personal rights. 'Abbās Maḥmūd al-'Aqqād (1889–1964) was a reputed misogynist. Iḥsān 'Abd al-Quddūs regarded women as mere bodies whose purpose was to provide men with pleasure and heirs to their wealth. And in his novel *Al-'Ayb (Shame)*, Yūsuf Idrīs (1927–1991) contends women's existence is validated only by their sexual identity and purpose, which defines all their moral and social codes.

In 1956, Naguib Maḥfouẓ (1911–2006) examined the complexities of men's demonization and vilification of women in his novel *Bidāya wa Nihāya (The Beginning and the End)*. In the novel, Ḥasanayn is both tyrant and victim. Instead of trying to change the conditions that oppress him, he strives to avenge himself against the class responsible for his oppression by sexually penetrating a woman of that class, which, he believes, will make him dominant over those who oppress him. "When I penetrate her," he thinks to himself, "every part of her warm body will call me 'master.' This is all I want for in life. If I am able to penetrate one [woman], I will have penetrated her entire class" (p. 245). Similarly, Muṣṭafā Sa'īd, a character in al-Ṭayyib Ṣāliḥ's classic *Mawsim al-Hijra ilā al-Shamāl (Season of Migration to the North)*, is typical of the tyrant-victim whose tyranny and victimization are best expressed in his distorted conceptions of women and sex. He surrounds himself with mirrors in his bedroom in order to imagine that by invading the body of one Englishwoman, he is penetrating all Englishwomen (pp. 43–48). The sexual relationship with a woman here acquires significant racial and class dimensions.

In her important study, *Min Ṣuwar al-Mar'a fī al-Riwāya wa al-Qiṣaṣ al-'Arabiyya (Images of Women in Arabic Novels and Short Stories)*, Laṭīfa al-Zayyāt (1923–1996) addresses this issue and explores its causes. It is worth quoting at length:

> Women as they emerge in this selection of novels and short stories are sexual objects engaged either in the procreation of children to ensure a safe transference of private ownership from one man to another or to provide pleasure for men, and in both cases the woman is seen as a "thing" owned by man. The concept of sex in these writings reflects the multiple distorted concepts that prevail in the Arab world. Yet this notion of sex sums up to a great extent the ills of Arab reality and offers a disturbing comment upon it. The man who considers sex an act of aggression, a trap, invasion, triumph and humiliation is a man who himself is a victim and who is deprived by his social order of freedom and positive action. He is a man who instead of pursuing creative and purposeful action has indulged himself in false battles, scoring phony victories that can only amplify his frustration and impotence. If such conditions incapacitate Arab men, their effects are doubly disastrous on women. There is no salvation except through an increased awareness on the part of both men and women. (p. 80)

In this study, al-Zayyāt examines some of the most widely read and most influential novels and short stories in Arabic literature. She discusses works by Zakariyyā Tāmir, Naguib Maḥfouẓ, Iḥsān 'Abd al-Quddūs, al-Ṭayyib Ṣāliḥ, Tawfīq al-Ḥakīm, 'Abd al-Raḥmān Munīf, al-Ṭāhir Waṭṭār, Yūsuf Idrīs, Ismā'īl Fahd Ismā'īl, and others. Al-Zayyāt's findings may best be summarized in the titles of her chapters: "Woman as a Personal Possession and Means of Production," "Woman as Object," "Double Standards Regarding Woman," "Love and Marriage," and "Woman as Victim." Al-Zayyāt concludes that women are reduced to being mere sex objects, and sex itself is considered sinful, base, and dirty when its purpose is not solely to produce children. The woman as mother emerges as a symbol of altruistic love and self-sacrifice, which, though positive, imposes the moral requirement of self-denial. The study also suggests that the debasement of women within the family is a deliberate attempt to sustain the dominant patriarchal political order.

Yet when Arab women writers challenge this pervasive image of women as sex objects or women as wives and mothers with no other dimension to their lives, they are accused of not only being selfishly concerned with their own gender but also failing to embrace the paradigms of the social and political lives of people in their own countries. I, however, argue that Arab women novelists see the issues concerning their gender to be central to the social and political problems in which their countries are immersed. These women see in women's salvation the deliverance of their peoples.

The dilemma of Arwā, the heroine in Widād Sakākīnī's novel *Arwā bint al-Khuṭūb (Arwā, the Daughter of Upheavals)* is that of a woman who refuses to prostitute her body for any reason. After refusing to have sex with her brother-in-law, 'Ubayd, while her husband, Nu'mān, is out of town, she is accused of committing adultery, brought to court, sentenced, and then stoned. A series of attempted rapes at one point pushes her to kill her attacker: "She stood motionless in disbelief at what social injustice had made of her" (p. 58). All her ordeals show there is an unbridgeable gap between her image of herself and society's perception of her. She recognizes her beauty as the source of her tragedy "and wondered how to coarsen her looks and impair her feminine attraction" (p. 40).

But the other, more fatal, reason for her ordeals is the general assumption that all women are potential adulteresses and that they all enjoy being raped, no matter what they may say. When Arwā speaks, she is accused of lying, and when she keeps silent, her silence is taken to signify consent. She realizes there is a problem of communication that makes any discourse with her adversaries pointless. Most of the men who try to rape her are so immersed in their prejudices against women that she cannot convincingly portray her point of view. She is in a state of shock and disbelief at how men in all places at all times are only able to prove their masculinity by possessing women's bodies (p. 56). The conditions she finds herself in are so awful she is even unable to scream.

In *The Color Purple*, Alice Walker's Celie speaks not just for herself but for Arwā, too, when she says: "I can't speak. Every time I open my mouth nothing comes out but a little burp" (p. 125). There is no doubt that an Arab critic who found Arwā "fierce, anti-male, and Freudian" could not even begin to conceive of her agony and ordeal.[6] Arwā's body and beauty become her curse and make her prey in men's eyes. As Alice Walker's heroines were to do thirty-three years later, Arwā turns to God after failing to find a place on earth where she can function as a person without immediately being sexualized. Her inner purity and resilience remain unshaken. Eventually she becomes a saint, able to heal her brother-in-law's blindness when he comes to her with her husband, Nu'mān, beseeching her to restore his eyesight. Her other assailants also arrive. She recognizes them, and when they know who she is, they learn something more. They realize how mistaken they were to harass her and to accuse her of being an adulteress:

> When Arwā started to speak they were so ashamed of themselves, none of them could lift his eyes and look her in the eye. They held their breath, each of them secretly wishing he had died before coming here to meet their victim, a living martyr sent by God to expose their mischief and the enormity of their ignorance of women's nature.[7]

Bereaved and disconcerted, men kiss Arwā's feet, asking for her forgiveness. Commenting on this point, Ḥusām al-Khaṭīb wonders why

Widād Sakākīnī makes "men kiss a woman's feet; is this a compensation for her heroine's sexual frustration, or an escalation to it from below?"[8]

Nu'mān tries to win his wife back. She excuses herself to say her prayers, at which point her soul departs. She is mourned publicly, and on her grave is written the epitaph: "Here forever rests woman's sanctity that has been forever defiled by men."[9] The fact that the novel ends at this point is significant: it stresses the fact that the message has been conveyed and the truth is known.

Speaking of her novel in 1990, Widād Sakākīnī said,

> The reason my heroine turns to God is because she is exposed to horrifying social injustice prompted by blind habits and ignorantly inherited concepts of women. She cannot function because everyone treats her as a sex object. By turning to God she is at least able to preserve her dignity and self-worth in her own eyes.[10]

That Arwā ends up being superior to all the men who mistreat her is the high point of the story. Once this point is made, the story ends.

Like Widād Sakākīnī in *Arwā bint al-Khuṭūb*, Flannery O'Connor (1925–1964) concentrates on the spiritual dimension of human life and its often grotesque distortions, particularly in short stories such as "A Good Man Is Hard to Find" and "Good Country People." O'Connor is often indirect, showing what faith is *not*, as well as the perverse consequences of being faithless in contemporary society. Sakākīnī's strategy is to show what faith *is* by tracing the life of Arwā, a woman who flees human society, turns to God, and eventually becomes a saint sought out by people from different faiths. Arwā defies social injustice through an inner resilience, and eventually her strong belief not only in her innocence but also in her particular vision and perspective allows her to become a saint with healing powers.

In the final analysis, Arwā realizes herself, not as conceived by men but as she has always perceived herself to be. Although she dies, her achievement is unquestionable: she is not only accepted but cherished by everyone. In its fictional quality, in the atmosphere it creates and the beauty of its Arabic phrases, this novel approaches the quality of *A Thousand and One Nights*. The author exercises impressive flights of imagination, which some critics have unfortunately described as "fabrication and impossible to believe." Had Sakākīnī written nonfiction, doubtless it would have been similarly dismissed for being "autobiographical."

Sakākīnī's biographies of two exceptional women, Rābi'a al-'Adawiyya and Mayy Ziyāda, confirm our understanding of her novel *Arwā bin al-Khuṭūb*. In *Al-'Āshiqa al-Mutaṣawwifa: Ḥayāt wa Afkār*

Rābi'a al-'Adawiyya (First Among Sufis), Sakākīnī again constructs the life of another woman saint, this time a real one, who lived in the eighth and ninth centuries AD. Rābi'a was a fourth, unwanted female baby in a family with no boys. Her unorthodox, uncompromising views brought her hardships and adversities during her lifetime, but once she died, her simple house and grave became religious shrines. Now the people of Iraq, Syria, Saudi Arabia, and Palestine claim her origin and even her tomb.

In this biography, men are made to consider the spotless life of a woman who was very much wronged by them, who opened a path for other women, and who proved that the birth of a woman should not be lamented. Rābi'a al-'Adawiyya demonstrated that women have souls, pride, dignity, and self-esteem. Sakākīnī's concluding paragraph of her biography reads as follows:

> Rābi'a realized an ideal: she pointed it out for the righteous and the sincere. She lived that ideal with vision and knowledge and truth. She left for women an open door that was honorable and worthy of esteem, never to be closed again. She was a woman heading the ranks of the dedicated ones. And she became their living proof both in worshipping and in loving God. (p. 85)

Sakākīnī's biography of Mayy Ziyāda is a serious and compassionate effort to absolve yet another wronged woman. Indeed, her book *Mayy Ziyāda: Ḥayātuhā wa A'māluhā (Mayy Ziyāda: Her Life and Work)* is the product of careful research. Ziyāda was a female pioneer who had her own literary salon. She was accused by some male misogynists of being flirtatious, and during the last year of her life her family deprived her of her wealth, accused her of being insane, and sent her to a mental hospital where she died, many believe of a broken heart.

To Widād Sakākīnī's regret, she arrived in Egypt two years after Ziyāda's tragic death. She spoke at length to everyone who knew Ziyāda intimately, read all her works over and over again, visited her house, and constructed a biography that is both a creative and heartening account of a writer, sister, and comrade in a common struggle. Reading the book, one can feel Sakākīnī's heart beating when Mayy was happy and pounding when she was afraid. She even imagined that Ziyāda's spirit was moving her pen. Sakākīnī writes:

> If it were not for fear of being accused of spiritual incarnation, physical rebirth, and philosophical solutions, I would have claimed that my soul, which [has] accompanied her memory since her departure, is writing with her pen about her, joining me in defending her from malice and awarding her the place her work and talent have long earned her. (Introduction)

Mayy Ziyāda devoted her time and talent to ensuring that Warda al-Yāzijī, 'Ā'isha al-Taymūriyya, and Bāḥithat al-Bādiya were firmly placed in Arab literary history. Similarly, Widād Sakākīnī made a sincere effort to dispel the myth surrounding Ziyāda's life and death and award her the literary recognition she so deserves.

Sakākīnī's mastery of the Arabic language was beyond doubt. In 1937 the author won first prize for a short story published in *Al-Makshūf* newspaper. She was one of the best and most capable (though least acknowledged) writers in the Arabic language. Sadly, even though she wrote and published twenty books, not a single book has been written about her in Arabic. The reason may be found in the feminist consciousness expressed in all her writing. Writers and critics did not appreciate her feminist perspectives. Indeed, Sakākīnī had a reputation of being a strong, sharp-tongued feminist who is much too daring and outspoken.

As a literary critic, she was well aware of the stalemate in literary criticism in the Arab world:

> Our literature today, in its poetry and prose and all its fictive and dramatic genres, is neglected without any constructive criticism. There is no objective criticism of our literary output. There are no devoted, objective scholars who are bent on studying and evaluating our writings.[11]

She long realized she was the victim of biased, opinionated criticism, primarily because of her feminist vision. Like Ziyāda, Sakākīnī was aware of the history of Arab women's literature and devoted all her energies to form another link in this heritage. Her collections of short stories, novels, biographies, and essays are all informed by one single motive: doing women justice. As early as 1938, she wrote in her feminist treatise, *Inṣāf al-Mar'a (Doing Women Justice):*

> I refrained from what male writers excel in, directed my attention to our contemporary women's lives with all the concerns and needs prevailing there, and allowed my pen the liberty to write stories about women and explore the minutest details in their lives. . . . I believe that once our life obtains a better rhythm, women in the Arab world will have their own literature with its special art and output. It will enjoy its own merits, prosper in its seriousness and feminism and participate with men's literature in art's grand message of benevolence and beauty. (p. 99)

In *Inṣāf al-Mar'a,* the first book of its kind in the Arab world, Sakākīnī confirms my reading of her novel *Arwā bint al-Khuṭūb:* that her literature, although it is about women, is in fact addressed to both men and women. For only by reforming both sexes may a better world eventually emerge:

> This book is for women. They shall find in it what concerns them in their current lives. [It is] for young women to learn about the history of their mothers and for sincere men to find in its pages the truth about women, away from what has been fabricated by women's enemies, away from the false accounts made deliberately to impede women's progress and undermine their objectives. There are many instances where a good word has pointed the way to the right path. (p. 20)

Widād Sakākīnī did not set out on this course alone. Other Arab women novelists, too, were examining different aspects of Arab women's experiences, and their response was not so far removed from that of Sakākīnī. In Lebanon, Palestine, Syria, Egypt, and Iraq, Arab women novelists such as Hind Salāma, Fatḥiyya Maḥmūd al-Bāti', Hiyām Nuwaylātī, Colette Khūrī, Amīna al-Sa'īd, and Ḥarbiyya Muḥammad were striving to remodel the image of women in the public mind and retrieve it from "the curse of the body."[12] Their overall attitude was neither angry nor emotional; rather, they sensitively examined gender roles and concepts in the Arab world. Novels about love, marriage, professional life, and equality concurred that the construction of gender roles in the Arab world in effect erases women from the social arena and denies them their most basic rights as human beings.

In 1953 and 1954, Iraqi writer Ḥarbiyya Muḥammad published two novels, *Jarīmat Rajul (A Man's Crime)* and *Man al-Jānī (Who Is the Culprit?)*, in which she highlighted the way men rule like kings, collecting and discarding women as they please. A few years later, the Syrian novelist Hiyām Nuwaylātī published her first novel, *Fī al-Layl (At Night),* in which she examines the fate of a talented woman who tries to achieve professional parity with men.[13] Her heroine, whose name is never stated, is a talented and ambitious student of music. Gifted and self-confident, she tries to establish a working relationship with her elderly music teacher, whom she admires. But no sooner does she find herself alone with him than he starts to make advances to her and harasses her sexually. Resenting her rejection of him, her teacher fails her in her music exam and ruins her future plans. She wakes up from a nightmare to find that she has lost her eyesight. She leaves the country and becomes a famous singer in Egypt.

The literary critic Ḥusām al-Khaṭīb is puzzled by the heroine's rejection of her teacher's sexual advances, which later become sexual harassment, and cannot see the issue of power that plays very strongly in such an instance. He blames the heroine for allowing her teacher to believe she is interested in him. He claims she was a masochist—the only explanation he can find for her behavior (1976, p. 82). Such a reading, however, which has unfortunately influenced generations of students, totally ignores what the novelist is trying to achieve. Nuwaylātī puts forward the case of a woman with artistic talent trying to make her way in the world. The heroine is subjected to sexual harassment and penalized professionally for resisting sexually, and her life is completely shattered because she has refused to prostitute her body in order to advance her career. Her loss of eyesight is metaphorically intended to highlight the magnitude of her affliction. Perhaps it should be pointed out that today, over forty years after Nuwaylātī's novel was first published, millions of women all over the world and in all kinds of professions still complain of sexual harassment at work. It has to be emphasized that this is in no way a masochistic novel; rather, it is a balanced, well-crafted, and daring cry for professional parity.

As the novel draws to a close, by chance the heroine meets her teacher's son. She gives him her diary and asks him to pass it on to his father. Acting on the premise that the "sins of the fathers may be visited upon the sons," the son asks if there is anything he himself can do for her. She asks her teacher's son to name his first daughter after her. Husām al-Khaṭīb finds this "a very stupid and naive request as a price for all her suffering and ordeal" (March 1976, p. 79). Yet another reading is surely plausible. By giving her name to the granddaughter of the man who ruined her career and effectively her life, the heroine leaves hope for future generations of women. The hope is that the struggle against "the curse of the body" will continue, and that everyone, including the descendants of previous antagonists, will join in this struggle.

Sadly, *Fī al-Layl* quickly disappeared from the bookshops and went out of print. A decade later, the author returned to the literary scene with a less direct literary genre: poetry. One explanation for this might be that poetry in the Arab world has lately become a less accessible genre than the novel, despite the fact that it was the dominant—in fact the only— literary genre in the Arab world for centuries. Nuwaylātī might well have reckoned that fewer people read poetry, and fewer still understand what it actually says.[14]

Both the Lebanese writer Hind Salāma, in her novel *Al-Ḥijāb al-Mahtūk (The Profaned Veil)*, and the Palestinian writer, Fathiyya Maḥmūd al-Bāti‘, in her novel *Mudhakkarāt Zā'ifa (False Memoirs)*,[15] agree with Sakākīnī that men need to be re-educated about the nature of women. They also agree that attitudes about women need to be sifted and sorted and that a representative image of women corresponding to the way women think and feel needs to be established. As in *Arwā bint al-*

Khuṭūb, the target audience in both novels is men and women, and the objective is to change men's attitudes toward women. At the end of both novels, the male characters realize they are the victims of entrenched misconceptions of women they have failed to consider and question.

The atmosphere prevailing in Salāma's novel *Al-Ḥijāb al-Mahtūk* is reminiscent of that which prevails in Jane Austen's works. Salāma has Austen's insight into her (upper middle) class background; she understands the social codes, the peculiarity of the class culture, and the position of women within it but does not have Austen's mastery of the art of fiction. Salāma's Arabic sentences are subtle, smooth, and, at times, moving, but her method of developing her characters and changing their social and financial status is not always convincing.

Al-Ḥijāb al-Mahtūk can be read on several levels, each of which reinforces the author's endeavor to promote a better understanding between the sexes. Throughout the novel, two different perspectives, two different approaches, and two different interpretations of women's actions are presented. Here, women are neither saints nor sinners; rather, they are the products of their social conditioning.

At the beginning of the novel, the author depicts Lamyā' as a woman who appreciates herself:

> In a room where chaos prevails, and clothes are scattered on an elegant couch, on the floor, and near the bed, an almost naked woman stands in front of the mirror combing her long hair. Her eyes move on the mirror from the chestnut hair to the dreamy brown eyes, the white face, small nose, pretty mouth and chin. In a deft move she lifts her hair and pins it up. Then she puts on a lovely dress that highlights her sensuous body and stands on the balcony of her luxurious flat. (*Al-Ḥijāb al-Mahtūk*, p. 5)

Hani arrives and announces his plans to marry his chaste cousin, leaving Lamyā' pregnant with his baby, Madeline. Lamyā' refuses to have an abortion because she believes in what she is doing. Hani gives her some money and never sees Lamyā' again. After her mother dies in childbirth, Madeline is sent to a convent. It seems likely that Madeline's mother had to die early in the novel because of the unbridgeable dichotomy between an unmarried, single mother who seemed quite happy with herself and a society that cannot tolerate such a woman. But having had no children with his wife, late in his life Hani seeks out his illegitimate daughter, Madeline, and leaves her his fortune. (His wife does not inherit his wealth because she did not bear him children. After Hani's death, she has to leave her home and return to her family.)

Thus all three women, Madeline, Lamyā', and Hānī's wife, suffer from varying displacements because of a patriarchal system that circum-scribes women in so many different ways. Here it should be noted that the discrepancy between the actual life men lead and the public image they try hard to convey sharply contrasts with women's courage and ability to live up to their convictions, even when they face social disap-proval and chaos in their personal lives.

Upon receiving her inheritance, Madeline immediately joins Lebanese high society, with all its predilections for the fads and fashions of the 1960s. Before her marriage to her beloved poet, Fayyad, she has a relationship with a cousin whom she does not love and therefore refuses to marry. This cousin, Sāmī, is unable to understand how Madeline can refuse him after they have had sexual intercourse. It is usual for a man to reject a woman who "surrenders" herself to him before marriage, but not the other way around. Madeline, however, like Rīm in Colette Khūrī's *Ayyām Ma'ahu (Days with Him)*, believes that when women give men their bodies rather than their souls they have given them their "second best." That, however, is not the way men feel. Men assume that once they have penetrated a woman's body they have "conquered" her and thenceforth possess her, both body and soul. They also think they have the right to dispose of her as they see fit.

Despite the intimate relationship between Fayyad and his wife Madeline, when she is accused of betraying him with her cousin, Sāmī, he immediately believes the allegations made about her. As a result, their life together is shattered, and she goes back to the convent for good. When the truth is revealed to her husband, he seeks her out and tries to win her back, but she refuses. "Finally," she says to him, "I have found peace" (p. 151). This statement encapsulates the heroine's objec-tion to the social paradigm that does not permit her to survive and feel at ease. The quintessential message of the novel is conveyed through Fayyad's reaction. Casting a last look at the convent before starting his lonely journey back home, he mumbles to himself:

> Women, whatever your lives might be, some of you remain spotless and loyal, devout and merciful. You are the source of compassion, of love, affection, and good deeds. Like flowers you infuse the world with fragrant perfume and like horizons you grant us clarity and space, though there are some among you who undermine relationships and impair human happiness. (p. 152)

In the last sentence of the quote, Fayyad is referring to the sister who plotted against him and his wife and jeopardized his marriage. Here the author is questioning society's willingness to accept generalizations and malicious gossip about women (something that Widād Sakākīnī was eager to highlight in her novel *Arwā bint al-Khuṭūb*). In an epigraph to *Al-Ḥijāb al-Mahtūk*, Salāma writes: "Not all women are the same; some of them are flowers, others are thorns."

A similar theme informs Fatḥiyya Maḥmūd al-Bāti''s *Mudhakkarāt Zā'ifa (False Memoirs)*, in which Laylā sacrifices her career for the man she truly loves, but social malice leads her husband, Rashād, to think she has betrayed him. Without making the slightest effort to check the truth of what he has been told, he beats her so severely that she loses her eyesight and the child that she is carrying. Yet Laylā still refuses to give evidence against her husband in court, believing that he is just as much a victim of society as she is of his abuse. Rashād learns the truth about his wife once it is too late for Laylā; the damage he has caused her is too grave to heal. Even so, as the novel draws to a close, Rashād is once more uttering unfounded generalizations, this time about Sāmīyah, the woman who becomes his wife and the mother of his child after he divorces Laylā. Laylā herself reminds him of the important lesson he should have learned from her own disastrous experience: "Do not judge her before reading her letter" (p. 238). And Sāmīyah's letter proves him wrong once again.

The language of this social realist novel is particularly accessible, the development of events is logical, and the characters are credible human beings. The author's message is subtly conveyed and deftly handled throughout.

All the novels cited above expose the injustice in the misconception of women as potential adulteresses. (The theme is not new, of course; Desdemona in Shakespeare's *Othello* was one such victim.) Arab women authors demonstrate that changing men's attitudes is the first step in achieving social reform. Notably, in spite of all the suffering inflicted on the heroines in these novels, the women bear no obvious hatred toward men. As champions of a greater cause than their own personal salvation, they offer genuine forgiveness and the ability to overcome their ordeals. Most important, the novels provide insight into women's ways of thinking, women's perspectives, and women's vision. Yet whether women genuinely forgive and forget the ills men perpetrate on them is very much open to question.

In'ām al-Musālima's *Al-Ḥubb wa al-Waḥl (Love and Mud)* seems to follow logically from the novels discussed above. In it, Dr. Aḥmad represents the consequences of men's behavior and attitudes toward women. He falls in love with a female colleague, Īnās, who has foresworn romantic involvement ever since the man to whom she was devoted betrayed her. Dr Aḥmad seems to have experienced the revolution in thinking that women have sought, believing in gender equality and in the need for woman's companionship. In the reader's first encounter with Dr. Aḥmad, we discover that he does not see women as sexual objects. He writes to a friend: "I used to deny Eve intellectual parity with men. I used to see her as a pretty, silly doll. Getting to know her closely has liberated me from such terrible attitudes and encouraged me to respect her. I wonder who has changed, me or her" (p. 20).

Dr. Aḥmad describes this change in himself as a triumph over his own weakness: "Having overcome the human weakness in me and having failed to find a male mentor, I decided to be the pioneering example in my attitude to women" (p. 21). Despite all social temptations and pressures, he refuses to marry any woman who fails to command his respect. When a friend of his is paralyzed, he finds even more reasons to cling to his beliefs. Looking at his friend's grief-stricken wife, who is unable to offer her husband either help or solace, he remembers his beloved Īnās: "If she were Īnās, she would have encouraged her husband and helped him to preserve his dignity and pride despite the loss of his legs" (p. 121). The message here is that both men and women are better off with strong companions rather than weak dependents.

Īnās, however, is beset with a different set of problems. She was the only child, and everyone felt she should have been a boy so that she could inherit her father's name and wealth: "At home, on the streets and at people's houses I hear people mumbling 'had she been a boy . . . if only she were a boy'" (p. 78). In spite of the shame and humiliation these comments invite, she later begins to understand that her family did not want a girl for other sound reasons. She says, addressing her deceased father, "May God bless your soul; you didn't want a girl because you didn't want your daughter to be a prey to wild beasts, may God bless you and forgive me" (p. 97). Elsewhere she argues (pp. 92–93), "Instead of dreading the birth of a girl, why don't men change their attitude to women, all of whom are their sisters, wives and mothers, and stop treating them as sex objects?"

Īnās is acutely aware of her status as less than a man's equal within the rigid, patriarchal structure she inhabits, so she decides to command her society's respect by developing a masculine mask and denying herself all expressions of femininity:

> I am a woman who wanted to be man's equal, so I have to suppress all my feelings and smother my emotions and live a dreary life. I am a woman, but can't lead a woman's life; I look like a man, but I don't feel like one. I am always concerned that my smile might be slightly

broader than expected, that I might have stood with a male colleague one minute more than I should have. Eventually, they called me a "hermit" and a "Sufi." I was neither. I was full of feminine passion and feeling but I wanted to keep my self-esteem and pride so badly. (pp. 86–87)

Thus, in her endeavor to avoid being denigrated as a person, she has to reject what is most precious and essential to her as a woman: her emotions and feelings. Dignity and respectability are male traits, and to acquire them, women have to assume the character of a man, even to dress as men, to pass as men, and thus achieve great success.

Another Arab woman writer, Su'ād Zuhayr from Egypt, examines the different nuances and consequences of just such a situation in her novel *I'tirāfāt Imra'a Mustarjila (Confessions of a Masculine Woman)* (discussed in detail in Chapter 4). The theme of the masculine woman as the only woman allowed professional equality with men recurs time and again in Arabic literature. Apart from the many works by Arab women, some male Arab writers, such as Tahar Ben Jelloun in his novel *Ibnat al-Rimāl (The Sand Child)*, also propose that women adopt a masculine veneer so as to be able to function on an equal footing with men.

The deeply entrenched notion of the inferiority of the female and femininity is detrimental to women's very existence. At its root is the assumption that femininity is the antithesis of professionalism and respectability. Thus masculinity becomes a prerequisite for any meaningful activity. That is why feminists have argued that women's ways of doing things, though different, may well prove to be as valid and as useful as men's methods. In other words, instead of being defined by the already dominant male culture, feminists claim that women should be allowed to embrace their femininity so that its benefits may be experienced by both men and women. In this context, it should be noted that the veneer of masculinity adopted by men is diametrically opposed to genuine feminist values.

In *Al-Ḥubb wa al-Waḥl*, Īnās is deeply aware of the magnitude of her deprivation caused by her wish to be treated as a respected equal. When she eventually sheds her masculine mask for the man she loves, he abandons her without justification. The only apparent explanation for his behavior is that he may have loved her as a strong, masculine woman, but when he discovers that she has feminine traits, he changes his mind. Men fear that feminine women may be "oversexed" and therefore prone to adultery. That is why so many women are reluctant to express their emotions freely, even to their husbands, for fear of suspicions that might arise in men's minds. Īnās once more withdraws into her shell, determined to protect herself from further emotional upheaval. She decides never again to become emotionally involved, "not because of my love for the man who had left me, but as a measure to preserve my dignity and self-esteem" (p. 98). For this reason, she refuses to respond to Dr. Aḥmad's earnest advances and departs to live with her mother. The novel closes with Dr. Aḥmad still awaiting Īnās's return.

Some critics have described Īnās as a sick, masochistic, convoluted human being who enjoys torturing herself and others and rejects love for no obvious reason. Ḥusām al-Khaṭīb, for example, claims this novel is an excellent example of women's literature that reflects women's perverted psychology (March 1976, p. 81). In fact, the heroine is trying to stress that she has achieved professional equality, but at the expense of her precious femininity and values. Īnās wants a place where she can be both professional and feminine without being considered inferior as soon as her femininity becomes apparent. It is notable that as early as 1963, al-Musālima was searching in her novel for a place where women could function as *women* rather than as honorary men, and she tries to liberate femininity from its second-rate, second-class status. This realist novel is a novel of protest like *Anā Aḥyā (I Live)* by Laylā Baʿalbakī and *Ayyām Maʿahu (Days with Him)* by Colette Khūrī, but the protest here is about obtaining the right to resist a humiliating social system; it is a type of passive resistance.

Problematically, the author never quite makes up her mind about her technique. She starts with an epistolary method that is soon abandoned. Nevertheless, the novel is both socially and psychologically realistic. It probes the depth of both male and female psychology and exposes the social hypocrisy that forces men and women to uphold double standards in order to perform gender-determined roles.

By abstaining from marriage, entering a convent, or facing their own death "happily," these heroines make a statement. They protest a social system in which women have no place to function on their own terms. The use of suicide and migration as a means of escape does not mean, as many male critics have suggested, that the "heroines [have] ended up where they started" or that "the novelists are convinced that this is the logical result for such a behavior."[16] The problem is that such misinterpretations are passed down from one generation of students to the next, and they sometimes quote these interpretations without reading the text to which they are referring.

Women novelists have often allowed their heroines to commit suicide when there seems to be no way out, just as women in real life have, much more often than men, resorted to suicide to express their fundamental objections to the circumstances of their lives. Thus, women in central Asia are still expected (often encouraged) to burn themselves to death as a means of cleansing a social shame.

Just as in *The Awakening,* Kate Chopin's heroine committed suicide in the late nineteenth century, "E," the heroine of Evelyne Accad's *L'excisée (The Excised),* finds no way out but to kill herself in the twentieth century. A mature, aware, and strong woman, E still surrenders her pregnant body to the sea after family, lover, husband, and society have crushed every living nerve in her:

> E. looks at the woman, the children, the sea. She is not able to swallow what she has on her plate. A constriction in her throat makes eating impossible. She looks at the ship and the passengers climbing the gangway. Will she at last succeed in coming to the end of the road? And Nūr, will she truly find the sunlight? How often must one cross the seas to understand? She wonders. (p. 80)

Accad's exploration in *L'excisée* of the limitations imposed on a woman who flees her father's house with her lover, only to discover that her lover has become an oppressive husband, is very reminiscent of Kate Chopin's *The Awakening*. In the latter novel, Chopin looks at the constraints on a woman's identity in Creole society in New Orleans at the turn of the twentieth century, and at the difficulties of trying to create a real space for the development and fulfillment of a woman's personal and artistic potential. Edna Pontellier moves out of her husband's house to "a room of her own," a place where she can be alone with her thoughts and develop her talents as a writer, free to love whoever she pleases. She finds, however, that although she can make choices for herself, she cannot change or escape society's values and expectations. Condemned as immoral by a world that had once revered her and ultimately finding her lover as narrow-minded as her husband, she walks to her death into the sea in a final exhilarating statement of defiance and despair.

How many generations of women will despair to the point of choosing death over life before we all begin to understand why women choose to commit suicide? Having lost the last shred of hope, after a history of resistance, defiance, struggle, and sacrifice, E in *L'excisée* unhesitatingly "goes into the waters which close over her. She goes to her rest. She goes to the silence" (p. 81). Edna Pontellier in *The Awakening* does exactly the same thing. An important difference, however, between E's suicide and other suicides encountered in earlier novels is that E has opened the way for other women: she has left the banner with Nūr. Nūr says:

I hope she will be proud of me, for she has saved me. Thanks to her I have seen the sunshine and the light. Thanks to her I shall never wear the stifling mask on my face. I was called Nūr[17] at my birth, but without her I would never know the light of day. I must live to help my other sisters. That is what she would have wished, isn't it? (p. 85)

When I asked Evelyne Accad why E was not allowed to live, she confirmed my own understanding of the novel by saying: "She committed suicide instead of me. I was on the verge of committing suicide, and by writing this novel and making E do it I seem to have saved myself."[18] How many other women novelists have written a novel to save their own lives?

Suffocating social and historical conditions have turned Rāniya into a pawn in Emily Naṣrallah's novel, *Al-Rahīna (The Pawn)*, seemingly without any good reason. Having been donated since her babyhood by her poor parents to their feudal master, Rāniya feels a moral obligation to fulfill her parents' wishes. Her father had always been indebted to the *Bayk* (feudal lord) "for his life and subsistence, and used the chance of promising him his daughter in order to pay off his debt" (p. 127). Her parents owed the *Bayk*; she was the only payment they were able to afford. Hence, rejecting the *Bayk* would forever enslave her parents to him and visit upon them social, financial, and moral bankruptcy. Therefore, she cannot say no.

Such selflessness is expected of women, but the moment they start to understand and interpret their roles and duties differently from this selfless ethic, they are objects of revulsion and denigration. Rayyā, the heroine of another novel by Emily Naṣrallah, *Shajarat al-Diflā (The Oleander Tree)*, faces a similar situation. Rayyā understands the abuse and harassment bequeathed on her in the name of love and care. When she tries to construct her own life differently from that which is expected of her, she is humiliated, socially denounced, and finally driven to suicide.

In Naṣrallah's novels, as in those written by Sakākīnī, Nuwaylātī, al-Bāti', and Musālima, the heroines are incapable of articulating their views or stipulating their innocence. One male critic asks why Arwā did not scream in the face of her attackers, why she internalized her struggle. Those who pose the question, however, do not know what it means not to have a voice or what it takes to acquire one. Mustering the courage to scream, to speak up, to reject or protest, is halfway toward winning the battle, but it is certainly not easy to achieve.

This pioneering generation of Arab women novelists has made a heartening plea for parity, but in a subtle way. What women sought, as these novels demonstrate, is not "sameness" but rather equal opportunity with men. The novels discussed in this chapter are samples of a literature yet to be discovered. The day will come when these writings by women will be part and parcel of Arabic literature and of school and university curricula.

CHAPTER 4

The Emergence of the New Woman

IN 1950 EGYPTIAN WRITER Amīna al-Sa'īd (1914–1995) published *Al-Jāmiḥa (The Wild Woman)* in the Egyptian series Iqra'. Books published in this series, edited by Ṭāha Ḥusayn (1889–1973), 'Abbās Maḥmūd al-'Aqqād (1889–1964), and Fu'ād Ṣarrūf (1900–1985), were distributed throughout the Arab world. The series was popular, read by all age groups and appreciated by all classes of people. Amīna al-Sa'īd was a pioneering educator at Cairo University who tutored generations of scholars and writers. Sadly, however, *Al-Jāmiḥa* has long been out of print and is quite difficult to locate.

The adjective *jāmiḥa* in Arabic means "wild." The masculine *jāmiḥ* is more frequently used than the feminine, often to describe a difficult, unmanageable horse. In Arabic the word is the antithesis of everything gentle or feminine. Yet in this novel it describes a woman, Amīra, an artist who has the heart of a poet and whose paintings rate among the best that have been produced in her country.

Because she is a woman, life has endowed her with a fine sensitivity and the emotions that might have sufficed for ten people (p. 6). It is interesting to compare the title of this novel, written in the 1950s, with those written by Arab women a decade or two later. Among the latter titles that come to mind are *Murāhiqa (The Adolescent)* by Mājida al-'Aṭṭār; *Widā' ma' al-Aṣīl (Farewell at Sunset)* by Fatḥiyya Maḥmūd al-Bāti'; *Mudhakkarāt Imra'a Ghayr Wāqi'iyya (Memoirs of an Unrealistic Woman)* by Saḥar Khalīfa; *I'tirāfāt Imra'a Mustarjila (Confessions of a Masculine Woman)* by Su'ād Zuhayr; *Ayyām Ma'ahu (Days with Him)* by Colette Khūrī; and *Anā Aḥyā (I Live)* by Laylā Ba'albakī. It is noticeable that these titles either express a desire for reform and change or suggest something unrealistic, "silly," or adolescent, apparently justifying the opinion that women have a different vision and style.

Al-Jāmiḥa is a social-psychological novel that provides an excellent critique of the idea of masculine as superior and feminine as inferior. It probes in depth the psychological and social life of its hero and heroine.

Amīra's prospects for artistic excellence and achievement are jeopardized because of her father's insistence on raising her as a boy. *Al-Jāmiḥa* may be seen as a psychological version of Tahir Ben Jelloun's much-acclaimed novel *Ibnat al-Rimāl (The Sand Child)*, in which the father announces that his wife has given birth to a boy and gives his daughter the name of a boy, attempting in vain to make her mind and body function like that of a man. In the end, she is neither woman nor man but a social misfit.

Amīra loses her mother at a very early age and is raised by a loving and caring father. He sees his daughter's femininity and artistic aptitude as signs of weakness, however, so he decides to prepare her for the harshness of life as an independent individual and sets out to rid her of her "female weaknesses." He models her upon himself, regardless of his daughter's own sense of self or of her instincts or emotions. She becomes confused and loses any sense of right and wrong. His well-meaning but harsh training of Amīra to be a man rather than a woman irreparably damages her character.

As an only child who has lost her mother, Amīra cherishes her mother's framed picture to which she tells her little girl's secrets and from which she tries to seek advice. When she attempts to learn more about her mother and asks whether the doctor can't bring her back, her father rebukes her for showing such weakness over the loss of her mother. He tells her time and again that he hates tears and other expressions of pain because they represent human weakness, and he does not want his daughter to be weak. She never mentions her deceased mother again.

Another, more decisive juncture in Amīra's childhood occurs when she breaks the neck of a favorite doll. She wants to see it mended so as not to lose her companion, but her father insists that there is no point in keeping a broken toy. She is shamed by her father's rational argument into throwing the toy away. The incident traumatizes her and finds expression in a painting she creates at a much later stage in her life.

As she is completely unable to challenge her father's will, Amīra resigns herself to doing his bidding, regardless of her feelings. She suffers from an alienation that continues to mark her adolescent and adult relationships alike. Her father acts with the best intent when he creates this emotional and psychological turmoil for his daughter. He wants her to be strong, so that she cannot easily be hurt. But having no power to be heard, much less listened to, she reverts to her mother's picture as her only social and psychological outlet.

Many female heroines in novels written by Arab women establish their closest relationships with inanimate objects—objects outside the human society in which they live. In *Murāhiqa (The Adolescent)* by Mājida al-ʿAṭṭār, for example, the main character, Lamyāʾ, establishes the only meaningful relationship in her life with a jasmine tree, so much so that the jasmine tree becomes the only object through which Lamyāʾs perspectives are given a hearing. Both Lamyāʾ in *Murāhiqa* and Amīra in *Al-Jāmiḥa* suffer from serious negative social conditioning, which means that they are unable to express their views, let alone enable them to be accepted as valid. Amīra finds solace in nature, wishing she were "a bird living in nature, free and independent, flying up and down as she pleases and following nothing but her natural, spontaneous free movements away from all conditioning traditions" (al-Saʿīd, p. 39). Similarly, in *Murāhiqa*, Lamyāʾ says: "Why am I not a palm tree to be moved by the wind, shaken by the storm, to be bent or even hurt but never broken or destroyed?" (al-ʿAṭṭār, p. 83).

Throughout her life, Amīra fails to have any meaningful relationships with colleagues, friends, or husband. She is confused and out of touch with her own feelings. She can only be herself outside the boundaries of society, which dismisses or denigrates her views. One evening, for example, she contrasts her relationship with her husband to her relationship with a star that she watches from her window: "The star is affectionate and understanding; unlike my husband, whose evaluative looks fill me with apprehension and fear" (al-Saʿīd, p. 156).

Her father's prolonged silences weigh on Amīra as much as his words and actions. When she breaks her doll, he sits next to her "for minutes which seem ages and says not a word, his face seen across the ascending smoke of his cigarette seems to her like a terrifying nightmare" (al-Saʿīd, p. 29). The scene is reminiscent of that in Evelyne Accad's *L'excisée (The Excised)*, in which the heroine speaks eloquently of the silence of her father, the agony of which can be more wrenching than physical punishment:

> He hardly speaks to her. These silences announce a storm and a tempest. She becomes more and more aware that he must know something. These attitudes, these looks, these prayers, these heavy and long meals, these silences are familiar things to her. He is preparing to do something. Something is going to burst out in the house. Something is going to explode in the city. The waiting is agonizing. She draws back more and more into the corners of the house to avoid Papa, to escape meeting his eyes, "to not to have to see" Mama brought to her knees, to no longer feel the menace and the reproaches following her everywhere. (Accad, p. 30)

The silence of Amīra's father finds expression much later in her life in a painting of a young child clutching a broken toy: "her face spoke volumes of misery, frustration and loss of confidence" (al-Sa'īd, p. 180). Salmā, the bereaved heroine of Fathiyya Maḥmūd al-Bāti''s novel *Widā' ma' al-Aṣīl (Farewell at Sunset)*, also resorts to painting to express her feelings about the tragic day in 1948 when an Israeli soldier killed her young son while he was lying on her lap. Painting, like writing, is a means of self-expression and sometimes of social protest. Amīra says of her painting: "The painting is not just about a child who broke her toy; it is about a woman whose happiness was absolutely shattered and who had to spend the rest of her life in pain and regret" (al-Sa'īd, p. 181). The child "who was confused in dealing with her toy becomes the woman who is unable to discern right from wrong" (p. 184).

Amīra fails to marry the man she loves; the man she does marry leaves her, and the novel closes with her back in her father's house, sitting on the balcony waiting for "another opportunity to rectify what has been lost" (p. 191).

The lesson to be learned from Amīra's experience is that what is logical for men can be fatally damaging for women. No argument should be needed to justify the way women feel. It is society's privileging the masculine as a source of strength and condemning the feminine as weak that is at issue here. The narrative does not hold the father guilty for trying to ensure the well-being of his daughter. When his parenting habits have the opposite effect from what he intended, he is revealed as a victim of society's misguided priorities. The novel questions social precepts and suggests we discard those that are detrimental to happiness.

Al-Jāmiḥa also invites the reader to reconsider his or her inherited notions of the "rational" as glorious and the emotional as disreputable. The novel's underlying message accepts and vindicates the existence of difference. Additionally, the novel testifies to the validity of human emotions, which raises serious questions about the habitual labeling of some emotions as expressions of weakness rather than simply indicative of being human. The novel's controlled and well-guided argument explores these themes through suggestion and example. The fact that Amīra is a seriously disturbed and certainly unhappy woman calls into question her father's effort to arm her against the "weaknesses" of her own sex.

Al-Jāmiḥa is written in the third person, which is in keeping with its controlled, yet profoundly feminist, argument. The author's stream of consciousness technique weaves a matrix of interactions and correlations between Amīra's different experiences. The characters are well-rounded mixtures of strength and weakness, good and bad. They are credible products of their society and the human condition. This forthright critique of the prevalent social ethos of feminine and masculine values paved the way for a more radically outspoken questioning of these values that caused a storm in the Arab world in 1958.[1]

In the Arab world, the 1950s and 1960s were the age of "isms." Societies debated the meaning and relevance of nationalism, secularism, communism, and socialism. Political parties and social movements emerged at that time to express the fervent social and political dynamism then prevalent. Nationalist political parties, such as the Ba'ath party in Syria and Iraq, had already captivated Arab audiences, and socialist and secular parties mushroomed. They had a great impact on the writings of men and women, especially those that focused on women's rights and feminist concerns, as an overview of some of the works published at the time demonstrates.

The first striking difference between *Al-Jāmiḥa* (1950) and the novels *Anā Aḥyā (I Live)* by Laylā Ba'albakī and *Ayyām Ma'ahu (Days with Him)* by Colette Khūrī, published in 1958 and 1959, respectively, is that the latter two are written in the first person. For the first time in these books, Arab women novelists provided their heroines with unorthodox, challenging roles and allowed them to refer to themselves. Additionally, in these two novels, women's perspectives are the paradigms according to which social and moral values operate. Both Līnā in *Anā Aḥyā* and Rīm in *Ayyām Ma'ahu* question every aspect of Arab women's lives, accepting nothing but the dictates of their own minds and feelings. The opening paragraph in *Anā Aḥyā* sets the tone for the entire novel:

> I thought, as I was crossing the road between our house and the railway station, whose is this warm hair scattered on my shoulders? Isn't it mine? Doesn't every living creature have his/her own hair with which he/she does what he/she pleases? Am I not free to despise this hair that attracts attention to me until my very being has become epitomized by its presence? Am I not free to grant the hairdresser the pleasure of cutting its locks and throwing them between his feet to be carried to a rusty tin? Am I not free to pay the hairdresser more than one visit, to please my eyes with the sight of his sharp instrument as it cuts, eats and kills? In the evening, once I come back from work I'll pull my heavy legs to the shop with the sharp instrument. I feel a passionate desire to hear destruction, to see bodies, to gaze at hard, rough and unmerciful fingers. (p. 1)

This paragraph sets the tone for the argument and the action of the novel. Right from the beginning, the heroine departs from the expectations of an Arab woman. To reject long hair, the symbol of femininity, is the first step toward rejecting social conditioning and patriarchal authority.

Anā Aḥyā is a social realist novel that uses monologue and stream of consciousness to expose different aspects of social reality. Dialogue is rarely used, though when it is, it emphasizes the deep sense of alienation that pervades the heroine's relations with all members of her society. Līnā Fayyāḍ, the heroine, carefully scrutinizes class, gender, social, and political relations, and her conclusions are always at variance with everyone else's.

The novel is written in a simple, poetic language that holds the reader's attention from beginning to end. Līnā is the main character, although the other characters, presented mainly through her perspective, seem credible. In a society in which social hypocrisy is rampant, the heroine is a woman who eschews hypocrisy to be herself in order to feel worthy of being alive. Hence the title, *I Live*.

Many writers throughout history have discovered that the truth is too difficult to accept, often too difficult to state or even acknowledge. For that reason, language is sometimes used to present difficult facts in a favorable light. The heroine expresses an unconventional viewpoint and suggests a very different approach to addressing various issues. For Līnā, life is only worth living if she faces up to the reality of her own condition. Early on, she makes the decision not to align herself with the hypocritical attitudes, beliefs, and values of the society she lives in, whether at home, at the university, in the workplace, or in the political arena. The source of her inspiration is her unshaken belief that the personal is ultimately political.

As the daughter of a wealthy man, Līnā is not expected to work. She seeks work, however, because she disapproves of the way her father manipulates political events and uses people to accumulate more wealth. The link between wealth and social respectability infuriates her: "In no time we've become among the wealthiest. My father is proud of his wealth and of his friendship with the French [colonial authorities]. As if his accumulated wealth is not cut from the subsistence of thousands of families who were only given barley and corn by the French" (p. 34). She also realizes that her father is responsible for the disappearance of certain basic commodities from the market. She is shocked by his lack of concern for his people and by his total absorption with his personal wealth and his children's future prospects, including their inheritance. She has no respect for him and feels sorry for her mother, "who breeds, cooks, and sleeps while he pursues his desires with other women" (p. 22).

Like Virginia Woolf in *Mrs. Dalloway*, Laylā Baʿalbakī in *Anā Aḥyā* uses the stream of consciousness technique to allow her heroine to observe what is happening, to move between past and present, and to comment from her own perspective. Just as events and characters are seen through Mrs. Dalloway's eyes, Līnā introduces readers of *Anā Ahyā* to Lebanese society. Like Mrs. Dalloway, Līnā walks in the streets, observes, remembers, reflects, and comments, but always as an external observer who is not governed by generally acceptable codes of behavior. Her objective is to explore the intricacies of the problems that cause her to be alienated from the society in which she finds herself. Seemingly these problems are personal, but in essence they are profoundly political. Although Līnā is disturbed by the tripartite aggression against Egypt in 1956 and by the unpredictable consequences of the nationalization of the Suez Canal, she acknowledges that she has no ready solution for the problems of Palestine, Kashmir, or Algeria. She stresses the personal as the quintessence of the social and political.

At a personal level she pursues simple rights, such as watching a movie on her own. She reveals the subtle nuances of the psychological harassment to which women are subjected, particularly those who aspire to live an independent life. Another problem Ba'albakī reveals is the male tendency to see a proud, independent woman as a loose, permissive woman. Līnā's experience with her colleague, who can see only her body, despite the extraordinary lengths to which she goes to demonstrate her parity with him, pinpoints the confusion in the minds of Arab men. They have not yet made up their minds whether they want women to be their servants or their equals. They do not understand women's quest for freedom as a basic human need, rather than a form of promiscuity.

In Līnā's opinion, it is not only men who are to blame for this state of affairs. She believes that women perpetuate their status by acquiescing in their given roles of dolls and fashion consumers. An impenetrable problem for her is that her colleagues only ever see how she looks but are never genuinely interested in what she says. In a sense, she is never taken seriously: "They wrangle with each other for a kiss or a touch of my breasts, but they never hear what I say about politics, Palestine, or Algeria" (p. 103). Here she raises a very interesting problem. Men have always read in women's writing what they want to read and have seen in women what they want to see. What they don't want to read and don't want to see, they ignore.

Līnā takes a stand not only on gender and class issues but also "on party politics, military alliances, religious beliefs and the future of the nation . . . I am thinking of clarifying my stand about all these issues" (p. 129). For Līnā, her personal fears stem from her broad social and political concerns, whereas her boss is concerned only about the possible repercussions of social and political changes on his own position and prestige.

Līnā has major differences with all the people around her about politics. Colleagues, friends, and her potential lover, Bahā', express loyalty to political parties and talk of ideologies and the masses. By contrast, Līnā believes that "our progress toward a better future should start with the individual" (p. 171). Men speak about millions of people and society; she speaks about the individual and the family. In this respect, *Anā Aḥyā* is a novel about the voice of an independent individual who endeavors to establish the dignity and sanity of the individual, set against party loyalty, class privileges, and family considerations. At the time this novel was published in the late 1950s, the Arab world, as well as the world at large, was awash with ideologies. This novel tries to discredit ideologies in favor of the individual's voice and freedom. Had it been published in 1988, when disillusionment with party politics started to set in, it might well have been welcomed as topical and timely. Unfortunately, it was written and published thirty years earlier, ahead of its time.

Līnā's protest against social and political precepts is analogous to her rejection of the stereotypical classification of women as objects with desirable legs, breasts, and arms. Her rejection of party politics stems from the same premise as her refusal to be part of the institution of marriage. In both instances, her reasons have to do with her concern for her own freedom and independence. She decides never to marry so long as the rules dictate that "I am the slave and he is the master, I carry out what he demands, I live the hunger and he eats, I wait and he decides the time of action" (p. 195). Instead, she looks for a man with whom she can share watching the news, reading books, going to a movie, smoking a cigarette, and setting a table. "I want a man with whom I can share both the pleasures and burdens of life, in a relationship in which there is no inferior or superior . . . Only then can I feel that I am truly alive" (pp. 196, 199).

As her experience in life broadens and deepens, Līnā discovers that she has very little in common with her family, friends, and colleagues. Even Bahā', who initially seemed to understand her own perspective, turns out to be essentially one of "them," leaving her to face the intractable dilemma of how and where she can function: "I cannot move, I cannot live in any place or any time" (p. 212). Here Līnā predicts the dilemma of 'Afāf, the heroine in Saḥar Khalīfa's novel *Mudhakkarāt Imra'a Ghayr Wāqi'iyya (Memoirs of an Unrealistic Woman)*, published in 1986. 'Afāf is portrayed unrealistically because no realistic social context exists within which she can function as her true self. She shares one major problem with Līnā: her views are often dismissed before they are even considered. Both novels use monologue and stream of consciousness, with very little dialogue. It is sad to come across 'Afāf, almost thirty years after Līnā, only to find her suffering from a very similar feeling of alienation from family and society, and to find that although time has moved on, no more space has been provided for women.

The outcry that followed the publication of *Anā Aḥyā* was enormous. Laylā Ba'albakī was accused of indecency and immorality. She was perplexed and confused and did not know how to continue. The introduction to her second novel, *Al-Āliha al-Mamsūkha (The Dwarf Gods)*, reveals that the negative response of the public weighed heavily upon her mind:

> If *Anā Aḥyā* was a spontaneous novel that challenges the familiar ways of writing long stories in which the problems of characters are discussed simply and clearly, I tried to make *Al-Āliha al-Mamsūkha* a more complicated novel with a difficult and elaborate structure. In contrast, the structure of *Anā Aḥyā* was organic, like a transparent, smooth silk thread that, though unseen, holds the novel together. Instead of one heroine who was the center of events in *Anā Aḥyā*, I created many characters in *Al-Āliha al Mamsūkha* and tried to endow them with a similar ability to control their own destinies. (p. 5)

Now, over thirty years after the publication of both novels, the superiority of Ba'albakī's first novel is recognized by critics, even though at the time she was accused of giving expression to her own ego at the expense of family and social ethics. In the introduction to her second novel, she defends herself as follows: "I do not deny that my writing carries my own voice, my own breath and the pulses of my own mind; it has the prints of my own fingers, but many a time I stand surprised at my own discoveries" (p. 6). It seems odd that a writer should feel the need to defend herself against having her own voice in her writing. Surely that is a most excellent attribute, one that has been appreciated from the time of Socrates to that of Max Fischer and Naguib Maḥfouẓ. Had Laylā Ba'albakī been spared the public outcry after her first novel, she might well have enriched Arabic literature with other comparable works that everyone might have found both pleasurable and thought-provoking.

In 1988, almost thirty years after the publication of Colette Khūrī's first novel, *Ayyām Ma'ahu (Days with Him)*, journalists still ask: "Did your heroines do what you yourself were unable to do at the time?" Or, more generally speaking, "Was this the function of literature written by women in Syria at the time?"[2] These questions epitomize the criticism of Khūrī's novels, a criticism that views Khūrī as an advocate of sexual permissiveness and her literary work as a deviation from Arab ethics and culture. Many critics referred to Khūrī as an upper-class woman who had no need to work and who therefore turned to writing as a means of spending time and shaking off the fetters of a woman's body. That is totally untrue. For Colette Khūrī, writing was a way to change the existing social order through scrutiny of its most significant and sensitive links. In most cases, criticism of her novels demonstrates the critics' failure to grasp their themes or to explore the dimensions and objectives of her writings. Ironically, the criticism often imposes values and precepts on Khūrī's works that the author specifically set out to undermine. Below I offer a reading of *Ayyām Ma'ahu*, Khūrī's most frequently discussed novel, which is considered both the best and most notorious of her five novels.[3]

Ayyām Ma'ahu can be read at three interrelated levels regarding the woman, the man, and society. At the beginning, it becomes clear that the pivotal level is that of the woman. Characters use both dialogue and monologue and enjoy a great degree of flexibility and freedom. They have their own distinct, independent worlds and sustain meaningful interaction with each other.

The novel comprises four parts. The first two parts and the fourth are of similar length, whereas the third part is the largest and most integral. In each, the relationship of the heroine, Rīm, with her lover, Ziyād, or fiancé, Alfred, assumes a new dimension and a different abode. In this sense the structure of the novel is instrumental in clarifying and heightening its argument.

The novel opens with Rīm, the heroine, questioning social judgments of her as a woman and contrasting her ambitions with the meager opportunities available to her as a woman in her social sphere. She asks herself: "Just because I am a young, candid woman and I write poetry, should I be condemned? Sometimes I start to doubt myself and wonder whether I am truly a woman who causes problems to her family, only because she is ambitious, she has dignity and wants to live" (p. 17). From this point onward, the novel explores Rīm's point of view, which is quintessentially different from that of her society. Rīm not only rejects the prevalent modes of thinking and behavior but also suggests alternative social and human values that might operate, thus introducing a new element to Arab women's literature. As a character, Rīm is all the more impressive because she refuses to reach her objectives through being a hypocrite. She candidly discusses her duty to herself and her society and tries to establish a logical relationship between the two. In the process she exposes hypocritical practices and calls for the adoption of a single standard in both the personal and public domains.

Rīm is deeply aware of both her potential and actual self. She is resolute about conducting her relationships in ways that fulfill this potential. Her first confrontation with her family is about her right to work.

Daughters of wealthy families such as hers do not "need" to earn their living. But work for her means something else. She screams in the face of her family: "I need my life, my personality, my individuality; I need to know that I live" (p. 27). For Rīm, as well as for Līnā in *Anā Aḥyā'*, to live is to be oneself, to have a voice and to have a say. Wherever she turns she has to fight a battle because the gap between her ideas of decency and righteous behavior and those of the society she lives in is far too wide.

As far as family and society are concerned, she is engaged to Alfred, who is in Paris continuing his studies, thus rendering her "unavailable" to other men. But she feels no obligation to Alfred or he to her, and they both agree to live their own independent lives. It is interesting to note that in her relationship with Ziyād, the man she loves, she exercises more genuine self-restraint than that which society requires from her with her official fiancé. She dismisses social control, exchanging it for a more meaningful personal compass that takes into account her dignity and self-esteem. Thus, the conflict between her vision and existing social practices grows as the narrative proceeds.

Rīm is as uncompromising with the man she loves as she is with her family and society. She understands that Ziyād is the product of his own society but is nevertheless determined not only to reeducate him but also to redefine femininity and masculinity for him. She says to herself: "This man is a child whom I understand and excuse . . . his approach is the result of superficial and misconstrued experiences. I'll grant him love and affection and prove to him that women can be friends and companions and that emotion is the gist of being human" (p. 92). It is evident that Rīm's argument also embraces men's emancipation from their wrongly held attitudes toward women. At the conclusion of the first part of the novel, the reader feels that a strong distinction has been drawn between social, masculine, and feminine perspectives, with the aim of establishing a degree of understanding and compatibility among these three different viewpoints.

The second part of the novel highlights the ambivalence that most Arab men still feel about women's liberation. Rīm's relationship with Ziyād shows that Arab men are still confused and conflicted about the new woman. In principle, they seem to be staunch supporters of women's liberation, but in practice they are all too eager to demonstrate that their wives, mothers, and sisters remain traditional women. The crux of the matter seems to be that such men still confuse responsible independence with permissiveness and immorality. Such an attitude throws women into confusion. If they do not respond to men's advances, they are accused of being conservative and cowardly, but if they do, they are taken to be promiscuous. This dilemma is still a major problem in Arab women's lives in the twenty-first century.

Rīm, however, decides to do what she deems to be correct and leaves it to men and the outside world to understand the new woman. In the process she sheds light on existing differences between men's and women's concepts of love, relationships, sacrifice, and emotions. She finds women to be more emotional but adds the important qualification that deeply felt emotion is a sign of strength rather than weakness because it is the most precious quality in human nature. Armed with this appreciation of herself as a woman, Rīm endeavors to liberate Ziyād from his negative ideas about women and their emancipation: "I'll teach him how to be a human being. I'll plant in his greedy eyes a taste for passion; I'll sow in his arid self healthy values and shake the burdens of negative history off his shoulders" (p. 133).

The third part of the novel explores a love relationship that aims to go beyond that which currently exists in order to discover what is possible. Rīm reiterates the age-old question that was asked long ago by Mary Wollstonecraft, Mary Shelley, and George Eliot: "Why don't we consider love rather than marriage as the basis for relationships between men and women?"

Confident and self-assured, Rīm refuses to do anything covertly and acts in a way that she herself defines as dignified. As a result, she alienates herself from a society that favors discreet behavior in order to maintain a facade of respectability and social honor. Her relationship with Ziyād proves to her that as a woman she is truer to herself than he is to himself, perhaps because she has a more vested interest in change and has less to lose. In contrast, personal advantage guides her lover's respect for social norms, which he adopts and eschews at will. Occasionally, he even tacitly participates in punishing Rīm because she has challenged society for his sake.

Like Baʻalbakī, Khūrī discovers a woman's world with its minute details and broad dimensions. What is new is the sense of pride Rīm conveys about the values that she holds, regardless of her society's evaluation of them. In a monologue full of despair, Rīm recognizes the unbridgeable gap between her views and those of Ziyād.

> What can I possibly say to a man who considers woman a toy, dough which he can hurt, throw aside or extinguish, and then, whenever he chooses, with a little effort restore her to her original shape? He fails to understand that my Self is like a transparent crystal; once it is damaged, his life-long efforts cannot restore it to what it once was. (p. 233)

Just before the conclusion of part three, an interesting issue is raised. Rīm's fiancé, Alfred, whom she likes but does not love, arrives. Family and friends try their best to create opportunities for her to do whatever she pleases with him, while they all condemn her for meeting with the man she genuinely loves. In her relationships with both lover and fiancé, she is governed only by her sense of what is right and proper. The puzzle here is that the reader does not expect Rīm to maintain her relationship with her fiancé once she has decided that there's no future in this relationship. That may present a measure of compromise on Rīm's behalf for the sake of family peace.

To her great disappointment, Rīm discovers that Ziyād only loves her when she plays the role of the traditional woman who fears people's opinion and doesn't dare appear with him in public. Because Ziyād fails to appreciate the new woman in her, she decides to end their relationship and devote herself to her art and writing: "I am at a crossroads; which one to take? And suddenly a third endless road appears; a road lined with stars, with smiles and roses. I look again at the stars and find them to be smiling letters. I feel the need to tread this way, tell it my secrets, to embrace my letters and live among them" (p. 348). Through a well-structured and convincing turn of events, the heroine liberates herself from both social pressures and traditional norms to the extent that the novel closes with Rīm realizing her self-potential and becoming fully in control of her life and destiny. Near the end she says to herself: "Ziyād today is as I have always wished him to be, but I am as I should be. We both have changed" (p. 359).

This change is neither abrupt nor sudden. The change becomes possible because of the writer's ability to probe in depth the inner lives of both men and women and to examine them through nontraditional lenses. In contrast to the prevalent image of women as weak, Rīm provides an example of women's singularity, audacity, and strength. The problem seems to lie in the fact that men are still unable to accept women as their equals and companions. Hence the novel is as much about Arab men who have not yet come to terms with the new woman as it is about the new Arab woman who is still trying to establish her identity. The novel clarifies that although the new Arab woman has definitely emerged, there is no new Arab man who is capable of accepting this woman as his companion. The novel is pessimistic with regard to men's attitudes toward women but optimistic regarding women's potential and capacities.

The characters are not static. They interact both with each other and with their reality and, as a result, continuously change their views and perspectives. The major female character, Rīm, has a very clear sense of identity and is undaunted in her pursuit of her objectives, despite all the difficulties she encounters. Her merit as a feminist is that she is neither bitter nor angry. She is working for a better future for herself, which ultimately will be better for men, too. She fully realizes that men, like women, are the product of their social reality and that therefore they need to be reeducated rather than confronted by women.

In her novel *I'tirāfāt Imra'a Mustarjila (Confessions of a Masculine Woman)*, Su'ād Zuhayr starts where Colette Khūrī left off. The core of this novel is the struggle of a mature feminist against gender differences and social attitudes and beliefs that denigrate women. Samīḥa, the heroine, demonstrates what happens to an Arab woman after she completes a successful journey of self-discovery and self-realization. How does this new woman perform, and how is she received in her society? In all her actions, Samīḥa presents her struggle as an example of what her mother, sisters, cousins, and friends have suffered. Her formative experiences include witnessing the burdens under which her mother falters and the exploitation of her sister by the family doctor.

Samīḥa first tests the power of her femininity by casually flirting with a neighbor. To her horror, instead of giving her a kiss and a cuddle, which is what she expects, he attempts to rape her. At the age of fifteen, she is married off to a man she does not love, leaving a high school sweetheart because he cannot provide for her. She has no respect for a marriage document that signifies neither love nor desire. Having sex with her husband is like being sexually assaulted every day. Hence she has no qualms about leaving him and going back to her lover.

All her ordeals originate in the fact that she was born female. She has a twin brother, and at an early age she experiences the effects of gender discrimination. He is the apple of their mother and father's eye, whereas she is "just a girl." From childhood she learns to compete, to be more efficient than boys, in order to meet with just half the approval society voluntarily accords young males. The example of her mother, who always asks, "Where can I go if I leave your father?" shows her the importance of career and economic independence for every woman. Yet experience teaches her that "it is not enough for a woman to achieve economic independence in order to become a socially equal person with her own free will if she does not change her position as the man's emotional subservient. This emotional subservience leads the most courageous women to accept living as men's inferiors" (p. 106).

Like Rīm in *Ayyām Ma'ahu*, Samīḥa has her own independent set of values that hardly correspond to socially accepted norms. Despite her desire to be a mother, she refuses to bear a child to a man she does not love, even though he is her legitimate husband. Once she divorces him, men regard her as sexually available. Both at work and on the street, she puts on a masculine veneer and appears wanting in feeling and sympathy. She finds it necessary to protect herself from sexual harassment. The masculine mask she wears becomes important because it is all she has to protect her vulnerable femininity.

The novel is a thoughtful construction of the gender problems that still plague Arab societies. Throughout the novel, the heroine makes it abundantly clear that her struggle represents the fate of all women rather than only her personal destiny.

Like *Anā Aḥyā* and *Ayyām Ma'ahu*, this novel is written in the first person, which gives it strength and directness. The heroine rejects the male view of her as a sexual object, preferring to be seen as masculine or even asexual. Her ideal is a loving and caring relationship with a man who regards her as an equal. The novel very clearly suggests that no love can exist between two partners who do not see each other as equals. Hence her search for true love becomes a pursuit of genuine equality between men and women, and her self-styled masculinity becomes the most visible protest against a social order in which femininity is humiliated. Only after she has fallen in love with a man does she realize that all that she wants in her life is love and affection. This realization gives her peace of mind and prompts her to dedicate her confessions "to the dear girl whom I wanted to be my daughter from the man who taught me how to love only after it has become too late for me; to his future daughter from any other woman" (p. 162).

The novel explores the nuances of gender that make women's lives a continuous struggle against the currents of societal norms from early childhood until their death. Clearly it was too much for Arab society to tolerate. In her preface to the novel, the author explains the difficulties she faced as a result of the publication of these "confessions," which were serialized in *Rose al-Yūsuf*, the highly respected and most popular Egyptian newspaper during the twentieth century. Questions turned to resentment, then to anger and threats:

> During the time of the publication of these "Confessions" tens of [thousands of] questions were directed at me from people who knew me and those who didn't. This angered members of my family, who threatened to take me to court if I didn't stop the publication and protect the family name lest people thought it was I who wrote them! (p. 5)

Su'ād Zuhayr claims that a dying woman gave her this book of memoirs and asked her to publish it after her death; even so, she was not absolved of responsibility for their content. Zuhayr expresses her admiration for the heroine, who bravely challenges conventional thinking and behavior and stands firm in defense of her principles and perspective: "She is a signpost and a pioneer in our march for freedom and equality" (pp. 6–7). Zuhayr identifies with the woman she says gave her the book and points to the work's importance for the cause of all women:

> My experience concerning the publication of these confessions and the social harassment this has invited have once more reinforced the message conveyed in these confessions: the message that there is a huge discrepancy between our view of men and women. My experience with this publication has proved to me that a literary presentation of a real experience is a right vouchsafed to men alone. What has to be acknowledged is that to be fully alive and free is the right of both men and women. When such a right is established, we have to discover new values in every aspect of our human lives. (p. 6)

Both Su'ād Zuhayr in this preface and the heroine of her book *I'tirāfāt Imra'a Mustarjila* are bent on foreshadowing a new world in which women will enjoy absolute equality and freedom with men. The dedication of these memoirs to the future daughter of the man who teaches the heroine how to love is significant. That signifies he is the new man needed to create a new reality for women. The new woman is alive and well and awaiting the birth of the new man. Only after his birth can the world become a better place for both men and women. Hence the dedication is for a new, liberated generation.

Like Virginia Woolf in her essay "Women and Fiction," Zuhayr argues that a literary work is bound to reflect its writer's experience in one way or another. She adds, "Nothing distinguishes a literary work more than its sincerity and genuineness" (p. 6). Thus she argues not just for new social and moral values that will improve gender relations but also for new literary evaluations.

The issues raised in the novels discussed in detail in this chapter are major issues with which Arab women still wrestle today. Contemporary Arab women novelists are concerned with many of the same themes that were discussed in novels published decades ago because none of the problems have yet been resolved. The gender differences expressed in Su'ād Zuhayr's work are still pervasive in Arab women's lives. For anyone who complains about Arab women today still raising "feminist" demands put forward by women decades ago, an answer can be found in the words of Amīna al-Sa'īd. In 1976, Sa'īd took a notable shaikh (a Muslim religious scholar) to task for making such a complaint. "Why . . . does he hold it against feminists that they—for as long as he has been living—continue to say what they said at the time of Hudā Sha'rāwī[4] [and will continue to say] as long as they are not granted their demands and as long as ills still exist which destroy the moral principles of our society?"[5]

CHAPTER 5

Women and Nation

THIS CHAPTER CHALLENGES the perception of Arab literary critics that women's novels focus only on love, family, and children. The latter are valid topics, especially if we take into account the fact that the personal is ultimately political and acknowledge that women's strongest attachments are to family and children. It is therefore natural for women to write about what they know best and experience most. But I do not mean to imply that women are indifferent to the political arena. The novels discussed in this chapter testify to the fact that women are concerned not only about family and children but also about the nation. In fact, it is notable that women's novels written in the early 1960s were essentially political. The aim of this chapter is not only to prove that women's novels were political at that time but also to demonstrate that their politics were quite different from mainstream politics, a fact that might well account for their marginalization.

The novels chosen for discussion in this chapter are *Al-Bāb al-Maftūḥ (The Open Door)* by Laṭīfa al-Zayyāt (Egypt), *Thulūj Taḥt al-Shams (Snows Under the Sun)* by Laylā al-Yāfī (Syria), *Fatāt Tāfiha (A Silly Girl)* by Munā Jabbūr (Lebanon), *Layla Wāḥida (One Night)* by Colette Khūrī (Syria), *Murāhiqa (The Adolescent)* by Mājida al-ʿAṭṭār (Syria), and *Ṭuyūr Aylūl (Birds of September)* by Emily Naṣrallah (Lebanon). The one thing these novels have in common is the awakening of women's political consciousness. Women analyze and criticize social and political reality. They demonstrate a new vision that lays the basis for the emancipation of both men and women and for the political survival and future prosperity of their country in particular and the Arab nation in general.

Al-Bāb al-Maftūḥ (The Open Door), by the Egyptian writer Laṭīfa al-Zayyāt, presents the struggle of a generation against the negative elements in Arab history. It is not, as is usually assumed, a historical account of the period between 1946 and 1956 in Egypt. Rather, it approaches this period from various perspectives (the personal, the social, and the political), at many points revealing important links between men's attitudes toward women and men's attitudes toward their country and nation. These significant themes are articulated in the story of Laylā and Ḥusayn 'Āmir. On the one hand, Laylā symbolizes Egypt and its future; on the other hand, she is a real woman who lives and negotiates with her reality. Therefore her position and role change according to the change in the narrative structure and the direction and purpose of events.

The narrative operates at three different levels as regards women, society, and country. These levels interact and intersect, one influencing the others. Throughout the novel, the themes of women and nation are inseparable, and the social dimension provides convincing proof that these two themes are permanently interwoven with each other. In this context, Laylā's disappointment with her lover 'Iṣām over his refusal to accompany her brother Maḥmūd to the Suez Canal to support his country is one example of this link. Also, her devotion to Ḥusayn 'Āmir, a nationalist, motivates her to overcome all family and social impediments in order to build a better future with him. Laylā believes that only those who understand women's emancipation and national liberation as two sides of the same coin are capable of building a better future.

Laylā throws away the engagement ring and turns toward Ḥusayn, her lover and comrade. After fighting the battle of Port Sa'īd, Laylā asks Ḥusayn whether this is the end: "Silence prevailed between them again as they viewed the flood of people both in front and behind as if they were a sweeping, triumphant, and vehement wave pressing ahead. Ḥusayn answered with eyes full of tears and said, 'This is just the beginning, my love'" (p. 353).

The novel explores social, political, and national realities in a serious and concentrated attempt to find an opening for social and political change, a beginning to which both men and women can contribute as partners. Seen from this perspective, it is easier to understand the reasons for Laylā's failure to create a new reality in a society where the ethics are diametrically opposed to the dignity of women, their individuality, and their aspirations. Laylā discerns a new way of functioning when she challenges the will of her family to demonstrate against the occupying forces as "part and parcel of the masses" (p. 45). But her optimism and enthusiasm fade as soon as she returns home, where her father beats her in full view of her brother, whom she had previously considered progressive and an ally. He urges her to acknowledge her mistake. "You know, Laylā," says her brother, "the important thing is to admit that you were wrong; once you acknowledge that you will not feel the pain you feel now" (p. 49).

Laylā is numbed by her brother's reaction. She has discovered a crucial difference between men's theories about women's emancipation and how they actually behave. Maḥmūd is an enthusiastic nationalist who speaks often and strongly of the need to emancipate women, but as soon as his sister starts to create her own destiny, he opposes her. Later, Maḥmūd fights for the liberation of the Suez Canal and also to rid himself of the weakness that prevents him from accepting his sister as a comrade and an equal. He ends up not only as a fighter against aggression at Port Saʻīd but also as a liberal-minded person who marries a woman of his choice and who supports his sister in her wish to marry the man she loves, a stand that provokes their parents' indignation. What is more, Maḥmūd's credibility is measured against his identification of national issues, on the one hand, with issues relating to women's emancipation and equality, on the other.

Maḥmūd's transformation is indicative of the change that all men have to undergo if progress, both on the social and political fronts, is to be achieved. When the actual social experience contradicts declared political aspirations, very little can be achieved, either in the social or political domain. If progress is to be made, there has to be a viable relationship between words and deeds, as well as strong links between the personal, the social, and the political.

Similarly, ʻIṣām's attitude toward women's issues brings his relationship with Laylā to an end. He fails to consider her as an equal, worthy of respect and independence. Time and again Laylā arrives at the same conclusion: that ʻIṣām sees women as sexual objects and personal possessions. ʻIṣām draws a very clear distinction between women relatives, such as his sister and his cousin Laylā (he is her guardian) on the one hand, and between other women who are permitted to be the subject of his sexual desire. He talks freely about women's emancipation, although in practice he cannot tolerate the emancipation of his female relatives—his sister, his mother, his wife—because they symbolize his "honor" and that of his family. Emancipation is only for women who cannot defile his personal honor.

In his morality, there are two kinds of women: the object of desire and the chattel (that is, mothers, sisters, and wives). A desirable woman can be obtained and discarded with the passing of that desire. She is to be conquered and seized by force, and men have every right to pride themselves on such a triumph. Decent men, however, do not desire their cousins; neither do they desire the sisters of their friends, because desire is linked to the body and the body is an extremely filthy thing (p. 63).

'Iṣām's attitude toward women resembles his attitude toward national issues. Despite his constant talk about duty, which makes it incumbent on all citizens to go to the Suez Canal and fight for their country, he himself backs out at the last moment, leaving his cousin Maḥmūd to go and fight on his own. Laylā's relationship with 'Iṣām highlights the urgency of achieving harmony between words and deeds, between the private and the public, between attitudes toward women relatives and women on the street; in effect, between the social and the political. Only then will the new man be born, and only with the birth of the new man can the real emancipation of women be achieved.

Laylā's relationship with 'Iṣām seems to prove that women cannot create a new reality that takes their voice and dignity into account unless men understand what is required and accept the need for it. From the outset, Laylā sees all the impediments to her equality and dignity; she nonetheless fails to combat these elements in her relationship with 'Iṣām. Only when she meets Ḥusayn 'Āmir, the man who shares her enthusiasm in rejecting the negative aspects of tradition and in consolidating women's status as individuals with rights equal to those of men, is she able to establish a strong foundation for her freedom and well-being.

"Where do I go?" is a question Laylā often asks herself before meeting Ḥusayn 'Āmir. It explains her decision to marry Ramzī, an inevitable result of her inability to create any social framework within which she can function on her own terms. Only when Laylā meets Ḥusayn 'Āmir does she become able to openly reject outdated values and instead live according to the values she holds dear. Only then does Laylā create new social and personal modes of operating.

The idea of the new man being necessary to women's liberation might not be very comforting for feminists who do not want their achievements to be conditioned on men's approval. But the fact is that if a new reality for women is being sought in which they are able to function freely and independently, such a reality cannot possibly be created in a vacuum, in total isolation from men. Women should not make men's mistake of ignoring the role and significance of the opposite sex. For women's lives to change, men as well as women have to change. That is the lesson to be learned from Laylā's relationships with the different men she encounters in this novel and from the impact of these relationships on her future feminist plans. The author's argument is not unlike that made by Simone de Beauvoir in her introduction to *The Second Sex*. Beauvoir argues that in order to change the destiny of women, the attitudes of both men and women toward women have to be changed.

From the beginning of the novel, Laylā reveals an understanding of social, political, and gender roles that differs from the concepts held by

those who surround her. In the process, however, her sense of direction
is blurred by one obstacle after another, as well as by a deeply rooted
internal fear. When she abides by tradition and consents to become
engaged to Ramzī, she soon discovers that corrupt people surround her
who have double standards regarding every issue. On the eve of their
engagement, her fiancé cannot avert his eyes from her cousin Jamīla's
breasts, and Jamīla herself commits adultery. These and similar
instances leave no doubt in Laylā's mind that

> They are all corrupt; Ramzī, Jamīla, 'Iṣām, Jamīla's mother as well as
> her own mother, who accepts living in a state of fear, the fear of what
> people might say. Laylā's father, also, who strongly believes in his
> own self-righteousness, is also corrupt; Laylā is now sure that they are
> all corrupt and that all their values are rotten. (p. 280)

At this point Laylā realizes that she does not have to suffer the fate of
either Ṣafā', who has been driven to suicide, or Jamīla, who has married
a wealthy man but nevertheless lives in an emotional vacuum. Rather, she
is able to see a third way; a way that translates her awareness into a reality and expels forever her fear of her father, family, and society:

> Everything is clear now, clear and sharp; there is no compromise any
> more. Her love for Ḥusayn, like her hatred for Ramzī, is deep and vio-
> lent. Her aversion to her own weakness and helplessness is even deep-
> er and more violent. Facts are facts for her now, naked and clear. Laylā
> looks at them with open eyes knowing full well that her way is dis-
> cerned and defined, once and for all. (p. 305)

Only then does Laylā feel that she belongs, and only then does she
become a dignified citizen with an individual voice. One night she
writes to her brother, Maḥmūd:

> It has been a long time since I felt what I feel tonight, as I listen to the
> address of Jamāl 'Abd al-Nāṣir. I feel I am strong, and capable of
> doing anything, literally anything. Do you understand what I mean?
> This feeling of pride that had for so long abandoned me has come back
> today together with the feeling that I belong. I no longer feel alone. At
> this moment I feel I am there with the masses making themselves
> heard in Alexandria, with you, with Sanā'. (p. 306)

Laylā asks herself why she waited so long to renounce her base values and devious principles, particularly because she had previously
shown early signs of social and political awareness. She looks at the difference between the way men and women are treated. For instance, her
father was overwhelmed with joy when her brother, Maḥmūd, shaved for

the first time, but he received the news of Laylā reaching puberty wailing and screaming, praying to God to preserve the honor of the family. The issues that previously prevented her from translating her feelings into tangible reality can be summed up as follows. First, her own innate fear paralyzes her ability to challenge and confront. Second, she challenges family authority with 'Iṣām, only to be disappointed when 'Iṣām's worldview proves to be similar to her father's. Third, she cannot communicate honestly with those around her. The last factor may be the most difficult dilemma that women face. Laylā says of her relationship with her father, "a huge wall always stood between him and me, as if we do not speak the same language" (p. 279).

Laylā here reminds us of Kate Chopin's heroine Edna Pontellier in *The Awakening*, who says to Robert, her lover, that she loves him but that she has decided to be an independent woman, responsible for her own life. He refuses to hear what she says, however, and she remains, in his opinion, just as she remains in society's opinion, the property of her husband. When she is sure that she has absolutely failed to convince him of the birth of the new person inside her, she surrenders her body and soul to the sea. The problem here is not the lack of women's awareness; rather, it is the lack of proper receptivity to it. Women often fail to obtain the hearing they need from men; they fail to secure an understanding of their perspectives and points of view. Many, perhaps most, men believe that it is in their interest to maintain the status quo, and therefore they are often reluctant to join ranks with women seeking to challenge tradition and create a freer and happier world.

The questions *Al-Bāb al-Maftūḥ* raise are important and pertinent; the turn of events at several levels of the narrative suggests that a concern for women's emancipation is a prerequisite for social and political liberation. Another important prerequisite is the courage to challenge corrupt values, no matter how entrenched they might seem at the time. When Laylā grasps these facts, she imagines herself rushing to the battlefield while the enemy retreats. She wants to see the enemy retreating from Port Sa'īd, and she can: "Nothing is impossible now; she can do anything she wants" (p. 343). Thus the enemy to be defeated is not only on the battlefield; it is within us, as well as within the social structures, traditions, and values that govern people's lives. Laylā believes that the first step on the road to victory is overcoming inner fears and "standing resolutely by what we believe is right" (p. 346). Indeed, defeating a foreign enemy might well be easier than surmounting our own human weaknesses.

This engaging novel has never been out of print since it was first published in 1960, and the secret of its popularity is that it addresses the real concerns of real people in the Arab world. In it, al-Zayyāt considers women's feminist consciousness and men's healthy attitudes toward women's equality as the only political measures for building a better society in which both men and women enjoy equality and freedom. The novel makes it abundantly clear that political achievement has to be built on a solid social structure in which women's status is of crucial significance. The author's ability to articulate the interrelatedness of social attitudes toward women and nationalist causes has helped make *Al-Bāb al-Maftūḥ* one of the most widely read novels in Arabic literature.

Like Laylā in *Al-Bāb al-Maftūḥ,* Rīmā, the heroine of *Thulūj Taḥt al-Shams (Snows Under the Sun)* by the Syrian novelist Laylā al-Yāfī, visits the battlefield in Port Saʿīd in an attempt to defend the Arab nation and in pursuit of a better status for women. She arrives in Cairo from Damascus just as the tripartite aggression takes place against Port Saʿīd. Rīmā joins the army defending Port Saʿīd because she feels the Arab nation has been divided by the colonial powers into artificial countries, the borders of which divide citizens of the same nation. Thus when Rīmā crosses the border into Lebanon, she asks herself, "Why should all these restrictions be put in the way of citizens of the same nation?" She imagines the Arab world to be a mansion that belongs to all who inhabit it, invaded by intruders who force its citizens to confine themselves to one corner. They obey the intruders' rules even after their departure. Rīmā is comforted by the thought that things will eventually be restored to their natural state and that the Arab nation will once more be united (p. 110).

Since early childhood, Rīmā's personal life has been subordinated to national and public events to the extent that her personal life is inextricably linked to the political. As a child she is kidnapped by a gang of Israeli spies and imprisoned in a stable in a border village. The gang plans to achieve their purposes by blackmailing her, and once its members are arrested, they level claims against her. A childless judge exonerates her, and eventually he and his wife adopt her (her parents were killed during the kidnapping). As a young woman with the prospect of inheriting a fortune, Rīmā focuses mainly on national issues and is obsessed with the reunification of the Arab world.

Through Rīmā's relationship with her cousin Ṣalāḥ, who has recently completed his studies and returned from Germany, we encounter the lurking confusion in the Arab world of women's liberation with women's promiscuity. Such confusion makes sexual repression in the East a symbol of morality and chastity. Ṣalāḥ, for example, considers women who smoke to be liberated women, and looks down on his cousin who does not smoke (p. 74). Moreover, when Ṣalāḥ tries to rape Rīmā and she defends herself with dignity and pride, he sees in her the spirit of a goddess in a myth. "He was mesmerized because he had never come across any woman who was so beautiful and who yet defended her chastity with the vigor and dignity of Rīmā" (p. 96).

The passage highlighting Ṣalāḥ's confusion of chastity with honor highlights a dominant Arab belief: those women who are chaste are also honorable. Conversely, this belief presupposes that Western women cannot be honorable because they are not chaste. The behavior of Ṣalāḥ indirectly points to the hypocrisy of Arab men, who like to spend time with sexually liberated and/or available women but would never consider marrying such women.

This distortion of Western women's liberation and the identification of women's liberation with sexual promiscuity do not serve the interests of Arab women. The enemies of women's emancipation have frequently raised a hue and cry against the deterioration of women's moral standards in the West, as if Western women's liberation were only concerned with sexual freedom. This stereotype of Western women held in the East may be compared to the Western belief that Arab women are docile creatures with no voice and no identity.

Rīmā's participation in the battle of Port Saʿīd raises her consciousness, not only regarding her social status as a woman but also regarding her position and the dilemmas that are faced by all Arabs. She discovers that colonization and foreign enemies cannot be blamed for the troubles Arabs face; the problem, rather, is Arabs' attitudes toward each other. She recognizes that the only solution is for Arabs to reach mutual understanding among themselves. The official Arab media has always blamed the lack of Arab unity on foreign colonizers such as the British and the French, but Rīmā realizes that the roots of Arab disunity can in fact be traced to the Arab nation itself. She argues, for example, that heated conflicts among Arab countries, which often erupt only in the name of national interest, stem "from self-love. There has to be a strong tie that unifies the hearts of the Arabs which were torn asunder by colonization for generations" (p. 142). Here it is noticeable that Laylā al-Yāfī joins Laṭīfa al-Zayyāt in diagnosing the problems facing Arab societies rather than joining the chorus of voices that use external forces as a scapegoat.

Interestingly, in the battlefield, femininity no longer signifies weakness because women have become warriors, as capable as men of defending their country. In Port Saʿīd, Rīmā was transformed from a peaceful dove "to a wild cat who knows no fear or caution. She is no longer the poetic, sensitive girl that she was. She is fighting with an eager spirit and watching women, young and old, and children, who are walking to their death courageously" (pp. 154–155).

As with *Al-Bāb al-Maftūḥ*, al-Yāfī posits that women's freedom and equality can be achieved only when men become capable of appreciating women's achievements. Ṣalāḥ, who tries to rape Rīmā, desperately desires her as a wife once he is able to accept her as a mature, strong, free, and equal woman. The difference between the two books, however, is that al-Zayyāt in *Al-Bāb al-Maftūḥ* builds the details of each event meticulously, with a deep psychological probing and understanding of her characters. In *Thulūj Taḥt al-Shams*, however, al-Yāfī focuses on the impact of national events without providing enough justification for the changes that take place in people's attitudes and positions and without providing the necessary details that make the development of events convincing. Al-Yāfī announces at the beginning of her novel that her aim is to deal with public events in the Arab world and to submit all that is personal to serve that purpose. She says, "My personal wounds are always submerged under public events which storm my great nation" (p. 3).

Yahyā Ḥaqqī, a well-known Egyptian writer, describes al-Yāfī in his introduction to her novel as "a woman who is extremely proud of her country and people, with a deep belief in love and good deeds" (p. 8). She takes her Syrian heroine to Egypt to defend an Arab land, and on every occasion she prays to God to unite Arab hearts to secure a better future for the Arab nation. The most prominent feature of this novel is its beautiful language and flowing diction. Although it lacks strong characterization and plot, it remains a truly enjoyable work. Ḥaqqī agrees with this assessment: "When I read *Thulūj Taḥt al-Shams* I forgot myself and felt as if I were moving from the burning sun to a cooling shade that took me back to my days of youth and life's occupations. Worries receded, allowing me to enjoy my trip from one country to another and from one event to the next" (p. 8).

In this novel, al-Yāfī addressed the issue of inter-Arab relations at a time when the entire focus of Arab governments was on external influences, from Zionism to imperialism. Forty-five years after the novel was first published, many Arabs have begun to discern the reasons for the Arab nation's weakness and have discovered that they are similar to those identified by al-Yāfī long ago.

In her novel *Murāhiqa (The Adolescent)*, Mājida al-ʿAṭṭār skillfully links Arab women's issues to the issue of Palestine, revealing the dangers of male hypocrisy in both instances. She simultaneously compares patriarchal authority in the home to the patriarchal authority of the state, concluding that both authorities lack sincerity and objectivity.

Lamyā', the heroine of *Murāhiqa*, relates the story of Arab women, showing them to be estranged individuals who are denied the right to live in equal human dignity with men. The novel gradually but shrewdly reveals the causes of their alienation at the personal, social, and political levels. In the third part of this novel, the narrative reveals an implicit relationship between the status of women in society and the status of Palestine in the Arab world. The turn of events also highlights the analogy between the hypocrisy evident in both patriarchal authority over women and political patriarchal authority over Palestine.

Ḥanān, a Palestinian girl, symbolizes both women and Palestine. The manipulation to which fellow students subject her resembles Arab governments' treatment of the Palestinian cause: none really champion it, but all use it for political mileage in the Arab nationalist struggle for regional power and prestige.

The tragedy of both women and Palestine stems from the dichotomy between what is said and what is done, to the extent that any identification between words and deeds seems impossible. This dichotomy prolongs the ordeal of both women and Palestine because it creates an illusion of a "good" reality and, as a result, discourages those who wish to work for real change. Both women and Palestine seem to be the objects of action, while the actors, who are usually men who control both the political situation and women, are not interested in allowing any change to take place because the status quo serves their interests. Lamyā', however, is not fooled by the pretenses of her peers. She has a clear insight into the most minute details of their thoughts and ultimate objectives.

Lamyā''s alienation begins early in her childhood, when she observes the huge gap between her parents' attitude toward her and their attitude toward her brother, Khālid. She realizes that she is only a girl in a house that dreams of having a boy. The birth of Khālid, therefore, saves the house from crisis and

> [p]lants the smile of satisfaction in my mother's eyes since she is now able to reclaim her confidence in herself both as a woman and as a mother. Khālid's birth also restores my father's pride and saves our family from the pathetic remarks from neighbors who used to pity us because we did not have a boy. We now have a boy; even my father who I never recall ever kissing me, bent toward the newly born boy and kissed him. (pp. 12–13)

This difference between a boy and a girl grows to be the difference between a man and a woman. Lamyā' enters into an emotional relationship with Fu'ād, only to find that her assumptions are very different from his. He can stay out late or steal a kiss from her, but she is a girl, the living embodiment of her family's honor, and so must behave accordingly. The older she grows, the more she finds the atmosphere at home suffocating. Reaching puberty becomes a real threat to the honor of her family. Thenceforth, her every move is closely watched and scrutinized by her family. When gossip circulates that Fu'ād has kissed Lamyā', her parents feel humiliated; the family loses the respect of society and is relegated to the bottom of the social ladder. Thus a private encounter becomes a social disaster, and a personal right is transformed into sheer pain. The kiss also signifies the sexual repression from which men suffer. Lamyā' recounts the encounter as such: "Fu'ād's lips were pressing mine violently, his teeth were clicking against mine and his fingers were squeezing my shoulder. I was searching in vain for the sweetness of a kiss but to no avail" (p. 73).

What the narrative reveals is that both men and women in the Arab world are victims of sexual oppression, despite the fact that men's sexual behavior does not encroach on family honor. The violence of the encounter reoccurs with Lamyā''s female teacher. When the scandal of the kiss becomes known, Lamyā''s father tries to prevent her from attending school. Lamyā' complains to one of her teachers, who asks Lamyā' to accompany her home so that she can give her story a patient hearing. Her teacher starts to hug Lamyā' and kiss her, and then

> [h]er active, soft fingers moved from my lips to my hair, and then they slid behind my ears and to my neck and then to my breasts. Through the dark blue cloud that stupefied my thinking I found myself making a comparison between these fingers and those of Fu'ād. I suddenly realized that there was something unnatural taking place here. The active fingers turned into tongues of fire all over my breast. I mustered my courage and looked into the face above mine; it was bright pink with two wild eyes. (pp. 138–139)

Images become confused in Lamyā''s mind. The memory of Fu'ād mingles with an image of her father sleeping with the family's woman servant, Ḥusniyya. She feels sickened by the mask of chastity that Fu'ād, her teacher, and her father wear. She thinks of committing suicide—one packet of pills to end it all—but restrains herself. Yet from that moment onward a deep, permanent sadness indicating that she is no longer alive possesses her (p. 145).

For Lamyā', to be alive is to be consistently oneself, both alone and within society, without having to behave or speak hypocritically. That is precisely what Līnā, the heroine of Laylā Ba'albakī's novel *Anā Aḥyā (I Live)* achieves when she rejects social traditions and values. Lamyā' rebels against negative traditions and customs. She is not discarding high moral values; rather, she is renouncing everything that makes truly moral behavior impossible.

It can be deduced from this novel that there can be no compromise between corrupt social habits that govern the fate of both men and women and an aspiration for a sincere and genuine way of life. Another way of understanding the novel is to see that Lamyā''s resentment is linked to that of Ḥanān, the Palestinian girl, who is totally devoted to her country but is appalled by the apparent ease with which Palestinians abandon their land. She says: "Shame on them; shame on their cowardice and weakness; I shall beseech my family not to depart from our home no matter what might happen; even if they were to die one after another" (p. 164).

Both Lamyā' and Ḥanān know only too well that the Palestinian exodus from Palestine is a historic national disaster, whereas the teacher at school was talking

> [a]bout the difference between Communism and Capitalism, the disadvantages of the one and the advantages of the other; about the danger that is threatening us as a result of the spread of the Communist virus. This naive and silly teacher does not speak about the looming danger of losing our homeland, Palestine. (p. 195)

Events in the novel take a new turn when Lamyā' and Ḥanān direct their resentment at the teacher who claims to be an Arab nationalist—at that time the only politically correct position to hold—while ignoring the Palestinian exodus from Palestine. Lamyā' senses that the attitude of those in positions of authority toward Palestine is ambivalent and believes there is no other explanation for their apparent willingness to ignore a catastrophe of this magnitude. Here again the hypocritical attitude of men toward women finds its echo in the political hypocrisy toward Palestine.

In the novel Ḥanān is both a real woman and a symbol of Palestine. As a symbol of Palestine, she finds herself without any real support:

> Even colleagues who sympathized with her and offered their services at the beginning stopped asking about her. They grew accustomed to her absence. Are they going to be as familiar with the absence of Palestine as they are with hers? And are they going to confine themselves as they did with Ḥanān to sweet words while doing nothing? (p. 202)

What is more, they all use Ḥanān for their own purposes. Even Lamyā' acknowledges using Ḥanān "as a means to reach my objective; sometimes in order to talk to 'Iṣām, and other times to accompany him to visit her; one wonders whether Palestine is going to be one day just a means for something else" (p. 203).

Ḥanān commits suicide. Lamyā' then realizes that the only solution for her as a woman and a citizen is to be herself, trust her own judgment, and have enough courage to challenge what is wrong, no matter what price she might have to pay. She says, "I have made a promise to myself never to live an illusion and avoid facing real life. I have made an oath to myself to be always frank and to live in absolute peace with myself" (p. 201). Only with such a resolution can the hope needed to solve the tremendous political problems facing the Arab nation be restored.

The development of events strongly suggests that Lamyā''s father's attitude toward the birth of his daughter matches his attitude toward Palestine. The stance of her lover regarding "family honor" is directly related to his stance with reference to territory, freedom, and national dignity. To define the honor of men and their families according to the sexual behavior of women has for too long hindered the emergence of a more elevated and comprehensive sense of honor related to territory, country, and nation. As long as the behavior of one woman can create a social crisis, then treachery against one's country can pass unnoticed.

Rashā, the heroine of the novel *Layla Wāḥida (One Night)* by the Syrian novelist Colette Khūrī, demonstrates a fervor similar to that expressed by Līnā in *Anā Aḥyā* and Lamyā' in *Murāhiqa*.[1] The heroine wants to be true to herself so that she can live in peace, even if only for one night.

Ironically, critical studies of the novel charge the heroine with the same misdeeds that the novelist has set out to subvert. 'Afīf Farrāj, for example, argues that the heroine "avenges herself of her oriental deprivations by a solitary tryst with a Frenchman she met for the first time on a train headed for Paris." He argues that the author does not explain her recklessness, except to say that she was entranced by the beams of light shining from her lover's eyes, "which apparently justifies the sudden indiscretion of a respectable married woman, leaving the reader stunned and unable to comprehend this free sexual choice."[2] The description of a serious and responsible literary work such as *Layla Wāḥida* as an account of a "night of sexual adventurism" reveals the critic's fundamental misunderstanding of the spirit and objective of the narrative. To interpret the sexual encounter between Rashā and Kāmil as the sum of the story is to misread all that Rashā and Kāmil have tried to do on both the social and personal levels.

Through her short-lived relationship with Kāmil—which is anything but a night of sexual recklessness—Rashā discovers her humanity. For the first time in her life, she experiences the sensitivity of a man who is interested in her character as well as her physical beauty. In addition to admiring her hair, her dress, and the color of her eyes, he takes account of her real interests and concerns. These small but important details are absent from her marriage, a dour relationship in which her husband considers her little more than a piece of furniture. The stranger's attentions rekindle her pride in herself and draw her attention to the lack of peace and dignity in her life. The discovery of the self in the other transpires between Rashā and Kāmil well before they decide to spend the night together. Rashā says, "He stared at me and muttered sadly, 'I now know that I was never happy.' He fell silent. The same feeling was quivering in my depths" (p. 142). Both Rashā and Kāmil discover that neither has known a genuine relationship until this moment; thus spending the night together in a hotel room is a natural culmination of their relationship.

The encounter was an epiphany for Rashā that might have materialized in other ways: through academic success or a relationship with a social or political group, for example. But the essence of the story would have remained unchanged. Critics have focused on the sexual relationship in this novel and Rashā's betrayal of her husband, because from a social perspective they provide easy points of attack, given Arab society's preoccupation with women's chastity.

I find such criticisms invalid because they do not address the actual content of the novel, which very clearly questions the individual's relationship to the wider society. I suggest that *Layla Wāḥida* should be considered alongside literary works that address conflicting loyalties, such as loyalty to self and loyalty to society; the choices that these loyalties impose on individuals; and the various consequences of adhering to one loyalty over another.

Rashā reminds us of Nora in Henrik Ibsen's play *A Doll's House*, in which the heroine discovers through her husband's illness and her desperate attempts to save him that she has no true significance in his life and has always been a doll in his house. Although no other man appears in Nora's life, she nevertheless leaves her husband and children in pursuit of self-fulfillment. Similarly, Clarissa in Virginia Woolf's novel *Mrs. Dalloway* is forced by society's insidious emphasis on social class to abandon the man she loves because he is from a lower social class than hers. When she encounters her ex-lover twenty years after her marriage, she realizes that she still feels closer to him than to the man she married. She asks herself why she should waste twenty years of her life complying with social rules that are so unconcerned with a person's feelings. There are many literary works in various genres that deal with the conflict between self and society, between individual rights and social duties. Yet the question remains: does one's duty toward oneself take precedence over one's duty toward society? It is a question that Rashā never fully answers.

Although Khūrī's novel emphasizes women's issues, it also offers characters who are victimized by social norms and traditions. The heroine, Rashā, carefully considers social issues and poses questions that are never fully answered, leaving the reader to consider the dilemmas raised by the novel. Rashā claims no right to violate laws or tradition; rather, she questions laws and tradition by, for example, pondering the meaning of betrayal. Every night she sleeps with her husband, Rashā feels that she is betraying her body and soul in sleeping with a man for whom her heart has never beaten, and that she is likewise betraying her husband. She asks herself whether her "affair" is treasonable, since for the first time in her life she has acted according to her true feelings. Rashā concludes that betrayal is a loathsome word:

> Its attributes become easy when compared to this feeling of exhaustion, the feeling that for 11 years I've been betraying myself. For the first time yesterday the meaning of "betrayal" completely disappeared from my conscience; for the first time in my life, yesterday, I was true to myself. (p. 196)

Rashā's frank approach to her problems and her candid discussions of her fears and weaknesses create an understanding and empathy between her and the reader.

In her novel *Fatāt Tāfiha (A Silly Girl)*, Munā Jabbūr creates a bold narrative from the very first paragraph. The heroine speaks in the first person and is undaunted by either men or society in a novel that reminds us of *Anā Ahyā (I Live)* by Laylā Ba'albakī and *Mudhakkarāt Imra'a Ghayr Wāqi'iyya (Memoirs of an Unrealistic Woman)* by Sahar Khalīfa. Nadā in *Fatāt Tāfiha* challenges the concept of femininity, which to her represents weakness, a mere ability to trap men and motherhood. She rejects this attribute of femininity because it is incompatible with independence. She reckons, "I want to be ugly. It is impossible to be a means of reproduction, a statue for beauty and a well for desire" (p. 6). She wants to be a truly independent person "who neither functions at the behest of others nor is looking for men's admiration" (p. 7). Her major goal in life is "to be free; I want to have my own independent identity" (p. 7). Her determination to be independent places her at odds with school, home, and society: "At school they call me pessimistic, at home they think I am mad, and in social circles they say I am 'odd,' as if they are spitting at me" (p. 8).

Nadā considers the use of language and questions its associations. She strips words of their familiar meanings and adorns them with new ones that are more compatible with her thinking. Thus she wages a war against concepts, behavior, and language: "I selected words, fleeing words, such as country, society, entity, masses, ideals and looked at them at random, searching for their meanings . . . nothing but a vacuum. Words are incomplete entities that need protection. Words are women" (p. 9).

Nadā's attempt to probe language and infuse it with new meanings implies her rejection of prevailing social and political paradigms and her resolve to remodel them according to her own perspectives. Because language is like women, manipulated and exploited, it needs to be set free and then rephrased in a way that is appropriate to women's independence. She also comments on the weakness of the feminine and the strength of the masculine in the Arabic language. Arabic grammar dictates that feminine words always follow the masculine because the masculine linguistic form is always the stronger one. Nadā asks why can't "she" have the same power as "he" and *tilka* ("that" for a woman in Arabic), the same power as *Dhālika* ("that" for a man in Arabic).[3] In this discussion of the feminine and masculine in language, Munā Jabbūr predates Western feminists by about fifteen years, as her novel was first published in 1962. Western women had written nothing on the subject of language by the early 1960s, and it should be noted that in the West at that time, masculine pronouns were still generic terms covering both male and female.

Besides this linguistic inquiry, Nadā also considers two other important issues: first, standards of feminine beauty and their consequences for marriage and motherhood, which have relegated women to a life of slavery, forced to act according to men's desires and whims; and second, rigid social mores and duties that leave little room for individuality. Nadā tries to alter the concept of "femininity" and transform it into a sign of women's strength. She consequently takes a very firm stand against women's traditional roles, claiming to loathe beauty and motherhood. Her rejection of these qualities creates its own dilemma. She begins to resent being a woman and fears that love that leads to marriage might automatically undermine her character.

Gradually, the narrative reveals that the heroine softens toward love, marriage, and children, but along the way, Nadā adopts a totally new perspective that differs completely from society's. After a while she realizes that she neither hates children or men nor opposes love and marriage; rather, she rejects the classification of these roles as inferior and embraces them as symbols of strength and power. Once she discovers these important new perspectives, she works to emancipate herself not only from the myth of being weak but also from her own self-delusion that she hates herself and her beauty. The question for her is, how can she be feminine and at the same time remain free and independent? When she discovers that resolving this paradox is nearly impossible, she considers the solution of last resort: suicide. She says to herself: "Here is a truck that is passing fast; a desire moves inside me to throw myself under its wheels, but I retreat; to be killed in such a way is to concede that I am weak and that in the end I even needed a man to help me rid myself of this life" (p. 30).

Nadā feels shackled and alienated; she lacks any sense of belonging to her society, her family, or even her body because the limitations and functions of her body have been designed for her by others. She therefore attempts to re-map her body and redefine its functions in a society that does not acknowledge the right of women to think in such a way. She asks herself, "Do I have the right to re-map my body as long as I am living in a body that is not mine, and in a house that is not my house and in a world that is not of my own making?" (p. 49).

Nadā's politics differ from those of her father. She opposes the French mandate and speaks openly of the benefits of sovereign democracy that bestows divine rights on individuals. Her father, by contrast, embraces the French mandate in the name of Christian interests. Nadā rejects restrictions on national freedom with the same gusto with which she rejects her own limitations as a woman. She compares her father's attitude toward the occupation with his attitude toward her as a feminist; his only concern is to be rich and to curb his daughter's activities: "My father is lost; he is a hostage to his bank shares, to the French mandate, to his fear for the French in Algeria. He feels suffocated by the freedom of others, but what really disturbs him is my challenge; that really infuriates him" (p. 46).

Nadā's father is only one example of generations of Arab men who have put family honor—always defined by women's chastity—above the honor and future of their country. Thus, although a woman's sexual behavior might well disgrace her family, a man selling out his country and people suffers no sense of shame. Few characters in the novel criticize Nadā's father, who champions the colonial powers at the expense of his people's and his country's independence; rather, they are content to gossip about his daughter, who has chosen to leave the family home in search of a job. Nadā's employment is another deliberate challenge to the social structure. She has no respect for her father because she sees him as the embodiment of social and political hypocrisy. Like Lamyā''s father in *Murāhiqa,* Nadā's father plays the role of custodian of his family's honor—while sleeping with the family servant. Nadā's mother, Vera, has sexual desires and needs, but they are unfulfilled. Even so, her father is considered to be one of the most upstanding citizens in town.

Nadā sees an echo of her own confusion in the political turbulence in her country and concludes that in both cases the cause is one and the same: "The papers are boiling with the air of revolution. Against whom? It is against us, against ourselves. When is the world going to take a rest? When am I going to rest?" (p. 77).

In her more self-indulgent moments, Nadā reiterates the question persistently asked by Līnā, the heroine of Laylā Baʿalbakī's novel *Anā Aḥyā*: "Am I alive? If I get my baccalaureate will I then be alive? If I earn 1,000 liras a month do I become alive? If a driver bowed to me and shined my car for me, would I be alive? Am I truly alive?" (p. 69).

Nadā fights her own battle. She leaves her family, goes to work, and earns her own living, refusing to accept the role society has prescribed for her. But it is a battle of few rewards: men still run the country, and people's disapproving looks make her feel that her behavior is not at all condoned. She understands that to challenge her own femininity will bring her no happiness as long as society refuses to accept her as an independent and equal individual. She resolves her dilemma by looking for a man who respects her and stands with her in her earnest pursuit of freedom and self-fulfilment: "I am looking for a man who can rid me of my feeling of alienation and leave me the freedom to smash a pile of dishes in my own kitchen, in my own home. I go on and on searching for the warmth of my breasts; I am still on the move not knowing my destination" (p. 219).

Nadā aspires to self-fulfillment within a social context that acknowledges women's equal rights and full independence in a manner similar to that of Munā, the heroine of Emily Naṣrallah's novel *Ṭuyūr Aylūl (Birds of September)*, also published in 1962. Both heroines conclude that women should not have to sacrifice their social and emotional lives to meet their educational and professional aspirations. Women should strive for equality by changing the concept of femininity rather than by renouncing the roles associated with it. In *Ṭuyūr Aylūl*, Munā tries to dissociate femininity from weakness, while expressing the view that women's freedom and equality should not be achieved at the expense of their natural abilities and emotional inclinations.

Ṭuyūr Aylūl is one of the few novels in Arabic literature that makes the village its focal point, expressing love for the earth and the people. The writer's conscience becomes one with the land to which she belongs. Her criticism of what is negative aims to create a better future for the community she loves and the land to which they all belong. The novelist charts the concerns of fathers, mothers, husbands, and wives and unravels the origin of these concerns in a poetic language that is neither direct nor didactic. In this way she reveals the social and economic stagnation that causes Lebanese youth to emigrate. The narrative suggests the urgent need to change modes of social thinking and to adopt values more congruent with the aspirations of the younger generation and the spirit of the times. The development of events, however, shows how Arab societies' emphasis on reputation smothers the possibilities for change and threatens the future of the people who live in these societies.

Through an indirect but vivid narrative, the reader is introduced to the town's two ignorant gossips, Ḥanna and Angelina, whose idle, malicious chatter ultimately chart the destinies of young educated women. Miriam, Najlā', Mirsāl, Angela, and Munā fail to realize the futures they have planned for themselves or to marry the men they love. Only Munā recognizes—and ultimately avoids—the destructive influence of Ḥanna and Angelina, who essentially represent both the enormity of the social power aligned against women and women's own complicity in undermining themselves.

The fate of the relationships portrayed—between Miriam and Fawwāz, Angela and Kamāl, Mirsāl and Rājī, and Rājī and Najlā'— offers an overt and effective criticism of the distorted concept of love that prevails in the village. It also offers a view of the limitations of relationships based on class and religion. Such limitations sometimes lead to tragedy, as in the case of Miriam's murder, or to enduring unhappiness, as in the case of Mirsāl and Rājī, whose true passion is brutally severed. Even Munā, who escapes misfortune, is never truly happy because she cannot be a whole person, either as a woman or as a professional.

Remarkably, most of the village's inhabitants are women; the men have emigrated to the United States in search of wealth. Their absences, their returns, and their newfound wealth create disturbed emotional and family patterns. Men who once would never have been considered an appropriate match for well-born girls suddenly find that their money can buy access to single women from high society, often without their consent. Women always remain the victims in a social system that denies them both the right to choose their partners and the right to a normal, healthy emotional life. The novel criticizes the social ethic that extols the wealth of the nouveau riche and makes the male members of this class a subject of admiration.

On his return, Sam'ān—called Simon by the village residents—suddenly finds that he is welcomed and accepted by those above his original social class. His new financial status allows him to name any woman he chooses as his wife. Meanwhile, the elevation of the returnees' social status comes at the expense of the men who have remained in the village and who, on account of what they have achieved, have previously been considered of excellent repute.

The effects of emigration extend beyond the boundaries of the village and past the city limits into the region as a whole. Arab society is shown to be a victim of its own social paradigms. The text therefore should be read as an invitation to readers to question the prevailing social ethics and to dare to prioritize what is right over what is socially acceptable or materially favorable.

Naṣrallah focuses on the meaning of "betrayal," which in Arab society is one of the harshest accusations that can be leveled at a woman. The author poses difficult questions: What is betrayal? How do we define it? Is it to betray oneself, one's husband, or society? A striking example of this dilemma is revealed in Mirsāl's letter to her friend Munā. Mirsāl marries John, only in the hope that she can travel with him to the United States in order to meet her lover, Rājī. From the United States she writes to Munā as follows:

> If I were leaving with Rājī I would not have been sad at all, and all my preparations would have had a different flavor. Now I live in the hope of seeing him there. You are going to blame me and say that I am treacherous. Yes, but I am now heading toward the greatest betrayal in my life; the betrayal of myself and my emotions. I am about to sell my body to a stranger called John. It is the price I pay for fleeing this reality and moving closer to Rājī. I shall offer John my body and betray my emotions; after this horrid act of betrayal what does it matter whom I betray? (p. 209)

Here Mirsāl makes a passionate plea to scrutinize the words we use and the concepts they refer to. In this novel Naṣrallah examines her society and discovers the roots of its social and political problems. With a clear vision and a deep sense of responsibility, she highlights the dangerous consequences of these problems and the need to address them with courage and conviction.

The novels written by Arab women writers between 1960 and 1967 demonstrate that Arab women did not just write about love, children, and husbands; rather, they delved into the heart of social and political problems in Arab society at the time. The novels closely link the concept of women's liberation to genuine political reform; they also compare men's attitudes toward women to men's attitudes toward important national issues. Through these novels, one can see that Arab women's writings are significant in literary, social, and political terms because they offer a different perspective than that held by men, thus clarifying aspects of Arab cultural life. The novels discussed here represent only a small sample of a huge number of novels written at this time by Arab women that reveal feminist, social, and political awareness. They all concur that women's emancipation is the first step toward any real social and political reform.

Women's War Novels

UNTIL RECENTLY, it was assumed that war literature was primarily a male domain because it dealt with the battlefield. Unless the story contained descriptions of battlefield action, it was either regarded as insignificant or was not considered to be within the genre. In mainstream literary criticism, a field still largely dominated by men, war literature is, generally speaking, that which deals with action on front lines, with tactics and strategy, shelling and blood, and defeat and victory.

Recent feminist scholars, however, have listened to other voices of war and have portrayed its multiple effects on human society.[1] Feminist critics acknowledge such literature as war literature, although few other critics agree with this assessment.

As far as the Arabic novel is concerned, the Six Day War in 1967 ushered in a new consciousness. The events of that hot summer created an earthquake that shook the entire Arab world. The war not only humiliated Arabs but also induced a breakdown of systems, institutions, ideas, and ideologies. The bitter contradictions that prevailed after the war tore Arab writers and thinkers apart and pushed them in one of two directions. They either veered toward accepting the status quo, having despaired of reforming it or figuring out how to manipulate it and benefit from it, or they went down the road of devoting themselves to creative works that enabled them to escape reality.

This sad environment provided fertile soil that nourished a generation of writers. They expressed frustration, disappointment, and disillusionment with the past, suspicion of the present, and despondency regarding the future. Although the 1967 war was not the only war fought by the Arabs since the 1950s, nevertheless it was probably the most drastic. The colossal sense of defeat created a deep sense of fear in the minds of writers.

Arab women writers were less involved with direct action on the war front and were more concerned with the repercussions of war at the social level. They therefore expressed themselves differently regarding their war experiences. Women novelists have been more interested in exploring the sociopolitical and economic factors that lead to war, as well as war's impact on the human condition. They spend hardly any time addressing the theoretical or ideological arguments that preoccupy their male peers. At first glance, therefore, women's writings about war might well seem less political and therefore less "serious," but in fact in a broader human context they are very relevant indeed.

The first apparent difference between male and female writers after the 1967 war could be seen in the discourse both sexes used to discuss the situation. Men called the war's outcome a "setback," whereas women bluntly referred to it as a "defeat." While the Six Day War (as it is often called) was taking place, most Arab broadcasting stations were assuring their listeners of a landslide victory. Within days, however, Arabs everywhere discovered that they confronted a humiliating defeat. Arab leaders, who had been largely responsible for misleading their public, quickly substituted the word *setback* for the word *defeat*, insisting, as did Egyptian president Jamāl 'Abd al-Nāṣir, that the outcome of the war was nothing more than a minor setback in the long war with Israel. Arab leaders everywhere started emphasizing that the war with Israel continued. Reaction on the part of the Arab general public was twofold: first, disappointment with the Arab governments who had misled them, and, second, a decision both to overcome the psychological defeat inflicted and to work toward a brighter future. But because the word *defeat* had been excised from official rhetoric, the causes and ramifications of events were never fully explored or even addressed. The bulk of the literature that was written about the 1967 war was called *Adab al-Naksa (Literature of the Setback)*, comprising a proud political spirit that did not fully acknowledge the reality of what had happened.

Fadwā Ṭūqān, in the second volume of her autobiography, *Al-Riḥla al-Aṣ'ab (The Most Difficult Journey)*, wrote about a prominent female casualty of the war whose death had previously gone unmentioned. Samīra 'Azzām (1925–1967), a Palestinian short-story writer and journalist, died of a heart attack as she was broadcasting the news of the Arab defeat. Ṭūqān paid a rare tribute to the relationship between Samīra's life and death: "Samīra was a dramatic character in both her life and death. Palestine was her first and deepest passion since the exodus in 1948. The Palestinian cause was at the core of her entire literary output. Palestine was always the focal point of her vision and discussions" (p. 62).

Al-Riḥla al-Aṣ'ab should certainly be mentioned in any discussion of war novels produced by Arab women, who have expressed their profound frustration with existing conditions in inspiring works of fiction. The approach they have adopted, however, has disqualified their works from the war literature genre. Among such writings are *Dimashq yā Basmat al-Ḥuzn (Sabriya: Damascus Bittersweet)* by the Syrian writer Ulfat Idlibī; *'Aṣāfīr al-Fajr (The Birds of Dawn)* by the Lebanese novelist Laylā 'Usayrān; *Sa Amurru 'alā al-Aḥzān (I Shall Pass by Sorrows)* by the Lebanese writer Bilqīs al-Ḥūmānī; *Al-Dawwāma (The Whirl)* by the Syrian novelist Qamar Kaylānī; *Widā' ma' al-Aṣīl (Farewell at Sunset)* by the Palestinian writer Fatḥiyya Maḥmūd al-Bāti'; *Wa Tushriqu Gharban (Dawning from the West)* by the Jordanian writer Laylā al-Aṭrash; *Laylat al-Milyār (The Night of the Billion)* by the Syrian writer Ghāda al-Sammān; and *Būṣila min Ajl 'Abbād al-Shams (A Compass for the Sunflower)* by Liyāna Badr, together with the second volume of Fadwā Ṭūqān's autobiography.

Syrian novelist Ulfat Idlibī is a pioneering novelist who portrays the ordeals inflicted on women in the name of love, family, and duty. Women's suffering is further amplified through the juxtaposition of the important political role they are encouraged to play in defense of their country and their subsequent social subjugation. Many Arab women novelists focus on that theme, particularly after having witnessed the experience of Algerian women, who played a very important role in that country's war of liberation (1954–1962). Once liberation had been achieved, however, men once again assumed complete control and mastery over women, turning a blind eye to women's demands for equal legal status and equal opportunities in the social and political domains. Since that time, Arab women have realized that if women play an active role at a time of national crisis, it does not in any way guarantee that their demands as citizens will subsequently be met.

In her novel *Dimashq yā Basmat al-Ḥuzn (Sabriya: Damascus Bittersweet)*, Idlibī presents the story of Damascus and the Damascene people during the 1920s and 1930s, when Syria was under the French mandate. The focal point of the story is Ṣabriya, who shoulders the weight of both nationalist and feminist struggles and who highlights, through her tragic fate, the dire conflict between her feminist aspirations and an oppressive family authority.

The Arabic word *Ṣabriya* is derived from the word *ṣabr*, which means either "patience" or "very bitter." Ṣabriya's story is that of a young Arab woman who is denied most rights while at the same time she is required to fulfill her duties as a daughter and sister, with all the servitude these actions dictate. Even when the rebellion against the

French begins, Ṣabriya, who is apolitical, pays a heavy price: she loses her favorite brother and her sweetheart.

Ṣabriya comes from a typical Damascene family and has three brothers: Sāmī, Rāghib, and Maḥmūd. She can't help comparing her brothers' freedom with the imprisonment imposed on her. Both her parents and two of her brothers make her feel like a wild horse that has been corralled, whose only task in life is to serve others. The only member of her family who has a different attitude toward her is her brother Sāmī. He treats her with respect, acknowledges her right to be in love with his friend and neighbor, 'Ādil, and is the only one who acknowledges his sister's right to have a romantic relationship. Of all the members of Ṣabriya's family, it is only Sāmī who genuinely believes in the need to fight against the French, and he pays for that belief with his life. Thus, true political progressiveness is shown to be consistent with a healthy attitude toward women, and therefore genuine revolutionaries are naturally feminists and advocates of women's rights.

Sāmī, along with 'Ādil, joins the resistance movement against the French. Ṣabriya makes her contribution to the movement by selling her gold bracelets to raise funds for the resistance. Once the French kill Sāmī, she starts to see 'Ādil secretly. At one point she compares Syrian life under occupation with the lives of women under patriarchal authority and asks herself:

> Why is it that the people of my country demand freedom and at the same time cannot grant it to each other? Half the nation is shackled in chains created by men. That is a wrong we refuse to acknowledge. When I tear this suffocating veil away, I shall be able to enjoy the light and the air. I shall go out of the house just as my brothers go out. Nobody will ask me where I am going, and I won't have to tell lies and devise ruses. The day will come when I tell them that I have got to know 'Ādil, son of the baker. He fell in love with me and I fell in love with him. We will agree to get married when we have completed our studies. They will give me their blessings and congratulate me on the excellence of my choice. When that happens we will really be in good shape, worthy of the freedom we vainly laud today. (p. 149)

Ṣabriya's philosophy, coupling political and feminist issues, exemplifies the stand of Syrian women at the time. During the anti-French resistance, Syrian women began to demonstrate against the veil, claiming that the political and the feminist were inextricably entwined. At the same time, the National Bloc leading the resistance asked women to demonstrate against an official list of electoral candidates organized by the French: "Some members proposed we involve the women this time. They will arouse pride and enthusiasm. The merchants are bound to answer their call. They will close the shops, and the strike, which we regard as very important, will take place. Everybody agreed to the proposal" (p. 162). Although women were used only when needed and were not rewarded for their role in the liberation movement, they nevertheless rejoiced in their participation. Ṣabriya describes her feeling during the demonstration:

> As I stood up in the car I felt I had sprouted wings that enabled me to fly high, in spite of the black dress that hung from my head to my feet and the thick veil that covered my face. I felt that I was a defiant wave in this sea surging in front of me. I was overwhelmed by a strange sensation. For the first time I felt I was a human being with an identity and an objective, in defense of which I was ready to die. I had absolutely no sense of fear. Indeed I felt capable of facing anyone and defying the world. I felt able to confront Father, Mother and Rāghib and to tell them, "I have been on a demonstration with the young men, in defense of my country. There is no power in the world that can get in the way of what I want." (p. 164)

This psychological transformation is short-lived, however; it only lasts as long as the demonstration. Upon arriving home, Ṣabriya is beaten by her father and accused by her brother, Rāghib, of meeting 'Ādil for a clandestine rendezvous rather than being at the demonstration. To prove them wrong, she tells them that the police held her and a few other women. But rather than exonerate her, this information creates further alarm for her family. They fear for their daughter's virginity and summon the nurse, Um Fawzī, to examine her. Ṣabriya finds this most humiliating. Um Fawzī leaves after confirming that Ṣabriya is still a virgin, and although her reputation remains intact, Ṣabriya runs upstairs to her room feeling "as if I had been torn to pieces by wild dogs. Degradation and misery oozed out of every pore of my skin" (pp. 171–172).

Ṣabriya and 'Ādil plan to elope, but the plan is aborted when 'Ādil's body is discovered. Her suspicion that her brother murdered her lover is eventually confirmed. After this ordeal, Ṣabriya becomes responsible for looking after her elderly, paralyzed father, a duty she performs willingly for years.

The novel actually starts near the end of Ṣabriya's life, opening with a crisis depicted between Ṣabriya and her two remaining brothers, Rāghib and Maḥmūd, on the eve of commemorating the death of their father. Once her father dies, her brothers emerge as powerful players and make decisions regarding the family, including the sale of the family home in which Ṣabriya still lives—without even consulting her. Nevertheless, without telling her brothers, Ṣabriya arranges for a *mawlawiyya*, a party in honor of their deceased father that gathers men together to sing religious hymns and perform holy dances. The task of arranging the *mawlawiyya* usually falls to the men, and consequently Ṣabriya's brothers are angered and humiliated. They are stunned to find that Ṣabriya has arranged for this to happen. Once the ceremony is over, they rebuke Ṣabriya for what they consider to be her rude behavior and inform her of their decision to sell the house, because as men they are entitled to the lion's share of their father's inheritance, while Ṣabriya is asked to rent a room elsewhere. Her brothers, who had never shouldered any responsibility in looking after their ailing father, have now become the decisionmakers in her life. She, who has looked after her father for the previous ten years, is asked to leave the only home she has ever known because her brothers want their inheritance. At this point Ṣabriya feels her life is devoid of all meaning and decides to end it by hanging herself that same night by the lemon tree under which she has previously spent many happy hours sipping tea. Her niece, Salmā, spends the night with her, and Ṣabriya hands her the manuscript of her memoirs she calls the "blue book," in the hope of saving her from a fate similar to that of her aunt, and hangs herself.

Through Salmā's reading of these memoirs, in the second and major part of the novel, the reader learns details of Ṣabriya's lifelong suffering. The novel thus falls into two parts: the first comprises about sixty pages, concluding with Ṣabriya's suicide, and the second contains the revelations in the blue book. Ulfat Idlibī uses memoir and flashback to fill in the background and to reveal the reasons for much of what has happened to Ṣabriya's family. Only Ṣabriya is aware of the extent of her ordeal; none of the men seem to notice her trauma. Her brothers are taken by surprise by her decision to end her life, completely unaware of the injustices that she thought were apparent to everyone. Her situation reflects the lack of social awareness of women's plight in Arab society and the lack of support for women.

Characters who encounter each other in the novel rarely have anything in common, and they talk to each other without genuinely communicating their feelings and concerns, particularly with regard to women's rights. Often, this issue is not even discussed. Through the stand taken by father, brothers, and neighbors, the reader perceives that none of the male characters consider women to be equal to themselves or deserving human beings.

The novel reaches its most important technical and thematic point when people from all social strata, both men and women, move to defend their country against the French occupation. At this juncture the reader might well imagine that the focus of the novel has shifted from feminist struggle to political issues. But the political theme turns out to be short-lived and disappears after claiming the lives of Sāmī and ʿĀdil, laying the foundation for Ṣabriya's tragedy. The political theme is in fact subordinated to the feminist theme, depicted in the story of Ṣabriya and to a much lesser extent in that of Nirmīn, Ṣabriya's friend.

Many Syrians have argued that Ulfat Idlibī has gone too far in writing about Ṣabriya committing suicide, that she has unnecessarily exaggerated Ṣabriya's tragedy. Idlibī told me in response to this accusation:

> I know of many women who have committed suicide because they can no longer put up with the kind of life they have been living. My mother and aunt once went to visit their relatives, who asked them to stay the night, and they accepted. When they were having dinner the son of the host said to his sister, "The food you have cooked is not nice." She replied, "No, it is fine." He hit her on the head in front of the guests. In the morning they woke up to find that she had hanged herself. My mother and aunt ran out of the house and came back home because they didn't want to be seen by police and have to answer questions.

Idlibī continued: "It is certainly true that many women commit suicide, and if people are ashamed of such a thing taking place they had better address the causes which lead up to it." She said that she had intended to write a follow-up to the original novel about the life of Salmā, Ṣabriya's niece, but that she had never actually managed to do so. It is notable that in spite of the criticism leveled against this novel, in the early 1990s *Dimashq yā Basmat al-Ḥuzn* was the basis for a television series aired on Syrian television and the Syrian satellite channel that reaches most Arab countries.

In this novel, Idlibī links political and feminist issues. A national resistance movement is seen through the eyes of a woman who considers men's political behavior to be part and parcel of their social and personal beliefs. No ideological debate is raised; rather, the text offers a realistic description of people's daily lives at times of political crisis and of the concrete link that exists between political and social attitudes.

Recently, genuine support for women's rights has been acknowledged by some as the best measure of true political radicalism, and it is notable that this novel does not portray a war of independence occurring in a vacuum. Rather, it is described in relation to people's lives and personal destinies. No clear line is drawn between the political, the social, and the feminist. All are woven together in a historical-realist novel that describes a part of Syria's history with the lives of women at its center.

Idlibī is regarded as one of the pioneering short-story writers and novelists in Syria. Her work is considered to be a genuine expression of the way Damascenes live. She has always chosen Damascus as the scene for her novels and reflects in depth on women's lives and the complexity of family relationships in a society that does not consider addressing family issues publicly to be proper behavior. Some of her short stories are taught in Syrian schools, and a comprehensive study of the novel or short story in Syria would not be complete without a consideration of Idlibī's work.

The Lebanese novelist Laylā 'Usayrān takes exception to describing the outcome of the 1967 war as a "setback" and opens her novel *'Aṣāfīr al-Fajr (The Birds of Dawn)* with the statement, "I write this novel on the eve of the 1967 defeat" (p. 5). The novel is divided into two equal parts of five chapters each. The first deals with the shock, deep disappointment, and disbelief with which the Arab people received the news of such a swift defeat, and the second addresses the Palestinian reaction to the war—a reaction that gave birth to active resistance to Israeli occupation.

The first part of the novel is full of confusion about the past and the present, between news arriving from the front via national radio broadcasts and news broadcasts by foreign news agencies. Six days was hardly enough time for people to understand all the misinformation that had led them to believe that victory was close at hand, when in fact Israel had captured and occupied Gaza and the West Bank, the Sinai, and the Golan Heights. They were shocked not only by what Israel had achieved but also by the misinformation put out by Arab governments. Within a few hours, events on the ground gave the lie to twenty years of rhetoric from Arab governments.

In Beirut, Aḥmad, 'Iṣām, and Miriam find themselves inundated with broadcasts of the defeat and overwhelmed by the shocking color of blue (a reference to Israel's flag). Aḥmad attempts to deny the reality in discussions with friends and relatives and tries hard to believe in the broadcasts and reports from the national media. "He tried to look confident and to believe that the battle had not yet begun and that all that had so far taken place was tactical, or strategic, or even just manoeuvres or plans. But eventually he found nothing to say to convince others." His belief in the claims of Arab governments that Israel was no match for the Arab armies and that Jerusalem could be liberated, evaporated over the course of a few hours (p. 24). Neither Aḥmad, nor indeed anyone else, is able to understand how Jerusalem fell into the hands of the Israelis.

The loss of Jerusalem, together with a considerable amount of Arab territory lost to Israel, disturbed the Arab way of both thinking and being. The outcome of the war was all the more shocking because it directed a fatal blow to Arabs' previous relationship to their past, their present, and their hopes and aspirations for the future. The earth underneath their feet was shaken and they were left dizzy, staring into a void. "Something more important than the war has happened to Aḥmad; a complete divorce has taken place between him and his past; he has rejected his past once and for all and is enveloped in a vacuum of alienation in a capital which he does not know well" (p. 27).

The shock resulted partly from the rapid turn of events; there was no time to believe or disbelieve, to defend or discredit; everything happened so quickly, and the outcome of the war seemed too tragic to be true. "All we wanted was to continue fighting for a month or two; instead three capitals have fallen within a few days, bringing to an end 20 years of waiting" (p. 30).

'Iṣām tells Miriam that "foreign agencies testified that the war was over from the moment it started" and sums up the destiny of the Arab peoples: "We are finished as people; everything is over" (p. 107). A climate of absolute frustration and utter devastation prevailed within the Arab world. The defeat struck at the pride of the entire Arab nation and generated a deep sense of humiliation. The war, therefore, could be perceived as a psychological death.

After 1967 and the disillusionment that followed, Arab peoples assumed the legitimate right to chart their own futures, regardless of the course their governments chose to take. Hence the birth of popular resistance movements against the forces of occupation. In the second part of the novel, the crisis metamorphoses into a strong, clandestine resistance to the Israeli occupation of Palestine, a resistance that has become the only hope for a better future. Māzin, Salmān, Khālid, Miriam, and others of their generation shed their dependence on their governments and their expectation that foreign powers might help them to reclaim their lost lands. Rather, they enroll in national resistance movements that count only on their own efforts to end occupation.

This disillusioned generation of fighters, however, starts to make the same mistakes as their predecessors, such as lionizing leaders and placing them on pedestals, above question or reproach. In the second part of the novel, *al-Khityār* (the old man), the leader of the secret resistance (who symbolizes the Palestine Liberation Organization leader Yāsir 'Arafāt) is idolized.

The novel offers few insights into the problems that face the resistance. Salmān has been abroad studying at university and secretly leaves his studies to join the resistance. Only once does he stand in front of his home, confused about facing his family on the third floor: "He felt that some things require more courage than the courage required to carry out any military task or mission" (p. 107).

Nonetheless, the birth of active resistance restores dignity and a sense of belonging to people, who as refugees have lost their sense of direction, hold little hope for the future, and feel ashamed of their poverty and statelessness. Miriam confides to her brother Salmān, "I lived my life shying away from being a refugee; I was a stranger who did not belong" (p. 124). Although acts of resistance claim the lives of many youths, women nonetheless celebrate their children's martyrdom, because death has provided their children with a dignity that their mothers have not been able to secure for them in life. Notwithstanding all the sacrifice and the pain, the novel concludes with the idea that something more important than the war has happened.

> Tens of thousands of gods have died, and all the thrones have collapsed, but every minute has ushered in a new day, and every hour a new month, and every month the *intifada* [uprising] of the love of people who have been born anew with a new God, a new faith and new concepts . . . Something more important than the war has taken place; something that has been sung by the birds of dawn saying: "a revolution until victory." (pp. 160–161)

For the generation that lived through the 1967 war, this novel will doubtless be read with great enthusiasm. For later generations it will probably stir up less interest, mainly because the characters are barely distinguishable from one another and the development of events is preordained. The language is that of political activists, and the author emphasizes political causes over narrative technique. For politically oriented minds, however, the novel is interesting, and it does sum up the consciousness of a generation of Arab people. The major problem is that the characters and the relationships between them are not sophisticated enough to justify the complex development of events at the political level. Even so, the novel does celebrate the role of women, not only in assessing the war but also in launching the war of liberation that was considered the only answer to the 1967 defeat. Thus, even as it recognizes the disastrous consequences of the 1967 war, the novel goes beyond the defeat and failure to what has emerged, that is, the will and determination of people who promise to usher in a new dawn for the Arab nation.

In her novel *Sa Amurru ʿalā al-Aḥzān (I Shall Pass by Sorrows)*, Balqīs al-Ḥūmānī adopts a different strategy by focusing on ordinary family life and concerns, the ultimate objective of which is to resist occupation and undermine its future prospects within Arab communities. The strength of this 500-page novel is that it conducts a dialogue between different factions, convictions, and viewpoints; it explores all future possibilities and makes the reader a witness to what has happened. The novel opens with a dedication to women's political struggle: "For you, my sisters: Fāṭima, ʿĀʾisha, Shādiya, and every woman martyr and fighter in our occupied land; I dedicate this story to you because it is your story; I learned it from you and I write it for you." From the first page, the reader faces the cruelty and horrors of occupation.

Salmā and ʿIṣām are newlyweds, happily in love with each other, but they have different points of view regarding how occupation should be resisted. ʿIṣām believes in active resistance and, after lengthy discussions, Salmā finds that she has no choice but to support him. Thereafter, carrying out resistance activities becomes a feature of their family life. As a result, they are able to steal only a few moments together, tinged with fear for their safety and that of ʿIṣām's comrades. Their house, which has become a haven for other members of the resistance, is watched and attacked. ʿIṣām is killed, and Salmā is taken prisoner.

Al-Hajj Salīm also believes in active resistance, whereas his son ʿAbd Allah, a chemistry teacher, believes that military resistance will not restore Palestine to the Palestinians. He believes that Palestinians should focus their energies on science and education because the enemy currently leads in those fields. ʿAbd Allah further believes that "military resistance has only one consequence: to give the pretext to the occupier to occupy what is left of our land and to expel or destroy the rest of us. This is what our enemy is doing and his pretext for that is the military resistance" (p. 100).

The dialogue in this novel critiques patriarchal authority and the disasters to which it has led. The son disagrees with his father, but each is prepared to listen to the other and discuss ideas. Difference is not understood as treachery, as it usually is in Arab politics. People have paid a high price for that attitude, and the lack of political insight and leadership has caused many of the tragedies and disasters that have befallen people under occupation. The novel reads smoothly and introduces extremely difficult political dilemmas within a simple, clear-cut net of relationships and cluster of arguments. It should most definitely be studied along with the rest of the literature about the events of 1967, but unfortunately, so far it has been neglected.

In Qamar Kaylānī's novel *Al-Dawwāma (The Whirl)*, the start of war is foreshadowed by a dream experienced by Mrs. Haniyya, in which a storm swallows an entire town, including its houses and trees. People begin to run down the streets, some of them naked and others laughing like lunatics. No one is left except a military brigade and a newspaper salesman who shouts as he chases papers being swept away by the wind (pp. 23–24).

The novel presents four active female characters: Sāmiya, Haniyya (her mother), Ṣafiyya (her aunt), and Rajā' (her cousin). Men are elusive figures. Karīm, Sāmiya's husband, never appears. We know only that he resides a long way away. Jabir, who loves Sāmiya, appears on moonlit nights to express his love for her and to advise her to abandon her independent lifestyle. The social dilemma from which Sāmiya suffers is that she is a married woman separated from her husband and living on her own. Their arrangement deviates from a "normal" marital relationship and draws criticism from friends and neighbors, which causes Sāmiya to feel even more alienated from her social milieu. Even when she talks to her cousin Rajā', she feels that "the Whirl" is subsuming her. She mutters to herself, "This is amazing, this is strange, the Whirl has reached [me] as well" (p. 95).

The Whirl is a psychological condition; it is a dilemma that dominates the lives of all the characters in the novel. Before the war, the situation seemed absurd: no one was happy or fulfilled, and nothing was governed by logic. No one seemed capable of directing his or her own destiny; instead, all fell victim to dilemmas not of their own making. None of the characters was honest or decent: "Jabir is a slave to his sexual desires, and Salem is only interested in women's bodies. Bāsil and 'Irfān are no better; the world is populated with false people, all false" (p. 219). Nonetheless, the writer does provide her characters with insight. When Rajā' switches the light on in the hotel and finds Sāmiya in another man's arms, she thinks to herself: "What a contradiction and what a deceit, then, in her character" (p. 243).

Everyone was trapped within his or her individual loneliness; only when war erupts does a moral awakening begin. The war breaks Sāmiya's self-imposed isolation and total lack of interest in others. The difference between her and her husband, Karīm, is that she focuses on her personal world, whereas Karīm concentrates exclusively on public events. "Sāmiya feels that she is the center of the universe; this is the secret of her life and of Karīm's failure and this is the source of their ordeal" (p. 255). Sāmiya's self-absorption, however, does not overcome her political concerns. Quite the contrary—she actually becomes more attached to the land once war is declared. The course of the war shatters many myths and changes attitudes and personal relationships. Sāmiya wishes Karīm had been with her: "Had he been here," she thinks, "the barriers between us might have broken in the face of this grave danger" (p. 259).

When Sāmiya becomes certain that the war has started, she looks for something useful to do. She is critical of the fact that even though people have been taught to love their country, they have not been taught how to express this love. She wants to do something during the war but does not know what. She thinks of writing for newspapers because she has always heard that "the word is as powerful as a bullet," but decides to undertake more traditional women's work in a hospital.

The attitudes of both Rajā' and Sāmiya, as well as Fādiya and Bāsil before them, show that defeat has broken people's psychological isolation. Defeat has also shown them the need to rid themselves of the self-conceits in which they had been entrenched for so long, of saying what they mean, and of meaning what they say. The war has burned away all falsehoods, all false feelings and false relationships. Only solid convictions remain. The novel suggests, therefore, that hypocrisy and self-deceit were partly responsible for the Arab defeat in the war.

Like the characters in 'Usayrān's novel *'Aṣāfīr al-Fajr (The Birds of Dawn)*, Sāmiya resents people's deluded belief that the Arabs are gaining the upper hand in the war. She knows the truth and wants to convey it to others but does not want to shock them: "She does not want to deprive them of their belief in the greatness of this nation. She should at least leave them their faith in the near victory. She speaks and speaks without conviction; words are empty drums, and even she who always meant every word she said is now sounding these drums violently, for nothing" (p. 275).

Like 'Usayrān, Kaylānī refers to contradictory war reports broadcast on national radio and to the discrepancy between Arab and foreign radio broadcasts. People are confused. They find it hard to believe that the Arabs are losing the war. Sāmiya recalls the words of her father, who told her that Arab victory was assured because the Arabs had a legitimate right to Palestine, but now, "she realizes that victory is hard work and not easy words" (p. 283).

Sāmiya watches women go out and enroll in different activities in support of those fighting to defend their countries. Workers, housewives, and career women volunteer to do anything required in order to save Syria from the blazing war. She has never before witnessed such force-fulness in women (pp. 277–278).

The fall of Qunayṭira, a Syrian border town, throws Sāmiya off-balance psychologically, and she suffers a loss of memory. She is admitted to the hospital, and now the only thing she can do well is to paint: "The war has occupied her soul, has quenched the lights from her spirit and left her in absolute darkness to express all that she feels through paint-ing" (p. 333). She paints a picture that reminds her of the dream her mother had at the beginning of the novel: a Whirl, at the center of which is a headless woman spinning round and round. After conveying the terrible dream in the painting, she sets the house on fire and leaves.

Here the novel has something in common with *Widā' ma' al-Aṣīl (Farewell at Sunset)* by Fatḥiyya Maḥmūd al-Bāti',in which Salmā, the main character in the novel, holds tenaciously to the land and her right to it, even though the land has cost the lives of her husband and her child. Eventually Salmā, like Sāmiya, expresses herself in painting as the shock of the tragedy throws her off-balance. She paints the tragedies that have befallen her country and people. In both instances the women show an extraordinary loyalty to their countries and iron determination to defend their soil against aggressors, no matter what the cost might be. They call upon people to stay put and reject emigration, whereas men who claim to be patriots retreat in the face of defeat. Once women lose their spiritual and psychological balance, they transfer their emotions and feelings to works of art that allow their cause to endure for generations. Both Sāmiya and Salmā paint extraordinary pictures that express their personal experience of the tragedy of war.

Widā' ma' al-Aṣīl is an interesting, readable, and wrenching novel that should be included in any study of war novels by or about women. The turn of events highlights new facts about women's actions in times of war and national crisis. The tragedy of Salmā is the tragedy of Palestine. Salmā embodies the pride of Palestine and the pride of digni-fied Arab women who eschew wealth and jewels to preserve their home-land. After both her father and brother have paid with their lives to pre-serve Palestine for Arabs, Salmā is raised by her mother as a dignified woman who believes in pride, honor, and patriotism. She is a sensitive artist, not at all materialistic. She regards her neighbor's luxurious home with contempt because they sell their national conscience to the enemy, and she refuses their son's proposal of marriage. Through her own stand she encourages her male admirer, Walīd, to reject his family, which has just sold land to the enemy, and to join her in the resistance.

Walīd's mother, Ẓarīfa, the wife of Shukrī Bayk, is the opposite of Salmā. She is materialistic, preoccupied only with accumulating wealth, even to the extent of selling the family's land to the Israelis. She encour-ages her husband to betray his country to support her luxurious, deca-dent lifestyle. By holding these two contradictory types of women, Salmā and Ẓarīfa, responsible for preserving or squandering the home-land, respectively, al-Bāti' seems to consider women to be not only the conscience of men, but the conscience of the nation and the only true navigator of its future.

In *Wa Tushriqu Gharban (Dawning from the West)*, the Jordanian novelist Laylā al-Aṭrash attempts a more ambitious work that encom-passes the partition of Palestine in 1948, the Suez war of 1956, the ces-sation of the unity between Syria and Egypt in 1961, the Algerian war of independence (1954–1961), and the 1967 Six Day War. The novelist explores the political and social reverberations of these events by examining family and social relationships before, during, and after the wars. The social relationships depicted are credible, covering areas of tension between men and women, husbands and wives, parents and children, progressives and conservatives, and pessimists and optimists, to the extent that the novel seems to be extremely realistic.

The setting is a village, ironically named Bayt Amān (Secure House) because there is nothing secure about people's lives in this village. Their past has been stormy, and their future promises more turbulence. There is hardly any political propaganda or any ideological statements in the novel; rather, the effects of political mishaps and political hypocrisy are shown in the lives of ordinary people and in the details of their relationships. The family of Shukrī al-Najjār, taken as an example of a Palestinian family of the time, consists of four sons ('Imād, Ḥusām, Bassām, and 'Aṭallah) and one daughter (Hind). The two elder sons, 'Imād and Ḥusām, leave for the United States to pursue their postgraduate studies and, as expected, neither returns. Bassām becomes involved in the resistance; he is arrested and put into an Israeli jail, where he is forcibly sterilized. 'Aṭallah, the youngest son, has an Israeli friend called Levi who is against occupation and believes in Palestinian rights. Hind excels at school and registers to study law at the University of Beirut, but she, too, joins the resistance after the 1967 war.

Hind's mother tries to secure the same right to education for her daughter that her sons had and tries unsuccessfully to persuade her husband to send the girl to the United States to continue her studies. The difference between the treatment of a boy and a girl hits hardest, however, when Hind, a Christian, falls in love with Dr. Marwān Naṣṣār, a Muslim. Her brother, Bassām, has already told her that he is in love with Rīmā Yūsuf, whom he intends to marry. Hind thinks he will be the first to support her, but she is surprised to find that he opposes her relationship. She writes to her two brothers in the United States, one of whom is already married to an American woman, but here the answer is also a clear-cut "no," justified by concerns about the threat to the family's honor and reputation if Hind pursues her intention to marry a Muslim. This particular incident is significant because it focuses on a contradiction in attitudes toward women that prevails throughout the Arab world: that women are granted the right to pursue their education, choose their careers, and defend their countries but are not allowed to choose their own husbands or make any other choice that might upset the patriarchal order. Women's academic achievements have not contributed much to a change in men's attitudes toward women's rights; equally, women's political achievements have not been translated into acknowledged personal and social rights.

Nevertheless, women are the first to defend their countries in various ways and by various means. Ḥasnā', a much-pitied character in the village, has paid with the lives of her five sons for Palestine and lives her life in a state of semimadness. She carries the key of their home in East Jerusalem everywhere with her, even to bed. When the West Bank is occupied, Hind is among the first to enlist in the resistance and carries out operations against occupying forces. In this domain, women are extolled, no matter where they might go and with whom. The strongest taboo, for women, is their sexuality or getting married to a man from a different religion or a different nationality. Men, however, may marry whomever they please, without bringing shame to their families.

National crises ease social differences. Men and women fight in the same trench because in a national crisis the focus is on duties rather than on individual rights. Whenever duties come to the fore, women are considered at least men's equals because they shoulder the same, if not greater, burdens. After the 1967 defeat (Laylā al-Aṭrash has no other name for the result of that war), Hind finds the men crying (p. 187). Hind, like almost all the heroines in Arab women's war novels, believes the Arab news agencies are responsible for the high number of casualties: "The Arabs have attacked; they have reached Haifa and [the enemy is] retreating under the force of arms" (p. 169). Such a declaration mocks the performance of the Arab armies and their refusal to acknowledge the worst defeat they have ever suffered.

Because people were not accurately informed about what was happening, they did not take adequate precautions to preserve their lives and properties:

> Ḥasnā' died when airplanes shelled Bethlehem twice. They flew over the people and rained their bombs on the market and shops during the third day of the war. People were still selling and buying as radio broadcasts assured them of an Arab victory. Thus people did not feel the danger. Warplanes roamed above and hailed bombs . . . people were pushing each other on stone paths absolutely terrified. Fractions of the bomb followed them and blood flowed down staircases; the bodies were scattered all round. (pp. 188–189)

People feel an immense sense of shame; in an instant, everything loses its meaning. Salmā wonders why people are making such a commotion about the resignation of Jamāl 'Abd al-Nāṣir, the Egyptian president and Arab nationalist leader who led the Arabs in the war. Salmā feels that 'Abd al-Nāṣir is just as helpless as she is and just as deceived and ashamed. But she believes her loss is greater than his: "He is merely sad, but she is a refugee; he is a miserably resigned president, but she is utterly lost" (p. 172). Here the narrative stresses that the fate of rulers, whether presidents, kings, or queens, is rarely as significant as the fate of the people who constitute a nation.

Nevertheless, despite the horrors, loss, and frustration that the war has brought with it to the Arab populace, it has some positive impact on social life. The Palestinians have learned from the experience of 1948, when they fled their land in order to protect their women from being raped. Hind's mother explains that people were torn between two alternatives: "to preserve their honor or to flee, but they decided not to repeat the experience of the 1948 war and not to turn themselves into refugees. They decided that they would not leave and that they would rather die at home" (p. 190). Thus it was as if the war had converted people and completely changed their social attitudes. Hind's mother, for example, who previously never believed that the marriage of Hind and Marwān would be possible, "pulled her daughter toward Marwān and put her hand in his and showered them with congratulations and best wishes for a bright future" (p. 255). It was a transformation like this that made Hind watch the sunset with Marwān and see another dawn, "as if the sun was dawning from the West" (p. 255). That metaphor shows that good may well be born out of evil and that a promising future may well emerge out of a humiliating defeat.

Wa Tushriqu Gharban is a political novel, but it is devoid of overt political statements and propaganda. It depicts politics in the home and discusses the freedom and future of the people as the wars of 1948, 1956, and 1967 and the Algerian war for independence were taking place. People respond to the conflicts within the context of their hopes, ambitions, and plans. The wars are not reduced to political abstractions, and neither do people's responses take place in a vacuum. The author never uses abstract political terminology but helps readers understand the impact of political events on people's daily lives. 'Abd al-Nāṣir is seen as a person who resigns and dies and who, like everyone else, suffers from frustration and disappointment, having been betrayed by his generals in the battlefield. The main focus of the novel is on ordinary people, who measure all political events by the effects these events have on their daily lives. Politics in this novel occurs where it should: that is, as an integral part of the political, social, and historical conditions of people's lives.

Laylat al-Milyār (The Night of the Billion) is a most unorthodox war novel. The Syrian novelist Ghāda al-Sammān addresses the hidden causes of the civil war that wracked Lebanon for fifteen years. In the novel, people living in Geneva discuss events in Beirut. The narrative aims not to offer an account of the war itself, but rather to explore its causes, and in so doing it discovers a web of financial and commercial relations. Beirut airport seems to be the only place where salvation can be found from an all-consuming war that has no apparent logic, purpose, or point of control. Although the scene of events is Geneva, Ghāda al-Sammān keeps all threads of the narrative closely linked to Beirut. To do so, she focuses on two major elements of the larger society: first, the loyal nationalists, who are forced to leave Lebanon and who follow the news minute by minute, awaiting the first opportunity to return; and, second, the arms' merchants, who sell weapons to all parties in the conflict in order to keep the war ablaze so that demand for their merchandise will be sustained.

By depicting daily contacts between these two groups, the author demonstrates the gap between genuine nationalism and the pretense of nationalism, between what is said and true convictions harbored in the depth of the self, between slogans raised for public consumption and real policies exercised on the ground. The novel operates at different levels to meet different objectives, encompassing the social, economic, and political aspects of human endeavor resulting from the complications of war.

Readers are shocked at first, when the novel unveils the unpalatable truth that those who are in command of their destiny are arms' merchants, drug dealers, and soothsayers, none of whom have any morality. Because this class of people controls the livelihood of all others, it is able to buy out some of those who are national icons, thus creating confusion in the ranks of nationalists, some of whom become vulnerable to the temptation of accepting financial inducements.

These politicians, arms merchants, and drug dealers attempt to strip the country of its last national symbol, the Palestinian coin, so that they can feel assured about their future. All they care about is money, and most people are intimidated by them. That is why Raghīd al-Zahrān spends a lot of money to buy an antique Palestinian coin from Laylā. The reader, however, discovers the shallowness of these people, supposedly nationalists whose devotion to their country is beyond doubt, and is angered by their ability to buy national symbols instead of adhering to their principles. Khalīl Durr', for example, tries hard to resist these unprincipled people, but as an unemployed exile, he has no choice but to cooperate with those whom he despises. Amid this state of despair, Baḥriyya arrives in Geneva. Her name derives from *baḥr*, the Arabic word for sea, and she is a symbol of Beirut (known as the City of the Sea). She is loved and cherished by genuine nationalists such as Nasīm and dreaded by arms' merchants and astrologers such as Shaykh Waṭfān and Raghīd al-Zahrān.

Bringing Baḥriyya from Beirut to Geneva strengthens the ties of people in Geneva with the home country and induces fear and confusion among magicians and merchants. Baḥriyya is the ultimate voice of truth that reminds people both of their origins and their purpose. She refuses to associate with unprincipled people and spend nights at riotous parties, and her presence in Beirut disturbs the corrupt class while at the same time helping the true nationalists to restore confidence in themselves and their future.

Bringing in Baḥriyya and the Palestinian penny strengthens the nationalist camp, but Khalīl and Laylā, who were previously known for their unquestioned nationalist stance, fall into the other camp for no logical reason. When Khalīl finds out that his wife, Kafā, is betraying him with his master, Ṣaqr, he realizes that she is corrupt and adulterous. Yet instead of releasing his anger on her, he remembers that he, too, is corrupt, because he also has betrayed the values and ethics in which he once believed.

Significantly, in this passage, adultery is not portrayed, as it usually is in Arab society, as the ultimate betrayal and among the worst of crimes. Betrayal of principles or conscience, and particularly betrayal of country, are seen to be far more serious offenses. The concept of betrayal is no longer confined to what a woman does or does not do with her body; rather, it incorporates other types of betrayal that are usually committed by men and that have more adverse social and political repercussions.

The psychological conflict in the novel takes shape most clearly in the life of Dunyā, the wife of Nadīm al-Faqīr. She remembers her art and creativity and attempts to gather together the remnants of a lost self. But in presenting Dunyā's inner conflict, the novelist offers no ready solutions. Dunyā's conflict remains unresolved, and for her, suffering remains a way of life.

Laylat al-Milyār is a novel on a large scale, rooted in the wounds of Lebanon, from which its characters were forced to emigrate to discover the source of those wounds. Here, as in her first novel, *Beirut 75*, al-Sammān depicts opportunists who treat their country's people as a commodity to be exploited for the accumulation of wealth and prestige. The message is clear: social and political immorality is responsible for the tragedy of the Lebanese civil war and the suffering of the Lebanese people. Throughout the narrative, al-Sammān highlights the interrelatedness of the political, social, economic, and national arenas, and concludes that no one can be both politically progressive and socially conservative. A true advocate of national freedom and democracy, for example, cannot be a domestic tyrant and an oppressive husband. This attempt to link aspects of men's behavior to politics is the most overt feminist argument in al-Sammān's works and is consistent with the ideas of other Arab women writers, such as Ulfat Idlibī above. Men have always tried to compartmentalize their political and social behavior and thus maintain the position of being politically progressive but socially conservative, particularly with regard to gender issues.

As I said above, *Laylat al-Milyār* offers a very unconventional account of the civil war in Lebanon, but it is one of the most significant because it unravels the origins of the Lebanese disaster. Many novelists have written about the Lebanese civil war, most of them recording the social effects of the war on individuals. Al-Sammān is the only novelist who has undertaken the task of unraveling the far-reaching circumstances responsible for its origin.

In *Būṣila Min Ajl 'Abbād al-Shams (A Compass for the Sunflower)*, the Palestinian writer Liyāna Badr finds there is no distance between the front line and the home front. The front line inserts itself into people's homes, into the most private details of their lives. For Palestinians in 1967, their homes, orchards, and streets literally became the front lines. They were forced to leave the towns and villages that held their history and part of their souls.

In this novel, Badr describes the moral, psychological, and physical violence of war. Jinan is asked to collect her memories and private belongings in five minutes because the call to go is so urgent:

> I'd rushed all round our house, confused and upset, and they'd shouted at me, "Quickly! All you need is nightclothes. In two or three days we'll be back." I felt sickened, thinking that this story of coming back in a couple of days was a pathetic re-enactment of what we'd always heard from those who'd left in the first disaster in 1948. "Two or three days," they said. "Until the situation improves." (p. 32)

Psychological violence mixes with physical violence caused by the shelling and uprooting of hundreds of thousands of people in the aftermath of the 1967 war:

> On the asphalt the body of a woman lay stiff and motionless in a black peasant dress. The black of her hair mingled with the black of the asphalt and the black of her dress. Only her feet showed, cracked and hard like the hooves of a goat. Nobody turned to look at her. Nobody seemed to see her. People jostled one another and surged forward bearing children and baggage on their shoulders and fleeing from the tongues of fire spilling out of the sky. (p. 31)

In this novel and in her novel *'Ayn al-Mir'āt (The Eye of the Mirror)*, Liyāna Badr reclaims the history of war, siege, and disasters that befell the Palestinian people in the 1960s and 1970s, both in Palestine and in Lebanon. With the eye of a journalist and the talent of a fine writer, Badr reproduces the physical, psychological, moral, and social history of violence to which the Palestinians have been subjected. She finds the front line in people's homes, on the road to Diaspora, and in the miserable conditions of the refugee camps. Her works are a worthy example of women's war novels.

The fact remains that women's war novels are very different from men's war novels. The difference can be summed up as one of perspective: men highlight the front line and the battlefield as central to the life they are trying to cover, whereas women weave a broad matrix of relationships in which the occurrence of war plays a vital role.

The war novels discussed in this chapter show that Arab women have been deeply involved in the destinies of their countries and peoples, as well as in their own battles against oppression and discrimination. To exclude these texts from Arab war literature is to impoverish the genre, both in terms of perspective as well as in the volume of available material. The novels make a significant contribution to Arab war literature and deserve to be included in any serious study of the literature written in the aftermath of the 1967 war, or of Arab war literature in general.

Most Arab women novelists writing about war make no attempt to speak the commonly accepted language of the time or to endorse the platitudes that were used to cover up the reality of the situation. Rather, every effort is made to show the truth as women novelists see it. There is no pretending that defeat is simply a setback or that the rhetoric of nationalistic fervor will somehow produce victory.

Revelations

IT HAS BEEN a revelation to read the more recent novels written by Arab women novelists and to witness the way they represented the subtle shades of social and political life in the Arab world. While reading these novels, I have found that Arab women novelists are not only perceptive but also at odds with the current social and political systems. Perhaps that is why their voices have been marginalized and their texts remain unread by the larger public.

Indeed, novels by Ḥamīda Naʿnaʿ, Ḥanān al-Shaykh, Hudā Barakāt, and Emily Naṣrallah mark a new stage in the history of the Arabic novel written by women. The fact that an impressive number of novels by Arab women have been translated into English has helped to enhance their popularity back home and among Arab readers elsewhere in the world; in 1995 alone, six novels by Arab women appeared in English. Arab critics and writers have considerable respect for Arab writers whose works have been translated into other languages, and therefore the translation of literature by Arab women has helped to enhance the status of both the works and the authors.

In this chapter and the next, I discuss a number of recent works by Arab women novelists and try to define the literary status of these writers and their work. I hope that a critical study of these novels will help both Arab and Western readers understand these novels better and contribute to a proper assessment of what Arab women have written.

I was surprised to discover how many Arab women novelists are concerned about national issues and how comprehensive was their understanding of the political situation in their countries. Their political approach depends on their conviction that the personal is ultimately political. The issue here, however, is not about equality; it is about difference. Such difference is to be expected, in fact, and more often than not it works for Arab women writers. Many of these women novelists successfully blend feminist concerns with national issues, but each approaches her subject matter with a different style and different technique, producing of course, a very different text.

Syrian novelist Ḥamīda Naʿnaʿ, in her introduction to the English edition of her novel *Al-Waṭan fī al-ʿAynayn (The Homeland)*, writes: "I have chosen *The Homeland* for inclusion in the Arab Women Writers Series, precisely because it brings the hidden history of the immigrant woman to the foreground" (p. v). Yet here, immigration is not just about the physical distance from home; rather, it relates to estrangement from colleagues, friends, and everything familiar.

The heroine of the novel, Nādiya, is an Arab woman who lives in Paris in the aftermath of her involvement with the Palestinian resistance, during which she carried out daring operations, including the hijacking of airplanes. But her convictions and political outlook develop in ways that prove inconsistent with those of her male colleagues. Sharp differences between them culminate in her expulsion from the political organization to which they all belong. Nevertheless, her expulsion from the organization and residence in Paris does not mean that she has abandoned the Palestinian cause. Even though she tries to isolate herself from political concerns, she finds that the Palestinian cause is something she carries with her all the time. The fate of her homeland is her foremost concern; her politics are a genuine commitment, not a formal obligation that she can drop as and when she chooses.

Nādiya has no simple answers. Life is not black and white, but something in between, and a nearly infinite variety of gray prevails: "The bread was the color of ash. The sky was the color of ash. Joy itself was the color of ash" (p. 122). Here the reader discovers the fundamental difference between Nādiya and her comrades: while they adhere to dogmatic, ideological statements, Nādiya chooses to think, question, and then decide. Gray represents her sentiment toward East and West, passive and active political struggle, men and women, and present and past. She realizes that most things are interconnected and interrelated and that flexibility helps her to discover the truth.

Nādiya's life, then, is a continuous journey of self-discovery during which her feelings, ideas, and understanding change and develop. Thus she is both a permanent migrant and a stranger. Many perspectives relating to East and West, men and women, crop up in the novel, to the extent that the reader feels its aim is to ask questions rather than provide answers, and it is here that the novel is very sound, both in theme and technique.

The events of the novel make clear that women's and men's political perspectives differ in fundamental ways. When Nādiya interacts with her colleagues, these perspectives come into sharp relief. The novel also compares the emergent Palestinian resistance organization involving both men and women that is in favor of defending Palestinian rights in Palestine, set against the rotten political system in place that neither grasps the present reality nor has any vision for the future. Family relations are another important theme. Nādiya's family urges her to live a "normal life," a phrase that implies marrying, bearing children, and looking after her family. Nādiya, however, feels absolutely opposed to adopting these duties and is much more at home with political activism.

The dynamic between East and West is explored through Nādiya's relationship with Frank. He is a revolutionary theoretician who lectures on the suffering and oppression of people in the Third World from the security of Paris, where he is sure of respect for his human rights and where he can enjoy living within a democratic system. As for Nādiya, she lives in conflict with political organizations at home, which cling to archaic ideological arguments, as well as with orientalists abroad such as Frank, who impose their own perspective on Arab people and take liberties in formulating theories about the Third World. Nādiya has no choice but to internalize her national identity in her heart and mind and try to protect it from external as well as internal harm.

The writer's use of the first person lends importance to Nādiya's point of view. The novel highlights the past and the present, the relationship between East and West, and Nādiya's attitude toward both. The narrative's movement between the present and flashbacks, brings Nādiya's internal conflicts into sharp relief. Essentially, Nādiya belongs neither to East nor West but sees the potential and limitations of both. She is also alienated from both cultures because she does not fit the archetype of either.

To escape the social and political restrictions this places on her, Nādiya designs a flexible language that helps her to express her vision of a new world, a world that refuses to submit to ideological paradigms that have seemingly become immutable. She begins to reconsider the use of language: "I looked at the word 'well' on the page. It looked like a decomposing corpse. I tried to believe it myself: We are well. I thought about how, without realizing it, we are governed by clichés and linguistic formulae, enslaving us to the word, although the word has little to do with the conditions and events of our lives" (p. 57).

Establishing a new language is critical for confronting reality and changing it. Because Nādiya believes that the language used is incapable of conveying reality, she looks at new ways of using language that might reflect reality more honestly and transparently. In discussions with her colleagues, Nādiya argues that times have changed, that what was once useful is now ineffectual. Changes in methods, attitudes, and policy are required. After a long conversation with her colleague Aḥmad, during which she acknowledges and applauds change as a sign of life, he condemns her for having changed. Nādiya thinks to herself: "I watch him spew up the lies of principle and revolution. I look in his face for an edge of truth, which I can lean on. There is nothing there. Nothing" (p. 83). In Paris, Nādiya reaches a point of complete disengagement with all those surrounding her: "The comrades remained entrenched in their positions. I had become a stranger among them. It was the first time that I felt like that in their company" (p. 91).

Once she reaches this stage, she decides to quit and keep silent. Hitherto, although she had been expelled from the political organization she held dear, she has nevertheless remained politically and intellectually active, but now she thinks of completely abandoning the cause.

> I stood in front of the building which we were occupying and said good-bye to each of the fighters as they set off. Abū Mashhūr came up to me and kissed me on each cheek without saying a word . . . no final requests. How futile our words are! All the words in the world could not convey what was in my heart at that moment. They went off into the dark. (pp. 93–94)

Na'na' is one of the first Arab novelists to focus on the role of language in supporting political dynamics. The author's rejection of the misuse of language in general grows out of her renunciation of political dogmas. The revolution in her convictions requires a new formula through which to express them and a new terminology to convey them accurately. For Na'na', the revelation of the centrality of language signals a fundamental shift in her major character Nādiya, who becomes a politician with a different vision and perspective. As such, Nādiya is alienated from the comrades of her youth, but simultaneously she emerges as a symbol of the homeland and as someone who is courageous enough to acknowledge the importance of the lessons life has taught her.

The woman as a symbol of the homeland is nothing new and has frequently been employed by both male and female novelists, but Nādiya adds a new and important dimension to this symbol. The misuse and misappropriation of language has for too long shaped and defined politics, history, and gender relations in Arab culture. Thus Nādiya discovered that part of what ails Arab societies is ideologues' use of language. She prescribed a "new discourse" as the cure, which she saw as a precursor to advocating an Arab cultural revolution. Now that Arabs are crying out for change, her stand may seem mundane, but thirty years ago it was nothing short of revolutionary. Nādiya highlights the need to evolve by demonstrating that to be static is to be dead.

To her surprise, Nādiya discovers that her "revolutionary" colleagues refuse to challenge authority and fear differences among themselves. When some within the ranks differ from others, their colleagues sometimes send them to their death or to prison. Meanwhile, they use a language that entirely alienates them from ordinary people. As a result, Nādiya no longer believes in ideology or ideologues, revolution or revolutionaries. She believes only in what is real and tangible.

> Instead of reading—devouring, I should say—the bodies of my friends, the poets and writers, I would go to my office in the morning and immerse myself in the everyday details of the lives of people who had remained, in spite of everything that had happened, unarguably real. One could always cast doubts on Aristotle and Heraclitus . . . *but you cannot ignore the onset of winter, or the threat of rheumatism and fever to the people of the camps.* (p. 115)

Near the end of the novel, Nādiya becomes certain of the impossibility of total revolution, "which will eliminate all inequities. Every example which you have given us so far has become a model of tyranny and dictatorship" (p. 146). What is more, she becomes convinced "of the impossibility of a revolutionary operating in a country other than his own, while part of your soul conspired to convince you of the impossibility of revolution itself" (p. 154). Thus the novel ends with reality triumphing over ideology and with honesty overcoming pretense and hypocrisy. Nādiya's only allegiance is to truth and the whole truth.

The novel strips reality of its pretense and glitter and bombast in an attempt to make a first step in the right direction. It resists ideologues, opportunists, and so-called revolutionaries and asks them to face themselves and the reality of the Arab condition honestly and truthfully. The heroine's most important achievement is her acceptance of the changes that have occurred in her thinking and her campaign to convince others of the need to effect change in the way they think, speak, and behave.

The medium the author uses—language—becomes an important means of rendering change because she recognizes that language both reflects and shapes thoughts and convictions. Thus the language and the structure of the novel help communicate its theme. Is it possible to conclude, then, that Nādiya's vision was different from that of her male colleagues and that her insight was more perceptive than theirs? Is the author suggesting that women have something very important to say, even in the political field, and that men have to take their views into account if something good is truly desired and to be achieved? Or is she foretelling, years before the collapse of the Soviet Union and the demise of communism, that the only way to remain alive is to acknowledge the need for change?

Apart from the very weighty issues explored in this novel, it is a pleasure to read because of the very real sense that Nādiya is conducting a dialogue with other characters in the novel. The narrative brings all the characters alive (especially Nādiya, whose opinions and vision prevail), and thus the arguments they raise engage the reader.

The Lebanese novelist Ḥanān al-Shaykh is not as overtly political in her writings as Ḥamīda Naʿnaʿ. *Hikāyat Zahra (The Story of Zahra)* is al-Shaykh's first and best novel. It follows a Shiʿite woman living in the south of Lebanon during that country's civil war in the 1980s. Through the life of this woman, the inherited but worn-out paradigms of social and political life become clear, and the suffering of mothers, daughters, and wives is explored in psychological, social, and political contexts.

The novel's namesake, Zahra, suffers from domestic and social oppression in a patriarchal society, as well as oppression stemming from the consequences of a complicated civil war that has drained the life even from the bread that people eat. Her life is dominated by fear of snipers; the smell of bullets; the smoke of civil war; and the confusion over values, norms, and traditions that war inevitably instigates. Nonetheless, Zahra tries to dream and to remain hopeful about the future.

Zahra's personal tragedy begins when her mother takes her, while still a child, on a visit to her lover. Zahra's presence serves as a shield that protects her mother from her father's suspicions. At an early age, therefore, Zahra begins to feel that her mother's relationship with her is dictated by self-interest rather than by love. She is sure that her mother is not only betraying her father but also herself when she locks her daughter in a room and joins her lover in the room next door. Such incidents provoke Zahra's anger and disgust. But she cannot speak about the issue in case she creates a scandal or, worse, causes a disaster for her mother or herself. For a child, it is a bitter pill to swallow.

Her feelings of hatred for her mother and disgust turn to pity, however, when she witnesses her father mercilessly beating her and sees her mother's face covered with blood. At such moments, Zahra is so confused that she doesn't know whether to blame or love her mother, or whether her mother's behavior might be justified.

In an attempt to escape all this, Zahra leaves Lebanon to join her uncle, who migrated to Africa a long time ago. The uncle's nostalgia for his homeland and family is expressed in his firm embraces of Zahra, although they remind the girl of a relationship in which she was sexually exploited. The only haven she finds in Africa is in the bathroom, where she can lock herself away from everyone. Her time in the bathroom triggers memories of her father's looks that suggested he knew she was no longer a virgin. But the bathroom is also where she can escape from those looks. She is afraid of men, of sex, and of sexuality.

Having trained herself since early childhood to suppress her feelings, Zahra is unable to discuss her concerns candidly. Instead, she holds her breath and swallows her tears. She cannot resist comparing her life to that of her brother, Aḥmad, who is the center of his father's attention, despite the fact that he is a complete failure. He is almost illiterate, having failed to learn how to read and write, yet even so his father dreams of sending him to the United States to complete his studies. Moreover, at the dinner table, the choicest cuts of meat are saved for Aḥmad, as are the freshest tomatoes and the plumpest olives. In fact, the only real difference between them is that he is a boy and she is a girl, and that is the source of her suffering at more than one level.

In Africa, Zahra marries Mājid in an attempt to escape her family, her uncle, and others. She expects him to be a savior and to requite her loneliness, but she is disappointed. Once she is married, she remains as lonely and as distraught as she was before. Neither her family, nor her uncle, nor her husband know the true Zahra, They treat her as chattel, as an inferior, and judge her by her sex and appearance. Thus all places become the same for her as she discovers that her relationship with her surroundings is the same in Beirut as it is in Africa. If all things are equal, she thinks, why not return to Beirut?

When she leaves her husband and returns to Beirut, she finds Lebanon consumed by a civil war fought in the name of religion, although religion has nothing to do with it. Zahra decides that the war "between Muslims and Christians" is really a proxy war between external powers, being fought by the Lebanese on their behalf. Those who stoke its fires are not close enough to feel its heat, and those who are watching the war on television know nothing about the inferno. War has two faces: on the one hand, it strengthens ties between people and increases intimate contact; on the other hand, people are freed from their customary social identities and mores, tribal and family relations, in such a way that they easily commit acts of violence and murder.

Amid the horrors of war, its contradictions and disasters, Zahra has a relationship with a sniper. For the first time in her life she feels really alive, as the sniper is the first man to awaken her passion. She is surprised to find that he is an ordinary man, with an emotional, quiet voice, who affectionately plays with her hair. Like any other ordinary person, he enjoys a plate of *ḥummuṣ* and *fūl* (boiled broad beans) and speaks not as a murderer but as a decent, even lovable, person.

Because the sniper is of a different religion than Zahra and the relationship therefore has to be clandestine, the war is both its cover and its foundation; without war the relationship cannot exist. Zahra's situation resembles that faced by Mother Courage in Bertolt Brecht's play, *Mother Courage and Her Children.* Mother Courage questions the value of life during peace and longs for war, when people enjoy a higher level of consciousness and responsibility. It is as if Zahra has emerged out of Brecht's play to ask, "What would I do if the war were to come to an end?" Because she discovers the importance and beauty of being alive through the relationship she has with the sniper, that relationship outweighs all the misery and cruelty of war.

Zahra is not alone in her need for the war. Her brother Aḥmad has also developed an interest in its continuation, because it has provided him with a salary and a gun, both of which he now finds essential for his identity and prestige. He begins to hope that the war will continue without end.

In her secret relationship with the sniper, Zahra sees herself as a replica of her mother; she relives all the feelings of fear and awe she experienced when accompanying her mother on her rendezvous with her lover. She relives the terror of her father discovering her deception and saying, "Like mother, like daughter" (p. 179). Her fear eventually drives her to insist that the sniper legitimize their relationship by marrying her, especially since she has become pregnant. Once she presses him to formalize their relationship, however, he becomes tense. She says: "My smile disappears in the face of the frown he returns" (p. 180). On that day, he keeps her longer than usual, until darkness falls, and then promises to visit her family the following day. As she walks back home she wonders whether he really is a sniper and whether she can't persuade him to do something else after they marry. Her inner monologue as she walks back home reveals the social, psychological, and political dimensions of the relationship:

> In all this relationship I never stayed out as late as I have done tonight. The evening has descended. The street is empty, except at the barricades. The rain falls. I stumble. I hold on to a telegraph pole to stop some force from dragging me down. My thigh hurts. It's hurting even more. I reach down to touch the place and feel something wet run down my leg, and on to my foot. Can it be the rain? It's surely not raining so hard. Am I miscarrying? I can't even walk, but must not stop. I must reach home. The pain is unbearable. I can't go on. I fall to the ground. (pp. 181–182)

As she collapses, she hears passersby shout that there is a sniper nearby, and she discovers that her lover has killed her:

> He's killed me. That's why he kept me there till darkness fell . . . It's as if someone is saying, "The sniper's still up there," as if they have retreated from me. I close my eyes that perhaps were never truly opened. I see rainbows processing toward me across the white skies with their promises only of menace. (pp. 183–184)

The political reality of evil prevails over every attempt to forget the sound and reality of war. The father of the child she will never see and the man who has discovered the hidden parts of her bright self has opted to kill her for reasons that are up to the reader to divine. Is it because she's asked him whether he is really a sniper and he fears that she might inform on him? Or is it because she has "defiled" herself by sleeping with a man outside marriage? Or is it simply that he does not want to become involved with the duties of marriage and fatherhood? Zahra thinks about the love and trust she felt within the parameters of their relationship and, as she dies, considers that love cannot coexist with war, that war's only meaning is mistrust, hatred, and death.

The Lebanese writer Hudā Barakāt chooses a very different narrative technique to describe the horrors of the Lebanese civil war in her novel *Ḥajar al-Ḍaḥik (The Stone of Laughter)*. She chooses a hero, Khalīl, rather than a heroine, whose daily life and behavior clearly illustrate how war distorts thoughts, morality, and character. Khalīl appears to be homosexual, though he is not. He simply doesn't know who he is, nor does he know the truth of his feelings. Unlike Ḥamīda Naʿnaʿ, who explores political theory and ideology, Barakāt prefers to study the effect of political events on the lives of ordinary people without ever mentioning those events. The language of the novel is coined in a daring and unusual manner. Cultural and political metaphors stem from a woman's experience in the kitchen and the responsibilities of a traditional woman at home. Rather than shying away from being categorized as a "woman novelist," Barakāt exalts in this status, to admirable effect. The reader is left with the definite impression that the author's creativity is intimately related to her gender. If we place Barakāt's experience in the context of the history of Arab women's literature, in which Arab women have often refused to acknowledge their gender and have insisted their narratives are similar to those written by men, we can appreciate the precedent that Barakāt sets. Perhaps she has ushered in a new phase of women's literature.

The novel observes the daily routine of the hero, or rather the antihero, Khalīl, weaving that with the understanding of war, its details and effects on people, and moving between the private and the public spheres. The reader has to understand symbols, suggestions, metaphors, and images to catch the meaning this forceful writer is trying to convey.

The story opens with a simple scene, highlighting the importance that will be attached to characters on the one hand and to daily events on the other. "Khalīl's legs were not long enough, while Nājī tossed his head, scattering raindrops. Khalīl panted behind him, on the penultimate step, stamping his feet to get rid of the mud on his shoes before he caught up and went into the flat with him" (p. 3).

Instead of resorting to a documentary style in describing the effects of war on people, Barakāt uses allegory: "Whenever a battle draws to an end, Khalīl feels the need for order and cleanliness, and the feeling grows, spreading until it almost becomes an obsession. After every battle, his room is clean and fresh again like new, as if the builders had just left. The tiles shine and the room emits a smell of soap, of polish, of disinfectant" (p. 11). It is as if by cleaning his room, Khalīl tries to cleanse himself of every trace of war and to rid himself of any feeling of guilt or shame. Thus his room becomes a substitute for the human self, and its cleanliness compensates for the inner peace and tranquillity that Khalīl cannot achieve. Cleanliness and tidiness help him to feel good, even happy. Such feelings are essential to resist the depression and sorrow generated by war.

Khalīl has few real social relationships and keeps mostly to himself. The few relationships he does have seem to be with people who are replicas of each other. Although most of those who stir Khalīl's feelings are men—Nājī, Yūsuf, Nāyif, Dr. Waddāh, and a character called "the brother"—it is not certain that he is homosexual. Time is distorted and social relationships are deformed; thoughts and concepts are warped. In an environment of abnormality, how can a person's feelings be expected to be "normal"? So in this complicated and distorted reality, Khalīl is unsure of his feelings toward Nājī.

> When Nājī is late, Khalīl feels cheated of the splendor of his ideas, their brilliant sparkle is dulled . . . Khalīl dissolves in emptiness, becomes like a hinge with a single pin which trembles and braces itself against the door, seems as if his body is split in two: one half says he's coming and the other says he's not. His mind stands in the middle, torn between the two, empty and piled high, abstracted and overloaded like Ibn al-Amīn in the story of King Solomon. Someone in this situation feels tired and weak only after he has made up his mind one way or the other . . . Khalīl, like a generous mother, came to prefer Nājī not to come full stop. Then . . . in the twinkling of an eye, his coming becomes a dire necessity. (p. 28)

After Nājī's death, and after his younger uncle moves into Mrs. Isabel's apartment above his room, Khalīl believes his cousin, Zahra, is in love with him. He starts to enjoy imagining her infatuation with him. At the same time, Zahra's young brother, Yūsuf, breaks Khalīl's heart, "shattering it like thick, glass dishes flung to the ground." Whenever Khalīl sees Yūsuf, "he would be stricken and feel faint. He used to say over and over again in his heart, or in his stomach, 'Oh my God, oh my God,' especially when they first arrived" (p. 90).

Khalīl's confusion over both Zahra and Yūsuf shows that feelings are not easily compartmentalized. Like everything else during a war, questions of gender are both confused and confusing. Khalīl is not certain of anything in his life, so why should he be expected to be sure about the way he feels toward Nājī, or Zahra, or Yūsuf? His conflicted sexuality is only one manifestation of his confused mind and life during a time of turbulence.

Once Yūsuf dies, the effect of his death on Khalīl is suggested through the latter's relationship with his body: "Khalīl's body no longer went with him anywhere. It began to refuse and dig in its heels like a stubborn mule, which is why he began to use it rather than work with it . . . Now the ugliness of his body and the pains in his stomach had begun to eat up his time" (p. 161). Subsequently, Khalīl feels the warmth of Dr. Waddāh's hands when the doctor is about to operate on him; he thinks that Dr Waddāh is like a magician who excises the pain and discards it, like garbage. But when, near the end of the novel, "the brother" tries to initiate a physical relationship with Khalīl, he shrinks, which might indicate that Khalīl's problem is mental rather than physical.

Khalīl's life story may be read as a journey in man's unconsciousness, translated into details that are rarely acknowledged, even by the person undergoing the journey:

> Khalīl knew that a fear of blood to the point of faintness, having short legs, a slight build, straight chestnut hair and large eyes, all these do not make a man a hermaphrodite, or effeminate, or any less masculine, or . . . queer . . . he knew that the temporary breakdown that he was suffering was only a psychological crisis that the mad world outside had imposed upon him. (p. 83)

Khalīl's suffering and the distorted life he leads are only two examples of the distortion that war creates for human beings. Khalīl is apolitical to the extent that he does not even know the names of government ministers or political parties. Yet he cannot protect himself from the effects of war on his most personal and private feelings.

Although the war is never mentioned, the author makes its presence known and tangible in the formation of people's thoughts and feelings and in the degree of isolation, distortion, and frustration that they suffer. Even when the writer alludes to war, she does so in an ironic or allegorical style. She shows how war distorts thought: "Then the area was relatively safe, and so allowed itself to be more serene since, it seemed, it had paid its share and it was time for others to take their turn. People on the opposite side of the street utter a sigh of relief that an explosion has taken place on the other side of the road and not on their side" (p. 35).

Hudā Barakāt makes a similar point in her discussion of martyrs and martyrdom, terms that have been deprived of their meaning by war. In *Hajar al-Ḍaḥik*, martyrdom has become a currency in which politicians trade, as they pay young men to lay down their lives. Political parties compete to raise the price of young men:

> The living costs of the young men became exorbitant during the war, so they were obliged to raise their wages and, accordingly [political parties] increased the reparations of the martyrs, each faction fearing that the other would beat it in the price race. And so the market was struck . . . Things settled down and prices appeared to stabilize, although there were some exceptions; some politicians paid in dollars to give their future martyrs some feeling of stability in the face of life's violent upheavals. (p. 47)

As martyrdom becomes a commodity politicians trade, war itself becomes a good investment that enables a few to accumulate wealth and future financial security. War is neither spontaneous nor accidental, as some would like to believe. Certain people have a vested interest in triggering and sustaining it for as long as possible.

People who live through war also experience chaos every day, and both time and place reflect their inner tension and frustration. Neither the time nor the place seems to have any depth or any future dimension: "The flat was, then, no longer a home because its internal time was time in a hurry . . . an upstart, not settled and quiet and reconciled to itself. The feeling of the family that they were temporary was not enough to make them scatter its time and mince it in that way, which made Khalīl feel sad" (p. 89). The political climate is equally tense and intermittent. Place often reflects the human psyche, and in that sense, cleanliness and tidiness reflect an inner psychological and emotional state of being that cannot be achieved.

On the other hand, war stimulates the imperative for survival, just as it does for Zahra and her brother Aḥmad in Ḥanān al-Shaykh's *Hikāyat Zahra (The Story of Zahra)*. People must obtain food, secure a salary or a weapon, feel secure, or at least feel capable of facing danger. Thus war, which by definition is a threat to all living things, becomes a pre-requisite for life, so much so that there seems to be nothing wrong with being involved in a war. "Is there anything wrong," Yūsuf asks, "in wanting to make sure that the needs of the house are met and to take a salary at the end of the month? I have to wear a uniform and have weapons' training for a couple of days, and do a bit of guard duty from time to time" (Barakāt, p. 114).

But when Yūsuf is killed, Khalīl discovers that those who send others to their death never explain to them what war truly means. They hypnotize them with ideology; they never mention the power cuts or the absence of bread from bakeries. Both war and death become necessary to rearrange the map of the city; ironically, they seem to be the only two elements that hold the city together. "Death sits at his desk. He cleans his spectacles thoroughly before picking up the long ruler and the pen to draw up a plan for the city as befits a great architect" (p. 152).

War and death become the daily bread for those who learn the art of becoming blood merchants. The horror of what is taking place is graphically portrayed in the description of Khalīl's body:

> Khalīl ponders his body again. He does not like his body, his weak, stiff legs, his chest, hollow as a frying pan without a handle, his arms, hanging down the sides of the chair like a pair of brooms without bristles, his skinny body, undone at the seams like a scarecrow planted in a bare, dry field, a scarecrow which scares nothing but the crows in his distracted eyes. (p. 159)

In this dire reality, differences between men and women seem to lessen. Like women, Khalīl desires men and carries out all the traditional tasks of women. The novelist's use of metaphors and similes, which outline in detail women's domestic duties to express political concepts or events, is impressive. The thread that is used to sew a cloth becomes the thread of days that pulls one day after another, just as tension pulls disturbed souls. Even speech becomes a plate to which hands are extended to share bread. The images used of women's work show that it is women who weave the main matrix of life and history. They are the pillars of human memory, culture, and civilization. It is through women that peoples of the world pass on their customs, traditions, and national crafts, and it is through women's wisdom that both death and life gain distinct identities: "Women," Khalīl thinks, moaning in envy alone in his room. "All the wisdom is given to women. Wisdom of life and death and wisdom of what is farthest from it . . . they're in touch with the world, they have a secret communication with it which makes anything that doesn't belong to them nothing but a flurry of dust" (p. 144).

Yet this novel isn't about the story of a woman or of a man; rather, it is the story of one of war's losers, who has been defeated by political, social, and even emotional authority. It is the story of a human being whose only concrete relationship is with his body, but even this relationship is confused and distorted. Khalīl says to himself:

> "I'm like someone whose dead have been stolen away, someone whose two dead have been stolen from him." Before Khalīl's buried desire to kill them makes itself clear they kill them and they steal away their corpses, leaving him only the inability to weep for them and the lack of will to bury them, to remind him, always, that he is not man enough to forge his world of dreams and not woman enough to accept. (p. 145)

Thus we have to read the novel with the idea that Khalīl represents the state of androgyny often found in the characters Virginia Woolf created. He is neither a man nor a woman, or perhaps he is a combination of both.

What the author tries to do in this sensitive and poetic narrative is to dissect the world of war with all its complications, interrelations, and reflections on the human self without approaching either the front line or the physical images of weapons, shooting, and destruction. Her ability to write about war is the result of her determination to write a new, serious text that internalizes war and analyzes its effects on the human mind and self.

> I'm not putting pressure on you, not with my eye, for how would you know what the look does to a person? Nor with my voice, for the voice is the direct ambassador of the soul . . . It's just that I martyr myself in my battle to write the best of what I see and feel and imagine, far from you, without making you feel any of the pain I feel. I give you the cream of my soul which I don't give to my wife or mother. (p. 126)

Through this serious and sophisticated act of writing, Barakāt is able to shed a unique light on the effect of war on the lives of ordinary people. She discovers that war brings neither justice nor triumph, for everyone who takes part in war, regardless of the result, suffers from social, political, and psychological defeat. In war there is no victory and no defeat, in spite of what people imagine, because war distorts human psychology, values, and morality. In that view, Barakāt is in total agreement with al-Shaykh, whose narrative shows that war means only death and destruction and, despite the temporary illusions it induces, can never provide happiness or security for anyone.

In her pursuit of the truth, Barakāt is not taken in by the nationalistic fervor usually felt at the mention of great national or political causes. She trusts her feelings and intuition as a woman and human being and isolates them from clichés, ideologies, and nationalism to find that "big causes" simply do not exist. What matters to most people is the detail of their daily lives and daily needs. Through her sensitivity to the importance of detail, Barakāt explores the selfish motives of power brokers that have nothing to do with either ordinary individuals, country, or future.

The writer most in touch with the lives of ordinary people, the names of whom history never records, is the Lebanese writer Emily Naṣrallah. In her novel *Shajarat al-Diflā (The Oleander Tree)*, she probes, as no other Arab novelist had done before, the meticulous details of village life, with special attention given to the lives of women who are not sheltered by husbands, brothers, or sons. Almās, whose husband has died, leaving her alone to raise their only daughter, Rayyā, suffers many types of blackmail, threats, and abuse. Bū Daʿʿās, who claims to be their protector and benefactor, tries to rape Almās and humiliates her daughter by marrying her off against her will to the simplest man in the village. Almās is torn between standing up to him and compromising with him so that she can continue counting on his support and protection.

Bū Daʿʿās is a frustrated man whose children have all emigrated from Lebanon but have never met with success. He invents stories about the great fortunes his children have accumulated beyond the seas, which he almost believes are true. He maintains his social prestige, especially with regard to Almās, whom he is trying to woo, by living a lie. Only his wife, Um Daʿʿās, knows the truth. Eavesdropping at the door, Rayyā hears Bū Daʿʿās making arrangments with her mother to kidnap her in order to marry her off. Rayyā understands well what Bū Daʿʿās is after and focuses on undermining his plans.

The narrative highlights a very subtle and important difference between private realities and public appearances. Bū Daʿʿās appears to be the caring and loving neighbor, but in fact he makes more than one attempt to rape Almās. The only two people who discover this discrepancy and reject it are Rayyā and Nājī, a young boy who throws stones at all who pass by him. Both are considered social outcasts, though in different ways and for different reasons. Both Nājī and Rayyā feel totally estranged from the social reality in which they find themselves and therefore try to support each other. Their alliance is short-lived, however, because Rayyā decides to elope with Makhkhūl, the simplest man in the village, leaving Nājī drowned in feelings of regret and helplessness.

The story of Rayyā and Makhkhūl is the story of a woman who is humiliated because she is a woman without male protection. She decides to rebel and challenge social norms, especially after hearing about the plan hatched by her mother Almās and Bū Daʿʿās to arrange for her engagement to Makhkhūl. "Rebellion is born like a storm; it descends from above; it falls on man like thunder. It is born out of years of oppression and injustice and of holding one's breath within one's chest" (p. 89). Rayyā wants to kill herself, but not before she has avenged herself. "A strange power moves in her chest, a power that cracks up like mountains and roars down as forcefully as waterfalls: 'Revenge, revenge,' a voice whispers in her ears. 'This is the road to destruction'" (pp. 84–85).

She decides to elope with Makhkhūl, ahead of the date decided on by Bū Da''ās for their engagement. Her scheme is an expression of her deep disgust for those who have made her life hell simply because she is a pretty young woman with no father or brother to act as her guardian. Bū Da''ās, who in the village is called *Bū al-Arāmil* (Father of Widows) has previously raped Rayyā in his own home when she came to borrow something, believing that his wife was home.

> She is filled with hatred for him, a deep hatred she does not know how to handle; she would like to set fire, to burn Bū Da''ās out of her life; she says to him: "I hate you." He laughs, twiddles his moustache, cocks his hat and makes a cold-blooded remark to her. She would like to tear his sly face to pieces, but she feels utterly helpless. She is overcome with the feeling that he is a cunning fox living next to a hen house, where her mother is a chicken and she a small chick who has no power because she is between the beak of the chicken and the claws of the fox. (p. 48)

Fleeing with a man she neither loves nor likes is the only possible way to escape. Rayyā's only two remaining friends are Nājī and nature. The villagers revile Nājī. Rayyā alone knows why Nājī uses stones to strike others; it is the only means left to him for self-defense (p. 66). Likewise, only Nājī knows how deeply Rayyā hates Makhkhūl, whom she intends to marry, and Bū Da''ās.

Almās is confused. She does not believe that her daughter is the delinquent Bū Da''ās claims she is and is not sure of the plans Bū Da''ās has for her. She feels uncomfortable with the plans she is making with him regarding Rayyā but reckons she has little alternative but to comply.

On the morning they plan to hatch their scheme, Almās and Bū Da''ās find Rayyā is missing. Bū Da''ās suspects that the girl has heard them plotting and has decided to flee in advance, but reasons that, even so, she would need a man to accompany her, and there is none other than Makhkhūl.

Makhkhūl has not grasped the meaning of his elopement with

Rayyā and tries to dissuade her by reminding her of the scandal it will create in the village. She cares nothing about this and orders him to make haste, wondering why she has to drag Makhkhūl behind her as if he is her destiny. They arrive at the village of Ṭurra, a two-hour walk from their own village, Jūrat al-Sindiyān, and are married by a priest. "The priest was stunned by the difference between the peaceful, simple Makhkhūl and Rayyā who is a revolution embodied in a woman" (p. 94). Makhkhūl can hardly understand what Rayyā is saying to the priest to justify their elopement, and he stands askance, wondering whether she is truly going to be his wife from now on.

When news of the two young people's elopement circulates in the village, the gossips give full vent, tut-tutting that "this is what happens" when there are no men in the house. Had there been men in the house, the villagers say, they would have slaughtered Rayyā a long time ago, and the entire predicament would have been avoided (pp. 98–99). Interestingly, Makhkhūl's family is untouched by the scandal; rather, all blame is placed on Rayyā and her family.

The priest who marries Rayyā and Makhkhūl, Father Jrays, acts as their host for two days because he falls in love with Rayyā and is torn between his religious duties and his passion for her. Rayyā does not allow anyone, not even Makhkhūl, who is now her legitimate husband, to touch her physically. She invents reasons for her inability to sleep with him. Nevertheless, Makhkhūl begins to act like a husband and orders her to get ready to return to their village. Rayyā considers the many generations of women who have never had a say in their own lives. She dreams of having wings to fly out of her reality. She speculates that men see only women's bodies and beauty but have no insight into their ordeals and the volume of thoughts and feelings locked inside them. Makhkhūl's physical advances remind her of the shopkeeper, 'Ammū (Uncle) 'Ūmrān, who sexually assaulted her when she was a young girl sent to buy things from him. Since that day she has felt that no amount of soap in the world could ever wash the dirtiness from her body. She sees 'Ammū 'Ūmrān's face in all the men who follow and harass her, though the only possible response available to her is the tears she generously pours on her pillow.

When they return to their village, Makhkhūl's family throws a party for them. As the attendees sing and dance, Rayyā considers how she can ward Makhkhūl off if he thinks of touching her. It is supposed to be her wedding day, the happiest day of her life. She looks at her mother-in-law and finds her to be a woman without feeling or will: "She wears every occasion like a dress and lives satisfied" (p. 138). Her mother-in-law is yet another victim, as are all the women in the village.

Rayyā has decided to take revenge on behalf of all these women by refusing to let any man own her. She has decided to be free. Because of her internal anguish she loses consciousness and is carried to the bedroom, where she is supposed to consummate her marriage to Makhkhūl. She pities Makhkhūl, and wants to tell him that she pities him, but she feels that those around him are laying one trap after another in her way. Every time Makhkhūl tries to touch her, she remembers the teeth and burning eyes of 'Ammū 'Umrān and she begs Makhkhūl to divorce her. He thinks she has gone mad.

Before they leave the newlyweds alone—if they ever leave them alone—the villagers clamor to see the sheet upon which Rayyā is supposed to have been deflowered to prove that she was a virgin. But because Rayyā won't let Makhkhūl touch her, the villagers begin to question Makhkhūl's manhood; he is advised to be violent with her. Rayyā recalls the names of the women who have paid the price with their bodies for their rebellion. She knows what will happen to a woman who rebels against social norms. She finds serenity only when she decides to kill herself. She compares herself to Um Makhkhūl, who follows her husband obediently, takes pride in the burdens imposed on her, and endeavors to live according to custom. Rayyā is the very antithesis of this type of woman, and realizing that she is unable to live in a world to which she does not belong, she commits suicide in the room in which she was raped under the guise of an official marriage. The marriage that both Makhkhūl and the people of the village wanted Rayyā to have was for her a death sentence. She had tried to avoid it by all means possible, but once inside the net she found that there was nothing else she could do but end her life.

The phenomenon of women's suicide is worthy of study and scrutiny, because in most cases it indicates a chasm that still exists between women and the society in which they live. What women need to do is challenge and change the reality that is oppressing them, rather than let it overcome them once and for all.

In *Shajarat al-Diflā*, Emily Naṣrallah has shown that it is impossible for a woman to live and function on her own in a patriarchal society without being fenced in by men. Rayyā's resentment is directed not only at the way she is treated but also at the hypocrisy that motivates the way men behave or even gesture toward her. Since her childhood, she has faced unending attempts by men to gain access to her body by any means, while they pretend to maintain an impeccable public moral stance. It is precisely this discrepancy between words and deeds that makes Rayyā's story a metaphor for the oleander tree—a tree that blossoms beautifully but bears no fruit. In spite of her radiant beauty, she lives a fruitless life and dies a fruitless death. Both her life and death are shocking examples of the deep and multifaceted oppression that women endure.

The novels outlined in this chapter show that Arab women have not been living at the periphery of social and political events during the most turbulent upheavals in the history of the Arab world. Rather, they have been deeply immersed in the fate of their countries and peoples. They make no attempt to speak the commonly accepted language of the time or to mask realities. In fact, they make every effort possible to strip the truth naked and leave it glaring in the eyes of Arab peoples, who have previously seen things through dim and artificial lenses.

Masters of the Art

AS THEIR CONFIDENCE GREW, Arab women novelists began to explore the past and articulate their own vision of national history. The novelists whose works are discussed in this chapter address subjects that were previously considered taboo in the social and political arenas: Leila Abouzeid (Morocco), ʿĀliya Mamdūḥ (Iraq), Aḥlām Mustighānimī (Algeria), Saḥar Khalīfa (Palestine), Samīra al-Māniʿ(Iraq), Maysalūn Hādī (Iraq), Nādiya Khūst (Syria), Raḍwā ʿĀshūr (Egypt), Zahra ʿUmar (Jordan), Laylā al-ʿUthmān (Kuwait), Hādiya Saʿīd (Jordan), ʿArūsiyya al-Nālūtī (Tunisia), and Nawāl al-Saʿdāwī (Egypt). Their novels have delinked the past and the present, exposing the roots of problems that had not previously been addressed because no one had dared to do so.

Leila Abouzeid is the first Moroccan woman novelist to write in Arabic and be translated into English. Moroccan writers either write in French or are first translated into French from Arabic, not into English. Leila Abouzeid is an exception to this rule. Despite her proficiency in French, Abouzeid wrote in Arabic as a symbolic expression of her commitment to Arab society. Her literary work focuses on the worries of the past, the complexities of the present, and people's aspirations for the future. It is a text punctuated with the sighs and hopes of simple people who silently sacrifice themselves and then vanish without a trace, leaving neither name nor testimony of their trials and tribulations. Abouzeid's outlook is that of a woman who is very sensitive to the political pulse of her people, someone who is prepared to challenge harsh realities that are considered to be unchangeable.

If Abouzeid's choice of writing in Arabic is evidence of her attachment to and pride in her origin, her choice and treatment of subject clearly express her faith in ordinary people, who are the true heroes and heroines of her work. The first indication of this commitment can be found in the dedication of her novel *'Ām al-Fīl (The Year of the Elephant)*: "To all those women and men who put their lives at risk for the sake of Morocco and expected neither reward nor thanks for it." The explicit mention of women who risked their lives alongside men sets Abouzeid's work apart from official Moroccan history, which excludes any mention of women.

Hers is one of few Arabic literary texts in which countless unnamed "little people" are provided with an identity, imbued with purpose, and acknowledged for their honorable sacrifices. The implicit claim that emerges in her narrative—that those who change history are neither kings nor presidents, but ordinary people such as housewives, technocrats, carpet merchants, spices sellers, and truck drivers—also sets her work apart from others.

Even the title of the novel, *'Ām al-Fīl*, evokes a popular memory rather than history as it has been written. Muslims consider the Year of the Elephant to be a pivotal date and refer to their history as having occurred either before or after it. Likewise, the popular memory in Morocco viewed 1956, the year of Morocco's independence, as equally significant, and began to mark history as happening before or after independence. Hence the Year of the Elephant is a metaphor for Moroccan independence.

Although national events constitute the novel's framework, they do not overshadow social or human interaction. Many themes overlap, creating a narrative that reflects the psychological, social, political, and moral complexities of life. Clearly, the author is a sensitive and highly aware woman who is prepared to redefine reality as she sees it, regardless of the extent to which her views contradict all that is customary and familiar.

The narrative focuses on Zahra and the everyday details of her life. Her childhood and marriage are outlined, as is her work in the underground resistance movement that leads to the triumph of the independence movement. The assignment of her husband to a prestigious position in the postcolonial government is also described, together with Zahra's subsequent divorce and her eventual reevaluation of the meaning of independence in her life.

In lieu of ideological statements or clichés, the author relates the story of a woman who is profoundly wise, in spite of her apparent simplicity. Like other Arab women novelists, Abouzeid finds that feminism and nationalism are very closely interrelated. She defies the orthodoxy that women have nothing to do with politics. For instance, Zahra is thoroughly immersed in the struggle against French colonialism but is ultimately left to reckon with the fact that political triumph against oppression does not necessarily signify an end to women's oppression.

After years of marriage, Zahra's husband, with whom she has shared the struggle for Moroccan independence, abruptly announces his decision to divorce her, telling her that her papers will be sent to her "along with whatever the law provides" (p. 9). The law requires her husband to remit her expenses for a hundred days. Zahra begins to consider how worthless a woman really is in the eyes of society, when the law simply permits her to be returned with a paper receipt as though she were a defective commodity taken back to a shopkeeper. "I feel neither sorrow nor hatred," Zahra reflects. I feel "nothing but a vague awareness that something inside me has been extinguished, has finally come to a halt" (p. 8). She feels that she has been "returned" because she does not function properly in Moroccan high society: "I don't eat with a fork. I don't speak French, I don't sit with men. I don't go out to fancy dinners" (p. 16).

Zahra joins the resistance after she witnesses the massacre of Casablanca, in which French soldiers fired on civilians. Although Moroccan tradition dictates that no woman should sell her property, Zahra recollects that in the wake of the massacre, "I happily sold my olive trees, my jewels, everything worth selling for the cause." Resistance supplants the role of emeralds and rubies in her life, until she ultimately feels "nothing but contempt for such trinkets" (p. 28).

Her husband's abrupt dismissal, however, reminds her that for women, security is rarely guaranteed, even in marriage. It brings to mind her grandmother's constant admonition: "A woman has nothing but her husband and her property, and husbands cannot be trusted" (p. 21). Thus she decides to take a room of her own, believing that decision to be one of the best and most significant decisions she has taken in her life.

In *'Ām al-Fīl*, readers confronted a woman who willingly makes sacrifices to help to secure Moroccan independence, only to discover that once independence has been obtained, Moroccan society has denied this woman the basic rights of an individual on the basis of her gender. Instead it subjects her to men's whims and to a law that has no respect for women's humanity and dignity.

Zahra participates in all forms of struggle against occupation, from collecting donations to organizing demonstrations, and discovers that many women are more capable and braver than her husband. She believes that a new Moroccan woman has evolved, a woman who abandons earrings and jewels and embraces arms in defense of her country and her people's identity.

Zahra's efforts, as well as those of other nationalists, are crowned by victory, as Morocco achieves its independence on November 18, 1956. After independence, however, Zahra is astonished to find that many of the social practices introduced by the colonizers persist. Zahra's husband, for example, does not like her to eat without a fork or to speak to the servants. His colonial elitism provokes questions in Zahra's mind about those who are expected to reform society. She finds such people to be hypocrites who hold double standards. She believes them to be more dangerous for the future of the country than any foreign occupation. They buy the country's property at a knockdown price, look down on the poor, and pursue a modernity that is "false" because it has been adopted wholesale from the colonial authorities without regard for Moroccan traditions and culture.

Zahra begins to ask herself what difference independence has in fact made to Moroccans. Moroccans believed that independence from colonial authority would provide a solution to every problem they encountered, but she concludes that in fact there is nothing left of Morocco's Year of the Elephant. She believes that independence has made very little difference in the lives of ordinary Moroccans. Women, for example, have retreated into the shadows, where they resided before their valiant involvement with the resistance. She is disappointed when she discovers that her fellow citizens do not share her views and comes to realize that national independence is not the important moment in time she had previously thought it was in the life of her country.

Thus the text uses Zahra to indirectly and subtly record the author's social, political, and intellectual response to political events in her country. As a feminist and nationalist, Zahra is concerned about the fate of men and women and the future of her country. It is true that only a woman, more specifically only a Moroccan woman, could have written the novel, but nonetheless the topics touched on are of importance to both men and women. Zahra is a heroine without bombastic mottoes or abstract ideologies. She is a salt-of-the-earth woman, and in her approach to most issues she represents millions of women in both the East and the West who rebel against the way they are treated and the laws governing their lives. Zahra's tragedy is both personal and political. On the one hand, her husband has abandoned her after many years of marriage and friendship, and on the other, she is disappointed with the attitudes and actions of her comrades and with the leaders of her country after the price she has paid for her country's independence.

Just as Abouzeid has chosen the Arabic language as her means of expression and the events in her country as a topic for discussion, she has also chosen to address the particular problems faced by Moroccan women. Any local problem that is candidly addressed, however, will most likely have universal application, as human beings experience many things in common. Nothing highlights these commonalities more than sincerity in treatment and expression. This novel is straightforward, easy to read, enjoyable, and impressive. Abouzeid has achieved what every writer aspires to achieve: honesty and courage in facing both oneself and others. She stresses the need for personal as well as political independence that should not be tainted by compromise or double standards. Although Zahra's starting point is her feminist perspective, ultimately she aims to provide for the welfare of her society and the country at large. In conclusion, women's perspectives are important for achieving national social and political reform. Her story is made all the more poignant by the intimate narrative used to convey the depth of her past relationship with her husband and his totally illogical and unexpected treatment of her. Abouzeid is a writer who trusts her reader's intelligence, so that she only suggests a way forward, leaving the reader the task of completing the scene and establishing its possible credibility.

Iraqi author 'Āliya Mamdūḥ focuses on the period immediately following Iraq's independence in her novel *Ḥabbat al-Naftālīn* (*Mothballs; Naphthalene* in the United Kingdom). "Mothballs" refers to the attempt to keep the stories of A'ẓamiyyat Baghdad fresh in the memory, even though there is no real danger of these deeply felt stories being forgotten; they are fixed securely in every individual's heart and mind, and constitute the subtext of Iraq's history.[1] The use of Iraqi dialect in the dialogue lends more credibility to the authenticity of the events described. Yet the Arabic used is smooth; it flows easily, leaving no room for complaint about accent or language.

More than any other novel written by an Arab woman, *Ḥabbat al-Naftālīn* explores in depth the real story of Arab women of varying ages and social status. The central character in the story is Hudā, the child and adolescent; the author moves between the first and third person to describe her life with an open mind, a brave heart, and a feminist consciousness. She is compassionate in her understanding of her mother, father, brother, and grandmother; compassionate in her approach to love and marriage; and compassionate in her spontaneous interpretation of crises, which always seem to be man-made.

The triumvirate of Hudā, her mother, and her grandmother comprises the summation of women's status in Arab culture, with all its inherent contradictions. The grandmother exerts absolute authority over her children, particularly over Hudā's father, Jamīl. She makes decisions and issues orders, with no consideration whatsoever given to male authority. She reigns supreme in the decisionmaking process, recognizing only too clearly the sanctity of her word and the duty of her children to respect and obey her. Iqbāl, Hudā's mother, however, is a completely different type of woman. Her husband, Munīr, abandons her, simply because she is ill, and, like any other commodity, she is replaced by another woman when she fails to fulfill her role of providing the requisite services. She suffers from oppression and lack of respect and sees her children impoverished and humiliated by their father's philandering. Hudā, the third generation of women depicted in the novel, is an aware and daring adolescent who is skillful in broadening the margins of her freedom and in manipulating the restrictions placed on her to advance her knowledge further and broaden her horizons.

Women predominate in this novel; they interact and complement each other in a way that shows that it is women who wield true power, whereas men, who are supposedly powerful, control nothing important in the lives of either their families or even in the life of the country itself.

Contrary to the customary belief that the relationship between a wife and a mother-in-law must always be sour, Iqbāl's mother-in-law allies with Iqbāl against her own son, because she believes that his behavior toward his wife is totally unfair and unreasonable. She refuses to acknowledge her son's second marriage to Nūriyya or even to see the children Nūriyya bears. Whatever reason prompts the grandmother to take this stand—perhaps her revolt against the gross injustices inflicted on women, her empathy with Iqbāl, or her rejection of male domination that atrociously manifests in the practice of polygamy—she nevertheless remains an independent actor, able to challenge entrenched male authority.

It is one of the paradoxes of most Arab societies that even though Arab women are reputed to possess a very high degree of authority within the home, nevertheless in the larger society they remain second-class citizens. The novel takes this paradox into account; male and female roles operate very differently from the way they do in other works of Arabic literature. Men are not always the unconquered masters, nor are women always the victims. Both are subject to tradition and a complicated set of social norms, which sometimes create frustration and dismay for both sexes. The uncompromising grandmother eventually longs to see her son, who has abandoned her, as well as his second wife and their children—all of whom she had once forsworn. The beauty of Farīda, an aunt, is shown to be only skin-deep: she harms both herself and Munīr. Iqbāl dies of neglect, frustration, and hopelessness. Her husband, Jamīl, lives in the squalor of prison and suffers the consequences of his marriage to Nūriyya and the wrath of his mother that accepts no compromise. No one is the absolute victor or victim. The only person who emerges truly triumphant is the author. She weaves a colorful matrix of family, social, and cultural relations in Iraq through her use of multiple voices and the distinguishing presence of women, in the process of which she proves that male authority is illusory. Her writing skillfully fluctuates between the classical Arabic language *(al-Fuṣḥā)* and Iraqi colloquialisms.

> The wind of *al-A'ẓamiyya* and Karbulā' blows at us, bringing with it the whispers of the grandmother with her grandchildren, the screams of the tyrant husband at his wife and the sighs of the infatuated Hudā with Maḥmūd. Baghdad is washed with the tears of its sad people, quivering with the deep coughs of Iqbāl; we see an Iraq resembling Munīr's face, displaying every contradiction. (p. 57)

Smoke mixes with the dust of Karbala, with the horrible atmosphere of the prison where Munīr works and recites the Qur'ān. We watch the Baghdad dawn like "the foam in Um Sutūrī's tub: the clouds were enormous, as if wearing gray and black cloaks" (p. 99). "The trees stood alone, naked, and dry, not moving as we passed them. Shops and garages were halfway open. Old, overturned automobiles, bicycles boys had dragged through the streams. Iraqi flags, limp in the heat and warm air, hung over police stations and official offices" (p. 115). The recreation of Iraqi women, men, air, and customs are tinged with political concerns and with an insight into people's feelings toward Jamāl 'Abd al-Nāṣir, the British, and the Iraqi king:

> Nāṣir came and infiltrated our vocal cords and set all our secrets free. We entered into the rapture and began to chant: "Curse the English, curse reaction, down with colonialism and the Regent. Say Palestine is Arab. Down with Zionism" . . . The picture of the King of Iraq deceived young and old people alike. He was handsome and sad, gloomy and unlucky.[2]

Caught amid all these social, political, and personal contradictions, Jamīl loses his strength and eventually his mind.

> He stands in the prison yard as the stars in the sky shine brightly overhead. In his hand is the picture of the crown prince. He opens his trousers and urinates on it. He does not look around; he only looks ahead. His legs are cramped as he crushes the glass picture with his nailed boots. The nails enter the head of King Faisal II and his successor. His urine is splattered on their medals and shoulders. He starts to run in the yard without screaming or chanting. He unlocks all the doors and shouts at the top of his voice, "Come on, get out."[3]

The preservation of this novel in fact needs no mothballs; it breathes the heat of the Iraqi summer and the complexity of Iraq's turbulent political history. It establishes the dormant contradictions in the status of Arab women, represented in the stark differences between the positions of the sister, wife, mother, and grandmother. This important work is true to Iraqi culture, politics, and society.

Both Leila Abouzeid and ʿĀliya Mamdūḥ set out to discover, each in her own way and for her own reasons, that foreign occupation is not the only enemy of freedom and progress. Both find they are constrained by the norms governing the home, in social relations, and within political mechanisms, all of which have to be questioned, reconsidered, and, perhaps, changed before it becomes possible for women to occupy their rightful place in contemporary Arab society.

Aḥlām Mustighānimī is the first Algerian woman novelist to write in Arabic. It is clear from the novel's dedication that the choice of language is not merely a technical consideration. Mustighānimī dedicates her novel *Dhākirat al-Jasad (Memory in the Flesh)* to Mālik Ḥaddād,

> the son of Constantine, who vowed after Algeria's independence not to write in a language that is not his. But the blank page overwhelmed him and his silence killed him, making him the first martyr [for the cause of the] Arabic language and the first writer who decided to die in silence but in love with Arabic; and to my father, may he find [in heaven] someone who is good in Arabic and who will eventually read this book—his book—for him.

The dedication shows the determination of a generation of young Arab writers to write in Arabic as a means of reasserting Arab identity and of expressing pride in that identity. The author's decision to write her novel in Arabic, then, is part of a struggle to restore Algeria to the Arab milieu, and since language is the most important signifier of national identity, Aḥlām Mustighānimī has played her part.

Mustighānimī's novel addresses problems that may be considered specifically Arab and looks forward to a future that embodies the dreams of a generation of Arab people. *Dhākirat al-Jasad* reconstructs the history of the Algerian revolution and its aftermath in a text that moves smoothly between dialogue and monologue, between present tense and past tense, and using flashbacks as a way to fill in the gaps.

The heroine, who carries the same name as the author, Aḥlām—also known to some as Ḥayāt—is both symbol and subject. She is the symbol of land and country and the subject of love and affection. One of the novel's heroes is an expatriate whose hand was amputated in the Algerian war of independence and who has been inspired to use his remaining hand to become one of the most important painters of his time. He was a friend of Aḥlām's father, Si Ṭāhir, an honorable and decent soldier who sacrificed his life for Algeria's independence.

A very subtle interaction between the human self and the identity of the country permeates the novel; in many instances the one seems to be a reflection of the other. Aḥlām is the woman the artist loves, and she also symbolizes Constantine (a city in Algeria) and Algeria at one and the same time.[4] He addresses her by saying: "Ye are a woman who wore my love as madness; gradually she took the shape of a city and the features of a country" (p. 13). Each character wears more than one hat: hence multiple symbols become apparent throughout the novel. They should be accurately interpreted so that the complex meanings the novelist intended to convey may be explored.

The novel's prevailing atmosphere is pessimistic; it sums up national sentiment following Algeria's independence and is replete with flashbacks to the sacrifices made for that independence. Writing such a novel means that heroes die, prompting Mustighānimī to state: "We no longer write novels to kill heroes. We have finished with those whose existence has become a burden on us. The more we write about them, the less they mean to us and the more opportunity we have for fresh air" (p. 18). This statement matters because it shows the discrepancy between the time of the war of liberation, when many people willingly laid down their lives for their country, and the postindependence era, when others started to use the sacrifices of those who died to advance personal interests.

The author is writing some thirty-four years after the announcement in 1954 by Algerians of the military struggle to end the occupation. She writes about what happens between then and "now," fully aware that "Between the first bullet and the last, there was a change of heart, objectives have changed and the country has changed as well" (p. 24). This novel, one of many examples of postindependence literature, is also, therefore, a final commemoration of these heroes and their ideals and values that are no longer revered. The text highlights a contradiction between the attitudes, beliefs, and values of the war generation and those who came after it and covertly unravels the process that might have sown the seeds of Algeria's long and bloody civil war.

Throughout the novel, Si Ṭāhir symbolizes the true independence fighters, who left their homes, family, and children and gave their lives for Algeria. In contemporary Algerian society, all that is left of him and his comrades are names on streets in Algerian cities and orphaned children. Si Ṭāhir's time has gone. Yet even Si Ṭāhir, symbol of another era that he is, sometimes longs to see his family and secretly cries, longing to touch his children. But he also knows that national symbols have no right to cry or miss their families. It is one of the contradictions of Arab politics that these symbols are raised to the status of Christian saints, but such human beings are no longer allowed to be ordinary mortals or express their humanity. They are therefore sometimes pushed to commit acts in secret that ordinary mortals would find unthinkable.

The hero, Khālid, who keeps up a dialogue/monologue with the narrator, is a former comrade of Aḥlām's father and remembers a great deal about the revolution. Khālid lives in the past, whereas Aḥlām, raised in the postindependence era and fed a steady diet of the revolution's legends, lives in the present. The interactions, comparisons, and tensions between these two periods form the backbone of the novel. People from Algeria can be divided into two categories: The first category of people comprises honorable Algerians who fought the war of independence, expecting nothing in return, and who indeed received nothing. The second consists of members of the postindependence generation who have abandoned the ideals of the previous generation and instead have devoted themselves to improving their individual destinies without regard for Algerian society as a whole.

The narrative focuses on these polar opposites and unravels two contradictory aspects relating to almost every issue, feeling, or person. Speaking of the golden past, Khālid tells Aḥlām: "I used to live in Tunisia, the son of that country and a stranger at the same time, free and shackled at once, both happy and miserable" (p. 60). Khālid's sentiments reflect the author's belief that life is rarely black or white; nor is it constant. Khālid, who lost his arm for Algeria and who used to carry his empty sleeve like a medal, is now, twenty-five years after independence, ashamed of it:

> Now after a quarter of a century you are ashamed of your empty sleeve which you hide shyly in the pocket of your jacket as if you were hiding your personal memory and apologizing for your past to all those who have no past. Your missing hand disturbs them, destroys their tranquillity and makes them lose their appetite. This time is not yours; it is the postwar era. It is the time of elegant suits and expensive cars and huge stomachs. That is why you are ashamed of your missing arm wherever you go, in the underground, in a restaurant, in a café, in a plane and at a party to which you are invited. You feel as if people are waiting for you all the time to tell them your story. (pp. 72–73)

Khālid's other dilemma is that he lives in France, a country that respects his talent but refuses to acknowledge his wounds, but he is a citizen of Algeria, a country that respects his wounds but rejects his talent. Which country is he to choose, therefore? "You are the man and the wound at one time; he is the spoilt memory of which this body stands as a physical manifestation" (p. 73). Through these interactions, in scenes that plumb both the past and the future, a romance evolves between Khālid and Aḥlām, he the comrade of her father and she the subject of Si Ṭāhir's love and longing, who has now become the symbol of hope for a better future.

In their dialogue and interaction, Aḥlām and Khālid depict the image of the relationship between Algeria's past and present. Aḥlām is both Constantine and Algeria, she is both a woman and the future for which Khālid and his colleagues, including Aḥlām's father, have fought, suffered, and died. While their love for each other grows, their frustration and disappointment with other people deepens: yesterday's comrades are the nouveau riche of today. The reputation these people had previously built for being obstinate nationalists is now supplanted by a reputation for being greedy materialists; the country for which they had all fought has become a cow that everyone wants to milk in order to become the first and best. Old values have died in the hearts of the men that Khālid used to know so well. Khālid looks at Mustafa, who comes to his exhibition, and thinks:

> The other man has died in him. At this moment he cares about nothing except possessing one of my paintings, exactly like other rich Algerians who recently have been struck with the desire to own art for reasons which often have nothing to do with art, but with a new corrupt mentality about art and with an obsession to become part of the elite. (p. 83)

The author questions many of the well-known myths about revolution: independence, martyrdom, and sacrifice. She communicates the feelings and sentiments of ordinary people, regardless of how contradictory they might appear. One of the myths of Arab history is that mothers do not mourn their children who die for their country; rather, they receive news of their death with ululation and joy. Aḥlām, however, relates a very different experience with her grandmother when the death of her son is confirmed in the aftermath of Algeria's independence:

> On Independence Day my grandmother cried as she had never cried before. I asked her, "Granny, why are you crying as Algeria is independent?" She replied, "In the past I was waiting for independence so that Si Ṭāhir would come back to me; today I know that I am no longer waiting for anything." When my father died, my grandmother didn't ululate as we read in imaginary revolutionary stories I read subsequently. She stood in the middle of the courtyard with a naked head (a sure sign that she had lost her mind, or she would not have left her head-cover off) screaming with a heartbreaking sadness, "My only boy, my love, Si Ṭāhir, why did you leave me?" (p. 107)

In the novel, the author discusses the choice of language in the form of a dialogue that takes place between Khālid and Aḥlām. He is surprised to find that she writes in Arabic, even though she speaks to others in French. So that she is not misunderstood, she explains to him: "I could've written in French, but Arabic is the language of my heart, and I will not write in any other language. We write in the language we feel most for and love best." When he remarks that she speaks only in French, she replies, "Because I am used to doing this; what is important is the language we use to speak with ourselves, and not the language we use to speak with others" (p. 91).

Regarding the issues of language, martyrdom, independence, sincerity, and honesty in Algeria, the author undertakes a comprehensive reassessment that questions old and inherited beliefs and values passed on from one generation to another. By so doing, she rewrites the history of the Algerian revolution and the following three decades. She writes from a totally independent perspective, with no deference accorded to authority or concern for gain, thus recording a genuine historical account without any falsification or exaggeration. The novel relates the authentic story of what actually happened since independence, a very different account of events than what is promulgated by the authorities. It is an enjoyable literary text, written in smooth, fluent, and captivating Arabic. It poses very difficult questions about patriotism and nationalism, together with the political manipulation of both, and unseats deeply established social and political convictions.

Mustighānimī is not the only Arab woman novelist who has concerned herself with rewriting the social, political, and, to some extent, literary history of her people and country. The first Arab woman novelist to do so was the Palestinian novelist Saḥar Khalīfa, who challenged Arab people to think differently about male, female, widowhood, national struggle, love, and marriage. In her novels she endeavors to rewrite the fate and status of the Arab people in their struggle against the Israelis. She also stresses the need to revolutionize ideas about the relative position of men and women and the treatment of boys and girls before being able to challenge the forces of occupation or restore political rights.

In her novel *Ḥabl al-Surra (The Umbilical Cord)*, Iraqi writer Samīra al-Māniʿ forays into the corners commonly overlooked or even deliberately ignored by historians, politicians, and political analysts and enhances the literary value of the text. The novel mirrors the lives of the Iraqi people from the 1960s onward, particularly during times of war, and focuses on their ordeals, both in exile and at home. The author's insight and experience have led her to question how the history of her country has been recorded. She also investigates the roots of domestic problems that are often blamed on external forces in an attempt to absolve those who have power of their responsibility to their people and their country. Throughout the complicated political process of a country whose politics are still a riddle to most people in the world, the writer explores the hidden aspects of women's lives that are usually considered of no social or political importance. People's low morale and lack of hope are manifested in their readiness to be agents and informers to the authorities, to the extent that friends and even brothers betray each other to gain favor with those who are in power.

Events take place in London, Iraqis' preferred city after their homeland. People fluctuate between Iraq and London, absorbing the impact of both places, sensing the agony of family members at home and of those estranged abroad. Their activities abroad reflect the situation and circumstances at home. No matter how long the exile in London, it remains a receptacle for Iraqis, who wait to be dispatched home at the appropriate moment. Amid this chaos, women keep the home fires burning, teaching the new generation of Arabic emigrants about their own experiences so that they don't lose their most important tie with their homeland. Women also play a role in literary movements in exile, but publishers, who are more interested in profits than in literature for literature's sake, are not interested in their daring texts.

Like Mustighānimī, al-Māni' discusses her writing experience, focusing on the importance of language and the difficulty of both creating convincing characters and a literary text that the writer finds satisfying. Madīḥa is an Iraqi woman who finds herself in London, looking for a job at a newspaper or journal run by the Iraqi opposition. She is disappointed to find that the supposedly radical opposition imposes restrictions on her writing that are as strict as those imposed by the authorities in Iraq. Just as an anxiety to maintain power governs the behavior of those who are in office in Iraq, an anxiety about the steady flow of funds governs the speech of the opposition. The experience of 'Afāf, an Iraqi student in Moscow, with Jalāl, her husband, comrade, and colleague, also highlights the discrepancy between theories that dominate men's public discourse and their treatment of their partners in the domestic sphere. Throughout her marriage, 'Afāf discovers that Jalāl, a communist leader striving to rid the world of injustice, poverty, and exploitation, is unwilling to listen to her or to hear her pleas for equality in their relationship. She wonders how he, who aspires to liberate the world, can fail to have any sympathy with his partner. This gap between what is preached and what is practiced lies at the root of most of the tragedies that have befallen the Arab states and their people. Referring to Jalāl,

'Afāf says, "His interest in the events in Latin American countries was much greater than his interest in cleaning his underwear; he would speak about political movements in Africa for hours instead of writing a letter to his anxious mother to put her mind at rest about him" (p. 80).

Events in the novel take place throughout the twentieth century. The narrative flows to the Iran-Iraq War and subsequently flashes back to the era of Arab nationalism and the governments of 'Abd al-Karīm Qāsim in Iraq and Jamāl 'Abd al-Nāṣir in Egypt. The author shows, particularly by depicting the competition between these two governments, how Arab written history has been distorted and the false accounts each country keeps of the history of the other. Motivated by grand ambitions to be the sole leader in the Arab world, the rulers of Iraq and Egypt endeavor to spread rumors about the apostasy of the other and to expose his treasonable activities. This petty, selfish craving for power lies behind many of the tragedies that have befallen the Arab peoples throughout contemporary history. The novel therefore calls for a rereading, or preferably a rewriting, of Arab history in a way that sets the record straight. It is only when Arabs manage to face up to and acknowledge the realities of their past, rather than be seduced by the false image that has been propagated, that they will be able to establish a better future for the entire Arab nation.

The author focuses on two taboos: women and religion. So-called progressive political movements, such as socialism and communism, have exploited women just as much as the most conservative regime. Leaders such as 'Abd al-Karīm Qāsim were brought down after being accused of apostasy, among other things, although they were not anti-Islam, nor did they challenge the *Sharī'a*. The novel exposes the gap between pretense and reality, between truth and what is claimed to be true by political parties, between the socially acceptable and the politically correct. Events in the novel cover most of Iraq's history in the twentieth century, focusing on the most important political events and weaving a social, political, moral, and religious tapestry of what was happening at the time. The novel shows that the political game remains unchanged throughout history, as do people's interests, concerns, and problems.

Throughout their lives, people are haunted by fear: fear of the ruler; fear of the informer, who might be a close friend; and fear of the death sentence that might be passed for a reason about which the condemned knows nothing. It is this fear that constitutes the biggest difference between East and West. In the West someone may be blamed or imprisoned, but rarely killed, for his or her political beliefs. The Iraqi people have lived through a bloody history for reasons unraveled in this novel, reasons that are very different from those recorded in the official history of Iraq.

It would be incorrect to call the novel a social history; rather, it is an enjoyable text that spells out the social, political, and moral complexities within the lives of the Iraqi people. The point is made that the Iraqi people have never been able to break away from their country completely throughout their long history because "they cannot part with their soil, despite the unbearable summer heat and the extreme poverty in villages and countryside. Iraqi people love their country and won't exchange it for any other; they love its sky; they love it just as a baby loves his mother without question" (p. 130). The novel embodies the immorality of the Iraqi government during the Iran-Iraq conflict in an Iraqi father, who is granted the Iraqi Mesopotamia medal because he executes his son who has fled the army. The man is considered to have set an example for all Iraqi fathers. 'Afāf's uncle asks a simple question: "What is the value of the homeland without my children? What is the value of Iraq without my children?" (p. 133). Amid the chaos that persists throughout much of the twentieth century in Iraq, Madīḥa finds that the only solution is to educate small children and to "bring them up to be decent, forgiving brothers and sisters according to her precepts and principles" (p. 138).

Both the problem and the suggested solution make clear the author's belief that the personal is deeply political and that once the political is completely divorced from the personal, it becomes inhuman, unethical, and sometimes criminal. The only measure of political correctness, as far as the author is concerned, is its effect on people's lives and its impact on their feelings and concerns. It is here that the author calls official Arab history into question. It has always been written from the point of view of men. In *Ḥabl al-Surra*, al-Mānic reinterprets history from a woman's perspective, an ordinary citizen who questions dramatic slogans and dogma, which in her opinion are partly to blame for inciting wars and inflicting human suffering.

Sometimes, she believes, war erupts simply because someone with power who makes sensitive political decisions is exhausted and nervous. She tries to understand complicated issues by examining their basic source and finds the answers by focusing on understanding the basic human motive behind the deeds. The interaction among political, social, feminist, religious, and moral values contributes greatly to the excellence of this novel. The narrative weaves many threads together and sets out to prove that no one thread is more important than another and that the interrelation and interdependency among different aspects of life is the essence of living and human nature.

Another Iraqi woman who reassesses a different war in the history of modern Iraq from a feminist and human perspective is Maysalūn Hādī in her novel *Al-ʿĀlam Nāqiṣan Wāḥid (The World Minus One)*. The author reviews the Gulf War from a human perspective, showing the effects of the shelling, killing, and destruction in the agony of two parents who are unsure whether their son has been killed or whether he has merely gone missing. They keep hoping he might return. The father of a pilot, who has been told that his son, ʿAlī, has been killed in the war, has a terrible dilemma. He goes to a village near the town of Sulaymāniyya on the Iranian border to fetch the body of his son. Extensive wounds on the body do not allow him to identify his son, but the military jacket and ʿAlī's identity card leave him in no doubt that the body is indeed that of his child. He transports his coffin to Baghdad and buries him in the family vault.

A few days later, as the father watches his wife washing and ironing clothes, he remembers that the deceased was wearing blue cotton long underwear, which his son never wore. The father then becomes haunted by the thought that the dead body is not that of his son, but rather the son of a Kurdish colleague who is supposedly being held hostage by the Iranians. What if the dead pilot was in fact the son of his colleague, while his son is the hostage? He spends sleepless nights trying to resolve the problem without telling his wife, so that no false hopes are created. He travels to the family of his son's colleague in the north and is heartened when he notices that the father is wearing blue long underwear similar to that worn by the dead pilot; that means that the body buried might be his colleague's son and not his own. The glimmer of hope he feels at the prospect that his son might still be alive, however, is extinguished when he observes his colleague's poverty, the family's kindness, and their innocence. Abū ʿAlī no longer cares whether it is his son or the son of these people who is dead. When he speaks to the family about the fate of their child, he finds that what has happened to the young man is more vague and sadder than what has happened to his own son. He asks himself, "Why am I keen to prove that my son wasn't killed, but a POW, which is not a happier fate anyway?" When he sees a picture of the other pilot, Abū ʿAlī shouts in surprise, "'Alī!" When the wife tells him that the boy is Munʿim, her son, Abū ʿAlī comments on the uncanny resemblance to his own child. The woman replies that all pilots look the same. Munʿim is the same age as ʿAlī and the same rank, and they look the same. Abū ʿAlī wishes the young man a safe return and goes back home to his wife, convinced that exchanging the fate of two young men is a meaningless exercise. He intends to forget about the dilemma that has occupied him for so long, but he can never fully remove from his memory the blue long underwear that his son might have borrowed from his colleague on a cold night.

Like the Lebanese women novelists who write about the Lebanese civil war, Maysalūn Hādī does not write directly about the killing or the shelling. Rather, she addresses a very subtle and sad consequence of any war: the loss of a son and the agony that war visits on parents. The fact that 'Alī and Mun'im look the same underscores the fact that all people whose children go to war suffer in similar ways. It makes little difference whose son is killed; they are all brothers in humanity, and the effect of war on them is exactly the same in each case.

Apart from the fact that this novel was written by a woman, it was also written and published in Baghdad. It is therefore unrealistic to expect it to be very radical in its assessment of the wounds the Gulf War has bequeathed. Nevertheless, the perplexed feelings and agonizing experience of Abū 'Alī and Um 'Alī are the highest price that human beings have to pay for a stupid war. It serves no purpose except the interests of the person in power, who hopes to tighten his grip on Iraq. While reading the deep sadness and insoluble dilemmas depicted in the novel, the reader grows both angry and frustrated and learns to resent wars and all those who initiate, fight in, or even support them.

In her novel *Ḥubb fī Bilād al-Shām (Love in Greater Syria)*, Syrian novelist Nādiya Khūst tries to restore to the people of Syria the collective memory they lost around the time of World War I.[5] She writes that she decided to reclaim the period of the beginning of the twentieth century for the Syrian people and bring it alive in her novel, because Syrians still experience today the consequences of the political decisions of those years, in which Western governments drew up the present-day map of the Arab world. Today, she says, Syrians suffer from bitterness, the seeds of which were sown at that time. There was a united conspiracy on the part of Western countries against the Arabs, adopted after World War I and the collapse of the Ottoman Empire. Arabs fought alongside the Allies in that war, only to find that in its wake the Allies had become their new colonizers. As an activist working to preserve the old city of Damascus, Khūst is good at sketching her characters in their historical context (customs, markets, cities, clothes, jewelery, etc.) and showing that they shared a very human experience. Khūst, and possibly other Arab women writers, use the past to understand the complications of the present that baffle most Arabs.

Khūst, al-Mānī', Mamdūḥ, and Hādī look to the twentieth century to provide solutions to the problems of Arab identity. But Egyptian writer Raḍwā 'Āshūr, in her novels *Gharnāṭa (Granada)* and *Maryama wa al-Raḥīl (Maryama and the Departure)*, appears to share the view of some Arab historians that the root causes of contemporary problems of Arab societies reach back in time to the fall of Granada in 1491. Many historians consider this period to be crucially significant in forming the modern history of the Arab world. 'Āshūr examines the period of the Arabs' exodus from Andalusia and the surrender of Granada after the November treaty of 1491. The novel does not deal with the lives of politicians or kings and queens. Rather, it explores the effects of their decisions on the lives of ordinary people who have to live during a time when they have been defeated. She covers the oppressive measures endured by the people during occupation (random arrests, destruction of houses, torture, rape, and other forms of humiliation), the burning of books, the revolution of Bayāzīn, and a witch hunt, by detailing the life of an Arab family living in Granada, a life that is full of danger, fear, courage, and caution.

In her trilogy (the second book mentioned above has two parts), 'Āshūr considers a period that some believe resurfaces at various times and in different forms in all Arab countries. 'Āshūr's trilogy triggers feelings of pain in readers, who cannot help but sympathize with a Muslim community that is subjected to the harshest forms of oppression—for no reason other than that its members were born Muslim.

Through a strong, exciting narrative, 'Āshūr shows that the problem that weakened Arabs five centuries ago—which she identifies as a failure to work together—also weakens them today and has also done so in the intervening period. Conflict and competition among Arabs was then blamed for the fall of Granada, just as it is now blamed for much of what is happening to Arabs today. The novel's main shortcoming is that historical events overwhelm the narrative at the expense of character development, making the characters appear less credible than they otherwise might have been. Nevertheless, by charting new historical territory, this trilogy constitutes a very important addition to Arab women's literature and to Arab historical novels in general.

A similar novel is *Al-Khurūj min Sosrowaka (The Exodus from Sosrowaka: The Epic of the Circassian Diaspora)* by Zahra 'Umar of Jordan. That book, about the Circassians in the Arab region of Syria, Iraq, Jordan, and Palestine, explores the history of a small ethnic group that retained its identity in both the Muslim and Arab worlds. It is impressive that many Arab women novelists are currently engaged with the history of their country and people through their writing. They offer a different perspective from the history relayed for decades in the Arab world. Are these attempts to rewrite history for future generations written from women's perspectives? It is certainly an important question to ask, although no straightforward answer may be possible.

Other Arab women novelists, such as Laylā al-'Uthmān of Kuwait, Hādiya Sa'īd of Jordan, and Arūsiyya al-Nālūtī of Tunisia, break different but no less important ground in their novels. Most of the themes they decide to address are still considered taboo in their respective societies. In her novel *Al-Mar'a wa al-Qiṭṭa (The Woman and the Cat)*, Laylā al-'Uthmān addresses one of the social problems from which Arab societies suffer, especially those in the Gulf. The reader first encounters Salīm in prison, where the interrogator is asking him to say who killed his wife, Ḥiṣṣa. As the story unfolds, we discover that Salīm is a young man whose mother was forced to leave his father because of a malicious aunt, who caused her brother to divorce three wives in succession, the last of whom was Salīm's mother. His aunt is a possessive and unloving spinster, who cannot bear to see her brother happily married. Because of her malice, Salīm grows up longing for the affection of an absent mother and a father who does not dare express love for his son. The only creature that Salīm grows to enjoy, love, and sympathize with is his cat, Dāna, who sleeps near his feet and keeps them warm in winter. One day the aunt discovers Dāna mating with a strange tom and decides to kill her. She dumps the cat into a cesspit, leaving her nephew absolutely devastated about the loss of his pet and dear companion. The insensitive aunt thinks her nephew should rid himself of affection for animals, which she considers a weakness.

As Salīm grows up, his aunt decides that he should get married. She finds a wife for him who happens to be lovely and deserving of Salīm's affection. But his boyhood experience with Dāna and the tomcat has left him impotent. His wife shows understanding and patience and, in spite of never having made love with her husband, tells him that she is pregnant. Salīm accuses his father (they both live in the same house) of impregnating Ḥiṣṣa (who never leaves the house). During a fight with his father, Salīm reveals that he is impotent, and his father subsequently tells him to kill Ḥiṣṣa in retribution for her apparent adultery. When Salīm visits his mother, she tells him that Ḥiṣṣa has told him that she is pregnant only in order to build up his confidence. His mother says that this is what a decent woman should do to restore her husband's self-esteem. Salīm realizes that his suspicions have been groundless, but by the time he returns home, his aunt and father have already strangled his wife. Salīm, however, is ultimately sent to prison for killing Ḥiṣṣa.

The characters in this novel represent two different kinds of people: those unable to love or to see love, and their victims. To Salīm, the killing of his cat is as serious an offense as the murder of his wife. As destructive acts, they have devastating effects on those who are still living, as does the forced exile of his mother. What is very noticeable in this novel is that women are both masters and slaves, the oppressors and the oppressed, whereas men are shadowy characters under women's thumbs. It should be stressed that such a relationship between men and women is the opposite of what is considered to be the norm, especially in Kuwait and other Arab Gulf countries, where it is believed that women are entirely controlled by men.

The novel raises a number of provocative questions. Why did the author decide to portray such a vicious and vindictive woman, and how could a woman visit such cruelty on her brother, his wives, and his child? Does she want to show that women who appear to be meek are in fact powerful? Or does she intend to show that because women are victimized, they automatically become the victimizers? Are Salīm's mother and wife, seemingly two decent women, victims of another woman, or are they in fact the victims of classical patriarchal rule? Is Laylā al-'Uthmān suggesting that the struggle is not between men and women but rather between the powerful and the powerless, regardless of their gender? Both men and women can be potential tyrants, or they can be victims. Women, like cats, might seem nice and soft, but they can hurt with their claws whenever they decide to do so. In a society that is almost entirely cut off from the rest of the world, it is common to find women who suffer from the results of other women's actions. Because these women participate very little in public life and live in their own worlds, it is not unusual to encounter power struggles between women that are more likely to be found between men and women in a more open society.

Jordanian Hādiya Sa'īd has introduced a new style, new technique, and the daring theme of adultery in her novel *Bustān Aswad (Black Orchard)*. Neither Arab male nor female writers normally dare touch on the topic discussed in this novel. Yārā is in love with a married man, 'Umar. Yārā has come to accept discussing Hayāt, 'Umar's wife, as an integral part of their relationship, while Omar believes that he is conducting two separate relationships and treats each woman entirely differently. Yārā often thinks of Hayāt because her own husband, Wāthiq, now dead, had also loved another woman, Rita. She spends a lot of time trying to find Rita to discover why her husband loved her. The novel does not mention adultery, treason, or betrayal; rather, every effort is made to show that both men and women are capable of loving more than one person and that it is normal for men to be in love with different women for different reasons. The novel is exciting both in its theme and in the language used. The author employs a brisk narrative style with short sentences that keeps the story moving. The work should certainly be rated as a very distinguished Arabic novel.

Tunisian writer 'Arūsiyya al-Nālūtī drives deep into Arab wounds, exploring disappointments, setbacks, and defeats in a symbolic way that is at once a revelation and a pleasure to read. The political, social, and personal combine elegantly in *Marātīj (Shackles)*. Al-Nālūtī's embracing vision concludes with a deep sense of frustration because nothing seems to be working: "Everything has become repugnant" (p. 72). According to al-Nālūtī, human pettiness has caused the general disaster:

> What do I do? Get out of my skin? Be haughty rather than petty? What skin can I enter, if all skins seem to be the same? What kind of person can I dream of becoming if everyone is short and ugly and is unable to carry his or her head?[6] Shall I do what others do, which is to use my reputation in order to feel taller, and ignore the human race as a sign of the fundamental state of loneliness similar to the loneliness of mythological beasts that disappeared owing to boredom and the absence of equals? What can I do when the world is more and more interested in the petty and insignificant? Perhaps the heroes of today are able to be as small as an atom. Why not? Everything is possible nowadays. (p. 72)

One of the most beautiful of Arabic texts, *Marātīj* is very much engaged with the realities of Arab existence. The author sees and focuses on shackles that prevent personal progress and development. But it is understood that the personal is also political.

The Egyptian writer Nawāl al-Sa'dāwī has written only a few novels. Nevertheless, she will be remembered for her fiery feminist writings, like a loud and effective scream in the mid-twentieth century to liberate Arab women from the confines of gender and injustice. In all her novels, al-Sa'dāwī attempts to liberate women from the evil trilogy of backwardness, patriarchal authority, and religious fundamentalism. There is no doubt that she has played an important and effective role in the process of Arab women's march toward freedom, independence, and equality.

Al-Sa'dāwī's *Mawt al-Rajul al-Wahīd 'alā al-'Ard (The Death of the Only Man on Earth)* is her best and most beautiful novel. It unravels the pretense of piety and patriarchal authority, throwing light on both a mentality obsessed with raping beautiful girls and the manipulation of the poor and needy in order to satisfy a "mayor" who is supposed to protect these people and their interests. Shaykh Zahrān, al-Hajj Ismā'īl, and the mayor conspire to satisfy the latter's desires. The conspiracy, however, leads to the destruction of the poor but pretty girl Nafīsa; pushes her father into prison; and destroys her sister, Zaynab, who is single. When Nafīsa marries her cousin, Jalāl, they send him to prison as well so that she can go to the mayor, who enjoys raping her every day. By the end of the novel, however, awareness and liberation begin to dawn, and the people of the village start to discover the source of all their agonies and ordeals. In a conversation between al-Ḥajj Ismā'īl and Shaykh Zahrān, who have spent their lives serving the physical desires of the mayor, Shaykh Zahrān says:

> But this time I feel that something is about to take place. I do not know what it is. But I am worried. People have changed. The peasant who never dared look me in the eyes is looking at me and also raising his voice. Yesterday one of the peasants refused to pay his dues to the local authority and addressed me, saying: "Shaykh Zahrān, we work day and night throughout the year and at the end we are indebted to the government." How can this happen? We have never heard of such a thing from them before. (p. 193)

Zakiyya, Jalāl's mother, finally figures out what is going on. She discovers who is behind the disappearance of Nafīsa and Zaynab, and the imprisonment of Kifrāwī and Jalāl. Even though she doesn't know quite what to do, she nevertheless carries her axe and goes out,

> her bare feet moved on their own out of the house; she left her home and passed the small area that separated her door from the iron door. The mayor saw her coming toward him and he thought that she was one of the women working on his land. When she got closer he saw her long arm going up with the axe at the end of it before the axe fell on his head to fracture it; he saw her eyes and lost consciousness. (p. 206)

In both her fiction and nonfiction, Nawāl al-Sa'dāwī empowers the weak and the oppressed and restores their voices so that they can scream in the face of injustice, although her main concern has been injustices pertaining to women. In Al-Sa'dāwī's novels, there is a great stress on content to the possible detriment of narrative. She has a cause, a mission in life, which is to uncover the pain, oppression, and ordeals to which women are subject. For that reason, she will be remembered as a feminist writer rather than as a great novelist.

Even so, no study of Arab women would be complete without a mention of Nawāl al-Sa'dāwī. She is a pioneer of the Arab women's liberation movement and has undoubtedly helped to pave the way forward for Arab women novelists and Arab women in general, to take their place in literature and other domains.

It would be fair to conclude that Arab women novelists have now taken the lead in novel writing in the Arab world in terms of both quality and quantity. This shift requires a corresponding, and substantive, change in the attitude of literary critics regarding Arab women's writing. The works cited in this chapter, especially those published during the 1990s, prove that their authors have mastered the genre and are daringly innovative with regard to both theme and technique.

Recent Novels by Arab Women

SAHAR KHALĪFA MAY RIGHTLY be considered the most important Arab woman novelist in the second half of the twentieth century. As a feminist, she has mastered the political novel, both thematically and artistically. She has been a prolific writer since the publication of her first novel, *Lam Na'ud Jawāriya Lakum (We Are No Longer Your Maids)* in 1974. Today she is one of the few Arab novelists known in most Arab countries and beyond. Both her two-volume novel *Al-Ṣabbār (Wild Thorns)* and *'Abbād al-Shams (The Sunflower)* were translated into German and then into English more than two decades ago, and most centers for Middle Eastern studies list her works in their curricula. After the publication of her novel *Bāb al-Sāḥa (The Door of the Square)*, and particularly after the publication of *Al-Mīrāth (The Inheritance)*, she became the most talked-about novelist in Arab literary circles.

In *Al-Ṣabbār* and *Abbād al-Shams*, Khalīfa probes the lives of Arab women in the occupied Palestinian territories. Here, women's gold bracelets are the best insurance money can buy as a hedge against difficult times; women are arrested, but men rest assured that women are more resilient than men are. Rebellion against occupation revolutionizes social relations. Basil, for example, accepts the relationship of his sister Nawwār with Ṣāliḥ, and advises her to inform their parents of the relationship so that they can abandon the search for a potential husband. When another man eventually proposes to her, her brother supports her in her choice of Ṣāliḥ in front of her parents. Nawwār says defiantly: "I shall not marry anyone but Ṣāliḥ, even if I have to wait a hundred years for him" (*Al-Ṣabbār*, p. 216). Likewise, when Līnā is arrested, 'Ādil feels ashamed: "Women are being arrested, and I am sitting here on this seat. In a few minutes time I shall sit at the table and eat just as others eat and drink my tea, smile, and then go to bed" (p. 206).

The conditions imposed by the occupation therefore had two important consequences for Palestinian women. First, they revolutionized women's social reality, which previously had not conformed to the active political role women had begun to play in Palestinian society. Second, as a result, women were empowered to impose demands on men.

In *Al-Ṣabbār*, the narration of events and characters is realistic, and nationalist sentiment is not exaggerated. The characters fight, hesitate, retreat, dream, revolt, become angry, and sometimes contradict themselves, sometimes remain consistent. Radicalism is considered the ultimate virtue of Palestinian women. The author shows that you cannot half believe in revolution; it is something that cannot be expressed in half measures. You cannot revolt against occupation by foreign invaders without having a revolt against backward-looking and negative traditions and customs. The true revolutionary is someone whose political, social, and personal attitudes are in harmony with each other.

In *'Abbād al-Shams,* Nawwār matures and finds her own path in national struggle. She refuses to follow in other people's footsteps and only agrees to participate as an equal comrade (pp. 10–11). Women in this novel possess strong wills and exercise authority, which men may well fear. Characters argue over the liberation of women and the liberation of land, and the true link that exists between both. Women insist that their issues are part and parcel of national issues, but men disagree. As far as women's emancipation is concerned, all men expect is free and unconditional access to their bodies. Women, however, reject such a puerile definition and try to establish a more meaningful and long-lasting concept of liberation.

Sa'diyya, the wife of Zuhdī, who killed himself in a suicide bombing mission, becomes the subject of neighborhood gossip once she is able to achieve a better standard of living for her children than her husband was able to attain during his lifetime. People begin to wonder how a woman can manage so well when men find it difficult to earn enough to buy bread for their children (p. 35).

This novel undermines two deeply entrenched beliefs about women: that they need men to protect them and support their families and that honor is related to sex.

> During a demonstration, the daughter of Abu Salem hurled a stone at the head of an army officer, injuring him. The officer grabbed her and said, "I know that today's girls are very rude. I know that you are not afraid of a beating, but I know what you do fear." The girl tore her dress wide open and motioned to her genitals: "You mean this? I do not fear anything about this either." God forgive us; such a rude generation. It is true that the soil is precious, but our honor is very precious too and we

are Arabs. Basil commented that after the honor of the country and the land there is no value attached to any other honor. (p. 49)

But this new reality that Palestinian women have created for themselves has not exempted them from traditional responsibilities; it has in fact supplied them with additional responsibilities. At some point, the new woman begins to look with envy at the traditional woman, whose life is more predictable and consistent and who is more at ease with herself, both physically and psychologically. Men have accepted what the new woman has to offer, but without relieving her of her traditional status and former responsibilities. Men want her to be a man, a woman, and a servant, simultaneously (p. 120). Men want her to be both aware and unaware, to see and to be blind, to speak and to be silent, all at the same time. Men want her to be both a revolutionary who supports them in the battle for liberation and an obedient housewife without any opinions or influence in her home.

What is important is that as the events of the novel unfold, women become more aware of their abilities and potential. They reject women's "weakness" as a myth, and through their own experiences they become more confident of themselves and their own abilities: "You are something, Khaḍrā, and they say we are women, each one of us is worth five shillings. God knows that each woman is worth ten men" (p. 166). As women engage in acts of resistance, their radicalism extends to their social status and self-definition. When the chief of the village calls to Saʿdiyya, "'*Yā ḥurma*' [Ay, woman], she responds, 'You are *ḥurma* [woman]'" (p. 279).

Saḥar Khalīfa's language becomes more poetic in her novel *Mudhakkarāt Imra'a Ghayr Wāqiʿiyya (Memoirs of an Unrealistic Woman)*. Among Khalīfa's works, this novel is notable for its few characters and its limited world. The novel focuses on the crisis Arab women face in their pursuit of social acceptance, which turns on their willingness to repress their inclination to be individuals and instead accept the roles of daughter and wife. The novel's first paragraph summarizes its theme and essence:

> I am the daughter of the inspector, and I remained so till I became the wife of the merchant; sometimes I am both. When my husband ridicules me he calls me "the daughter of the inspector" and when my father is angry with me he calls me "the wife of the merchant." (p. 5)

The tension between the inner self and the social self, which others see and accept, never goes away. Additionally, the novel shows the conflict between the new woman as she sees herself and the traditional woman as she is perceived and accepted by society. There is a tremendous gap between what the heroine sees as appropriate behavior and what others deem to be suitable. Thus she says, "Sometimes I had to pretend that I was stupid. I kept my impressions and questions to myself, and pressed my lips together" (p. 5).

Caught between self-fulfillment and satisfying social norms, women seem anxious and disturbed: "I am neither a good conformist, nor am I a successful rebel," says 'Afāf, the heroine of the novel (p. 7). That is precisely the predicament in which most Arab women find themselves. They have not revolted against custom and tradition, but neither have they submitted completely to them. 'Afāf wonders how she will endure the suffering caused by her discovery that marriage—ostensibly the noble objective of a woman's life—is actually making her very lonely. "When I am with him, I feel that my soul is fluttering like a caged bird, and I feel that his presence is prison bars" (p. 18). It is impossible for her to reach self-fulfillment and be consistent with her inner self once she discovers the most terrifying truth in the world, which is that "rude girls are killed, though she was not able to discover the limit of rudeness that deserves the act of killing."[1]

In the continuous dialogue between the girl as she shows herself to society and the girl as her true self, 'Afāf highlights the identity crisis of many Arab women who cannot be themselves, but who equally cannot be the women that their families and society expect them to be. The crisis becomes extreme when women reject their designated roles: "I loved a boy, who used to say to me, 'I am not a boy, I am a man.' I used to laugh at him and allow him to touch my hand. I used to feel that I was his mother, sister, and angel. I never felt that I was rude, or perhaps I am a different type of rude, a type that does not frighten me, but frightens them, so they kill me" (p. 25).

'Afāf resents the fact that she cannot fulfill her desires in the same way as men can and do and that she cannot be "a woman who loves, desires, and feels and who uses her husband exactly as the husband uses his wife" (p. 30). But she knows that women suffer the consequences of sexual pleasure, and suffer alone, whereas men bear no burden if they choose not to do so.

The heroine is accused of being an unrealistic woman because she rebels against the social concepts of

> rudeness, the girl's luck, and girl's honor. It was odd for a woman who lacks self-confidence, who is accused of belonging to the weaker sex, to have an unusual energy in resisting customary concepts of politeness, respect, and rudeness, to reject stupid images of women who only care about perfume and makeup and regard them as silly. (p. 40)

Resistance is the essence of the novel: women's resistance to the reality they have inherited. It dissatisfies them, but they cannot break free. Thus women remain torn between what they aspire to and the actuality imposed on them by the society they live in, between dream and reality. In the context of this discrepancy, marriage becomes martyrdom in order to remain a "decent woman" in the eyes of society, and life becomes a sacrifice to maintain "a realistic image of the self cherished by family, husband, and society . . . and why not, since everyone believes that the only place for women is their home" (p. 40).

Although 'Afāf knows that others share her experience, she begins to internalize the blame that society places on women for their misfortunes. She begins to understand her friends who ask her, "Don't you wish you were a boy so that you would not suffer menstruation or worry about your virginity or fear being rude and getting yourself killed?" (p. 52). Self-reproach supplants pride, and blame replaces analysis. "'Afāf begins to think to herself, 'If you were not childless you would have filled the house with children's noises, and he would have grown very fond of you. If you were not boring, he would not have been bored with you. If you were not ugly, he would not have tried to find others'" (p. 62).

In her novel *Bāb al-Sāḥa (The Door of the Square)*, Khalīfa reveals the extent of women's role in the *intifada*, the Palestinian uprising against the Israeli occupation of Palestine, and uses the uprising as a framework to discuss the concepts of honor, betrayal, love, and resistance. Mrs. Zakiyya, who works as a visiting nurse, knows the secrets of the homes she visits but is very discreet. She is considered the social compass of the village that points in the right direction. At first Mrs. Zakiyya does not answer Nazha's greetings. Nazha's mother has been killed by the resistance forces because she was accused of collaborating with the enemy, and she lives in a house visited by the Israelis. But when Nazha offers a refuge for Hiṣṣam once he is wounded, Mrs. Zakiyya changes her opinion of Nazha, and starts to visit her so that Zakiyya can supervise Nazha's wounded nephew.

The most enduring problem women face is fear: fear of violating the symbolism invested in them by society. A woman shouts: "I am not the mother, or the land. I am a human being. I eat and drink and dream; I make mistakes, I get lost, I suffer, I dream and speak to the winds. I am not a symbol: I am a woman" (p. 176).

The novel indirectly calls for a new image of Arab women, an image consistent with what actually takes place rather than with inherited notions and suggestions regarding what women are supposed to be, or what they are supposed to be doing. Women also call for solidarity and for accepting the idea of change: "Everything changes; positions change, faces change, even history and feelings and dates, everything changes. Life keeps moving; how could we stay at a standstill? Can we keep fighting for change, can we fight, challenge, and struggle for change?" (p. 193).

But the most important message of the novel comes near the end of the story, when fighters try to reach the door of the square and attempt to open a door in the stone wall. One after the other the martyrs fall, because every time one of them tries to climb the wall, he is fired on by the enemy. When Aḥmad, the brother of Nazha, is killed and they try to "groom him to his grave" as the spouse of Palestine,[2] Nazha says: "I want my brother, not Palestine" (p. 210), because she sees Palestine as being "like a volcano that devours and devours without ever having enough" (p. 219). Afterward, Nazha argues that as far as she is concerned, most of the sacrifices are either unnecessary or result from mishandling or a lack of vision. She asks,

> "Why should all these men die like sheep? Come here and I can show you a different way to reach the point you want to reach." She pulls a young girl's hand and pushes several others, and says loudly: "Come with me and I shall show you. You want to reach that point? Come and see; you want the flag? Come underground." She walks into the kitchen and then to the cellar and then to the secret stairs in the yard assigned for the animals, and then to the magic door of the square. Within minutes a huge number of women were flowing to the square from underground. (pp. 221–222)

It thus becomes clear that women do not fear dying or sacrificing themselves for their homeland, but equally they see no glory in sacrifice that will not bring about the desired results. That is woman's vision of resistance: it is resistance that minimizes losses and achieves objectives. *Bāb al-Sāḥa* reflects the powers of resistance from a woman's perspective inside the occupied territories in a way that no other Arabic novel has done previously.

In her latest work, *Al-Mīrāth (The Inheritance)*, Khalīfa discusses the dilemmas language poses for her writing:

> I found myself torn between local dialect, proper Arabic and people's concerns. I discovered an essential difference between proper Arabic and people's concerns, and between local dialect and people's understanding. We do not read [of] people's concerns in classical Arabic, because classical Arabic is the language of inspectors, inspectors of politicians and inspectors of conscience. Hence, classical Arabic lacks spontaneity and sincerity and local dialect lacks punctuation and question marks. I found difficulty in expressing what I hear, say, and feel. (p. 72)

Khalīfa's use of language in both *Bāb al-Sāḥa* and *Al-Mīrāth* is poetic, and I occasionally found myself reading passages aloud as poetry. Here's one example:

> Here they came,
> Here they arrived
> In ships that carried thousands of them
> And threw them with no mercy
> Here they settled
> If they were to leave, it would've been through the port and the sea
> Where's my father? Did he emigrate?
> Did his days take him to emigration again? (p. 38)

The title *Al-Mīrāth* implies social, political, family, and civil upheavals. Zīna, or Zaynab, who has emigrated to the United States with her father, lives there with inherited concepts of what a "decent" girl should be, together with memories of other girls who were murdered because they were not decent enough. When she returns to the West Bank to secure her inheritance, she finds that she is entitled to only a scanty portion of a huge inheritance that is shared by uncles, aunts, and grandparents. She discovers that she and the wife of her father will inherit only very small amounts of money simply because they are women. That is why her father's wife was encouraged to have a test-tube baby boy in order to prevent anyone else from securing the inheritance her husband left her.

Al-Mīrāth also refers to social mores, such as that which persuades Nahla to spend her youth working in Kuwait to pay for her brother's education. Nahla was once "young and pretty, full of love and emotion, but suddenly awoke one day to find herself at 50 years of age, [with] no refuge, no aim, and no fulfillment. She went back to gather the threads of her life and what is left of her reality, trying in vain to live" (p. 95). She spends a lifetime giving to her brothers, parents, and family, believing that "sacrifice for others is a great thing and selfishness is a dirty thing. Love for the country is the most divine thing in life, and benevolence is part of loving God, and loving God is part of loving your family. She gave her family all that she could, without expecting anything in return" (p. 115). But now that she no longer has much to offer, has no money to give to anyone, to buy a house, to pay the fees and receive nice words in return, she starts to feel lonely and humiliated. She starts to feel that she is a refugee and an uprooted woman, although she still has land and money in the bank. "Despite the property she has, she feels extremely humiliated because here she is in the guest room of her brother's house, and despite his welcoming remarks she feels humiliated.

Despite his generosity and attempt to fill her plate with all kinds of food, she felt debased" (p. 113).

The following day, however, after she refuses her brother's request to give him money, he considers her evil "and neglects her plate and does not invite her to eat, nor does he open his mouth to say a word to her any more, he only opens his mouth to eat or to say a heavy word to his wife" (p. 117).

The fate of Nahla represents the fate of Arab women in general, that is, women who are expected to sacrifice themselves unconditionally for any member of the family, but who at the end of their lives find themselves without support or status. That is Arab women's heritage. Women go to Kuwait to work in order to send money to their brothers who study, get married, build houses, and have children: "The mirrors in the rooms of these women are crowded with pictures of others, but what did they themselves get? They received the happiness of the brother who was groomed, of the brother who became an engineer and of the brother the hero, while they as women remain teachers with no children and of course no husbands or houses. They spend money to send all their brothers to schools and universities, but what did they themselves achieve?" (p. 161).

When Nahla decides to marry Abu Salem, a real estate agent, to escape her humiliating way of life, she discovers that her marriage is considered to be a family matter in which all and sundry believe they have the right to interfere. They wonder why Nahla should want to marry at age fifty, well past childbearing age, and imagine that she must want to marry only for the sake of sex—which is an illicit desire.

Al-Mīrāth is the only Arabic novel I know of that highlights the ordeals of grown-up unmarried sisters. In literature, women are usually treated as either daughters or wives, but the unmarried sister, who indeed is subjected to all types of oppression, has never previously been a major theme in an Arabic novel.

Al-Mīrāth also exposes Arab attitudes about wealth. Although displays of wealth are meant to convey virtue and status, they also conceal the origins of this prosperity: public money stolen to become private wealth. This lack of patriotism is indicated by Arab attitudes toward public property in contrast to their attitude toward private property: everyone jealously guards the well-being of the family, but no one cares about public institutions, streets, or the country. Public property is abused at will by anyone. Zīna comments on this phenomenon:

> I was shocked to notice the huge difference between the inside and the outside. [Outside] I saw only rubbish, dirty walls and streets that are swamped in sewage water and huge amounts of dirt. By contrast, inside

the home, the water is clean and flowers indicate spotless cleanliness. Afterwards I learned that this is the system of the country. (p. 45)

During the *intifada*, under the burden of national struggle and in a climate of intermittent war and peace, together with people's disgust with the poverty, starvation, and bone-breaking[3] that exist, "fast profit became the real issue. Everyone is in a hurry. You hear them everywhere repeating the same story: we are fed up with rhetoric and with words; only money acts" (p. 129). While the Palestinians were obsessed with financial gains, "the others" (as the author calls Israelis) were able to separate Jerusalem (al-Quds) from the West Bank. "Jerusalem became a different country with borders, cross points and inspection points and identity cards; what is needed is only the visa, and even this was invented, and they called it a 'pass'" (p. 138).

The Palestinian media says that Palestine will be a paradise, that peace is impending, and that the obstacles of settlements, check points, and all the other problems will soon be overcome. But what is actually taking place on the ground is diametrically opposed to the propaganda for the future promoted by the media. The media speaks about peace and coexistence but acts like snipers in the hills on the valleys and villages. They spread enchanting rhetoric about peace, but it is actually accompanied by oppression, coercion, usurpation of land, and the demolition of houses. All this is done in the name of peace, prosperity, freedom, and security: "they are still everywhere, controlling everything, expanding wherever they like, where is the Palestinian Authority for the Palestinians, which authority; is there a state without authority?" (p. 243).

In the West Bank the Palestinian Authority speaks about projects, prosperity, money, aid, and donations, but in fact the sewage project is an environmental disaster that has led to the spread of diseases, rats, and snakes. While members of the Palestinian Authority were at the height of their celebrations, "they did not notice that the castle became cut off [from] the rest of their world and that Wādī al-Rayḥān was surrounded with a new siege and new security forces" (p. 287). Thus the big question that loomed in everyone's mind was,

Is this an agreement? Is this a peace accord? And to which future will this peace lead? What is left for the people to look forward to? Now, this solution comes, and the forces of occupation come to do whatever they like, and Palestinian people are told that this is liberation, and that this is done for the sake of peace. This is an abrogation of the past in order to reach the future, but the present is not yours, and this is why we call it a cheat and not an agreement. (pp. 292–293)

Leaders are short-sighted and in a hurry. They do not think about the long-term future; they have no strategy; they want anything now, only now. One wonders whether they have heard of Nelson Mandela, of the struggle of people who fought and persevered until they achieved exactly what they wanted to achieve. Haven't they heard of China, where people work together patiently and ride their bicycles? "Patient people who are far-sighted. If only we could learn to be far-sighted, but our people want a solution that lands on them like a missile!" (p. 311).

All this confusion and incompetence at the political level has profound effects at the personal level. For example, during the delivery of her baby, Fitna starts bleeding. They take her in an ambulance to the hospital, but the Israeli soldiers stop the ambulance—even though the mayor of town is in it—and Fitna continues to bleed. Her mother says, "Fitna is dying; her life is in danger; we cannot wait long." She tries to convince the Israeli soldiers that the woman in the ambulance desperately needs to reach the hospital, but no one seems to hear what she is saying and no one responds. The mother takes the newborn and tells the soldiers, "Take the baby, it is yours." Fitna dies at the checkpoint. "Is this the heritage of peace that the Palestinian Authority wants to present to future generations? Is this what the Palestinian Authority has achieved? Is this Palestine's destiny? Does anyone accept this destiny?"

Al-Mīrāth is the only novel in Arabic that focuses on the faltering agreements between Israelis and Palestinians that restore neither rights nor land, nor achieve dignity, justice, or equality. The author pokes holes in the empty rhetoric of leadership and the bright picture the Israeli side wishes to promote while at the same time tightening its grip on land, roads, and water resources. People are confused; they do not know who to believe or which direction to go. Khalīfa believes that the future will reveal what she has already discovered: that Palestinians will gain nothing from the "agreements." Their future is being undermined for the sake of small and temporary gains for the Palestinian leadership, which has neither waited for a better, more lasting deal nor has seen the problem in its historical context.

Saḥar Khalīfa neither judges nor blames anyone; rather, in *Al-Mīrāth* she describes the situation as it really is, and concludes from what she herself has read that, following the Oslo Accords of 1993, a better future in Gaza and the West Bank is no longer possible. Darkness is absolute, with no stars and no promise of light. *Al-Mīrāth* is a nightmare that makes the Arab reader feel very angry, frustrated, and anxious.

It is interesting to note that Khalīfa's novel was published three years before the beginning of the al-Aqṣā *intifada* on September 28, 2000, and in many ways anticipated the explosion that took the world, including the Palestinian leadership, by surprise. It is a credit to Saḥar Khalīfa and her deep understanding of the pulse of the Palestinian people that her novels served almost as a precursor to the Palestinian movement.

The writings of Najwā Barakāt, especially her latest two novels—*Bāṣ al-Awādim (The Bus of Human Beings)* and *Yā Salām (Oh, My God)*—mark the birth of a new talent in the ranks of Arab women writers. The artistic tension in *Bāṣ al-Awādim,* a sociopolitical commentary, is exciting, and the characters are engaging. Barakāt's supreme command of Arabic enables her to use classical Arabic to denote and describe the most acute feelings and the most delicate and subtle circumstances. The use of classical Arabic, as opposed to a local dialect, does not detract from the authenticity of the dialogue or alienate readers. (This is a very controversial issue in Arabic. Some writers believe that classical Arabic can be used for the most common conversations, whereas others call for the use of simplified Arabic or for colloquial Arabic in conversations between characters. There is no right and wrong in this.) The story unfolds during a journey in which twelve characters are together on a bus headed for the same destination. The bus becomes a universe in which characters develop and events unfold, and, one at a time, the characters themselves—erstwhile strangers—reveal just enough to become part of a community united by ill fate on a journey that takes much longer than anticipated.

One of the most striking features of the novel is the detailed revelation of the inner worlds of the characters and their relation to the mundane reality within which the characters persist. The narrative is highly suggestive at many different levels:

> The wind massaged her hair and loosened the knot of her head-cover and threw it behind [her]. Long locks of hair were set free, and started dancing like fish that have just been taken out of the water. Khaddūja stood erect like someone who suddenly got mad. She reclaimed her head-cover from the passenger next to her, trying to cover [up] what had been revealed. "Please cover what has been revealed," she said to her daughter, and turned to the others with an apologetic smile. (p. 10)

When a storm forces the bus to stop at the roadside, the assistant lights the gasoline lamp he has with him and lifts it up. "A yellow light spread over the bodies of the passengers whose number was doubled by their shadows that promptly sat next to them on their seats, and spilled into the aisle in the middle of the bus" (p. 21). The characters' "imprisonment" on a bus liberates them from the restrictions of place and time, and it also grants the writer the freedom to be anywhere in the Arab world, at any imaginable time. Thus the writer has the freedom to discuss a wide range of topics, ranging from women's rights in Islam, to the partition of Palestine, to the security services that control people's lives like gods on high, unseen and accountable to no one. As the journey proceeds, relationships between the characters are intensified by the attraction and discord displayed between them. A woman delivers a baby on board, and a female atmosphere seems to pervade and override the male mood, with each eventually overlapping with the other passengers and sharing in the same suffering and destiny.

The writer is particularly skillful in building up and distinguishing her characters from each other. Each enjoys a distinct personality, and the suggestions and comments made both reveal the past and make a contribution to the construction of the bus community. Because the characters have different social backgrounds, the bus community becomes a microcosm of society. The reader is not surprised to learn that that the Lebanese Educational Society in Paris named this novel the best creative Lebanese text in 1996.

Barakāt's novel *Yā Salām (Oh, My God)* resembles a crime novel, a shift in genre that reveals the breadth of the writer's talent. Beirut turns out to be a city full of rats, and traces of the war can be felt through the psychological and moral distortions that have befallen almost everyone in the city. Salām, the novel's heroine, is rich and is initially a target for Luqmān, who wants both her money and her as a woman. But later he becomes interested in Lamīs Shīrīn, who might provide him with a residency in Paris, and encourages Salām to be interested in Najīb. Salām kills her brother, Sālim, who is addicted both to morphine and an incestuous relationship with her. After killing him, she puts his body in the basement, where she releases rats to devour the remains. Another very cruel woman, Lawrence, imprisons her son and opens a can of gas to suffocate and kill him.

The novel portrays Beirut in moral decay and without hope, the only hope for Salām being to change her environment. Salām therefore plans to leave for Paris with Lamīs Shīrīn, but that eventually proves to be impossible. Although the novel does not focus on war, or assassination, or on the action of snipers, it nevertheless depicts a place that is falling apart economically, morally, and psychologically.

The worst damage of the war is not to the city, its buildings, or its infrastructure, but to people's psychology and morality. *Yā Salām* may well be considered a new addition to women's war literature, in that it reveals how the traumas of war are manifested in a postwar era. Many of the characters in this novel have sinned, have committed crimes, and have been punished in one way or another. Their feelings of love, hatred, excitement, and disgust are so confused that it becomes difficult to justify entertaining any one feeling rather than another.

Sexual issues in the novel are taken seriously and are considered part of the moral and psychological matrix of society. Najīb and his crazy brother sexually manipulate Salām, but nevertheless the latter's virginity remains intact. In the war climate that obtains, Lamīs Shīrīn helps Luqmān get a passport after he satisfies her sexually. She marries him so he can get a visa and allows him to accompany her to Paris. From then on, he plays the lothario with her as often as he possibly can. Najīb physically attacks Salām, who seems to be proud of the bruises he inflicts on her. Thus the psychological distortion that plagues Salām forms part of the larger moral and psychological distortion within the city, expressed in the spread of corruption, frustration, killing, and crime.

The mother, Lawrence, at first tries to protect her son, Ilyās, who kills and tortures others. Finally, however, she decides to kill him to avenge all his helpless victims:

> I went down running, crying not in sympathy with your victim but in fear of you, of that face of yours, the face of a criminal, tyrant, pygmy, and a wild beast. I wished to cut off the breast that has fed you and the arms which carried you as a baby and the womb that bore you and the tongue that has prayed to God so that you may grow up and become what you are—cruelty and despotism. (p. 188)

Horrid crimes are accepted as a matter of course. As for Salām, she loses her mind. The author shows that crime only begets crime and violence can only breed violence, facts that call into question the general belief that punishment is necessary for social reform.

Yā Salām is a painful revelation of the devastation war inflicts on human psychology, morality, and relationships. It offers a horrifying picture of a city infested with rats and so plagued by corruption and decadence that it would seem impossible to redeem.

Another Lebanese novelist, Hudā Barakāt, also addresses the issue of war in her novel, *Ḥārith al-Miyāh (The Tiller of Waters)*, which won the 2000 Naguib Maḥfouẓ prize for best novel. (See Chapter 7 for a discussion of her novel *Ḥajar al-Ḍaḥik [The Stone of Laughter],* also about the Lebanese civil war.) The narrative probes the ancient history of Beirut in an attempt to show that the recent Lebanese civil war is only the latest chapter in a tale of war and destruction that has befallen the city, each time at the height of its prosperity and glamor. Barakāt contends that Beirut was born under the influence of Mars, a "harsh star" (p. 34). Every time the city is partially or completely destroyed, it is rebuilt again, not unlike other Arab cities that, the novel claims, carry no cumulative collective memory, since every decade wipes out what came before and starts anew.[4]

Barakāt has researched the history of Beirut, and that context is animated by the relationship of Hajj Niqūlā with Shamsa, a Kurdish woman. Through this relationship, the author explores the manufacturing and trading of cotton, the issue of the Kurds, and the relationship between creating the cosmos and weaving cotton and silk—both being acts of creativity and ingenuity.[5]

Through Shamsa, the Kurdish woman, the novelist tries to restore self-esteem to the Kurds, by recognizing their contributions to Lebanese society:

> Do you know that the Kurds were the first to weave cotton in this region? Yes, your people. The old Bilinos used to say that weaving cotton is honorable even for men, because it is far better than wool. The barbers were the Bedouins of the land, whereas the farmers were the ones who started urban areas. Cotton has become the coffin of the dead in their tombs: they used to wrap the dead in leather and bury them like a fetus. (p. 63)

The civil war in Lebanon is described as a link in a series of wars that have befallen Beirut every time the city has reached an irresistible stage of beauty. Part of the blame should be directed at Arab rulers who have lost many wars because they do not enjoy fighting wars. Then the narrative turns to seemingly unrelated concerns: cotton, silk, and knitting. It reveals, for example, that "the poor women in Belgian towers live off their needlework, away from the destruction of war and revolution, convinced that the Virgin Mary is the one who taught other virgins how to live off their needle work" (p. 117). The author indirectly but elegantly links war with destruction and distortion and knitting with peace, security, and development:

> Shamsa, because we forget and because we do not acknowledge our ignorance, we forgot that the weaver, wherever he is on this land, is entrusted with the secret of life and peace, and is the one who is always threatened with the triumph of death and war over him. Isn't disrobing, nakedness, linked to the first sin and to punishment and to an incessant quest for paganism? Look at the picture of the Goddess Athena, how she carries the loom in one hand and the dagger in another. In one hand, the wisdom of weaving, and in the other, the tragedy and destruction of wars. The wise Ghandi started to weave his clothes to be free of the British. According to Indian myth, the God Hingalaj asked people to transform themselves from fighters into weavers and knitters so that she could grant them the continuity of free existence and the blessing of the day dawning out of the darkness of night. (p. 130)

Perhaps the greatness of the novel lies in a subtle and balanced link between two levels that constantly differ: the imaginative and realistic, war and peace, illusion and reality, as the author seeks to find the truth somewhere between the two. If the weaver, as the author says, is the one "who weaves words and people wear his words" (p. 129), Hudā Barakāt has woven a narration that addresses past, present, and future; war and peace; love and life. The essential reason asserted for the continual destruction that besets Beirut is its residents' determined refusal to learn from history, from the experiences of their predecessors and their lessons and wisdom.

> The reason might be that what my grandfather related to my father remained a kind of rhetoric conveyed from one generation to another without morally affecting the people who inherit it. Hence, the entire story, the past and present, became irrelevant. No use is made of the lessons of the grandfathers and no advice is brought to bear on the future. Thus, people remember the lesson only after it becomes too late. (p. 165)

Beirut, therefore, is forever condemned to be at war, as is every Arab city, and the danger results from a lack of vision and a failure to make use of inherited wisdom. The novel conveys a new vision and a new historical approach to the issue of war, granting it a special status among novels written by women about the Lebanese civil war and among Arab women's war novels in general.

Egyptian novelist Salwā Bakr published *Al-'Araba al-Dhahabiyya lā Taṣ'ad ilā al-Samā' (The Golden Chariot)* in 1991. This novel relates the story of seven women in prison, introducing readers to the circumstances that led each of them there. We even learn the story of one of the jailers, which is not very different from the stories of the women jailed. Azizeh, one of the seven women, tells their stories according to her own criteria, ignoring masculine laws and their consequences. She would grant the women she chooses seats in her golden chariot, in which she will travel to heaven and liberate herself and others from the ordeals of this life.

This theme of an oppressed class or group of people (in this case, women) fleeing harsh reality to a pure, welcoming, and fair world recurs often in Arabic popular stories and myths. It is a manifestation of the alienation women feel and a symbolic rejection of its conditions. This concept has been used by Salwā Bakr as a framework or a common denominator among the women in the novel in a story that tries to imitate the narrative atmosphere of *A Thousand and One Nights*.

In her more recent novel *Al-Bashmuri* (1998), Bakr takes ordinary people as her heroes and heroines and broaches a controversial period in Arab history. Here, she discusses the Arab invasion of Egypt, a subject rarely considered in Arab history or literature. Her choice of topic is indicative of the boldness that Arab women novelists demonstrate in addressing difficult and controversial issues in their literary work.

The narrator is Bdīr, a Christian man, who abandons the Murky land (a place known as such in Egypt, located on the banks of the Nile) and becomes a priest in the aftermath of his beloved's suicide, which takes place the day before her planned wedding to his brother. Because the novel is written in the first person, all we know about Bdīr and Thawna (his traveling companion and a man from the church) is relayed through what Bdīr tells us.

Father Yūsab, the highest Coptic religious authority in Egypt, sends Bdīr and Thawna to the Bashmūrīn to ask them to become Muslims; in other words, Bdīr is to ask the Christian Bashmūrīn to stop rebelling against their Muslim rulers and convert in order to end the war. (History relates that the Coptic Church, which was Christian, supported the rule of Muslims against the rebellious Bashmūrīn. The church tried to convince the Bashmūrīn to accept Islam.) The journey of Bdīr and Thawna takes up most of the novel. They describe what they see on the road, what tribes do to them, and what befalls the rebels. The novel does not provide the Arab version of the story; the reader only learns about the consequences of their works and policies during and after the invasion. The author does, however, put thoughtful remarks about Islam into the mouths of Bdīr and Thawna, who are Christian:

> Islam requires people to do good deeds and warns them against doing bad deeds. No one denies that the Arabs are simple people who lead simple lives and who are neither lavish nor extravagant in their clothes or lifestyles. Their mosques hold no gold or silver; they pray to God in a truly devout fashion and in an extremely polite and simple way. (p. 93)

Bdīr and Thawna observe a Muslim as he performs his ablutions in preparation for prayer, inviting Bdīr to comment: "I had not known before that Muslims are so clean, as clean as we Copts are. This seems to me so similar to the necessity of washing your feet before you get to the holy statue and cleansing them from the copper pot that is full of purified water" (p. 112).

The novel focuses on the commonalties among religions, rather than their differences, but takes care to distinguish between people who are truly pious in any religion and others who use their religion in order to gain power, money, prestige, or authority. Thawna explains to Bdīr that the behavior of religious men does not always serve God; sometimes it serves human interests instead. That is why such men exaggerate their commitment to religion in front of others. Pious Thawna has a merciful heart as well as a broad mind, so he is able to understand and even forgive sins and ask forgiveness for the sinners from their God. He is an ordinary man who does both right and wrong and does not claim immunity from error.

In spite of its merits, the work has two major weaknesses: First, although the novel discusses the Arab invasion of Egypt, there is no single Arab voice or Arab character. We see the traces of destruction and hear the stories secondhand. Second, it is also strange that the Bashmūrīn refuse Father Yūsab's request to stop fighting, although Father Yūsab is the highest religious authority in the country. Perhaps it was an intentional omission: the writer has indicated that she plans a sequel to this novel, and perhaps these shortcomings will be addressed within it. *Al-Bashmūrī* nevertheless remains a very ambitious novel in both style and substance, because it addresses a complex and controversial topic in a fluid, informative narrative that makes it difficult to put the book down.

Aḥlām Mustighānimī's *Fawḍā al-Ḥawāss (Confusion of the Senses)*, the sequel to *Dhākirat al-Jasad (Memory in the Flesh)*, which was discussed earlier in this book, won the 1998 Naguib Maḥfouẓ prize for best novel and became one of the most popular contemporary novels in Arabic. Mustighānimī's capacity for dissecting some of the most unfortunate legacies of Arab politics—blackmail, treachery, exaggerations—was, I believe, what attracted Arab readers to this novel. The author suggests personal salvation as an option rather than political or collective salvation. She probes the relationship between citizen and state while chronicling the life of her mother, whose husband is martyred in the war for Algerian independence. After his death, she finds herself having to raise and feed her two young children alone, as well as being burdened with a big name. She carries on with

> a body that is not hers, and with a fate that satisfies the dignity of the state, the only force with the capacity to strip you of your dreams at any time, that stripped her of her femininity and deprived me of my childhood and then went away. The country that is still walking on my body and her body, on my dreams and her dreams, only with different shoes. It wore military boots with me while with her it wore an elegant pair of history's shoes. (p. 102)

In *Fawḍā al-Ḥawāss*, Mustighānimī also discusses the act of writing as a moment of revelation and subtlety in a person's life. After all big causes have been lost, writing remains vitally important, and after focusing on everything that is relevant to us, writing remains the most difficult to look at "without acknowledging that what is disturbing him is writing itself, as an act of confrontation, as a silent manoeuvering, he was not able, despite his intellectual capability, to spy on its credibility" (p. 96).

Big causes and big issues are what have made men heroic and dignified, but because all big causes have now been lost, all that is left today is the heroism and glamor of writing and creativity. Indeed, that is precisely the heroic status that Aḥlām Mustighānimī has been able to achieve, because she very clearly understands the sensitivities of Arab readers and what they like to read. Today, Arab readers want an honest, sincere analysis of all the reasons for their successive defeats. Also, they want to see a ray of hope, whether stemming from the inside or projected from another planet. In *Fawḍā al-Ḥawāss*, freedom flowers within the human self. After reading this novel, the Arab reader may attain a certain degree of harmony as a result of truly understanding what has happened in the Arab world, and why setbacks and defeats beset Arabs. The novel does provide the reader with a ray of hope, owing to the writer's ability to explore and enrich the inner world of her characters and to overcome the state of frustration and lack of direction that most Arabs feel today. The novel calls upon its readers to rid themselves of the illusions of the past and trust their instincts to lead them along a path where there is no blackmail, hypocrisy, or bargaining.

The public is skillfully linked to the personal in this novel, in a way that makes for a sound linguistic and political structure that excites the admiration and surprise of the reader. "I did not blame al-Shādhilī bin Jadīd [the former president of Algeria] that night for wasting my desire, as he has previously wasted years of people's desires" (p. 236). And when Muḥammad Bū Diyāf arrives in Algeria after spending twenty-eight years in a neighboring Arab country, the writer comments: "Is there only one hour between home and exile? Why did he then need twenty-eight years to cover that distance?"[6]

In her novel *Al-Bādhinjāna al-Zarqā' (The Blue Eggplant)*, Mīrāl al-Ṭahhāwī offers a text that rewrites all Arab defeats, setbacks, and feminist frustrations in a way that beautifully connects the private and public worlds. She uses symbolism to approach her topics; for example, she refers to the 1967 Arab defeat in the Six Day War as a "wild birth" that takes place under difficult circumstances. The author writes in first and third person, as if personally addressing the reader. The narrative probes the inner world of women and focuses on their hesitation among fear, doubt, perplexity, and courage:

> You say that after thirty years of crawling in dark psychological tunnels looking at a mirror that reflects the body of a child, your soul is

nevertheless in a great dilemma. It is your right to live and love. Do you feel that getting rid of your head cover is such a great sin that you deserve to have your small pleasures spoiled with doubt and confusion about your ability to love and give? . . . After give and take, hesitation and retreat, you put your mouth firmly on his and said "I love you," then you opened a new parenthesis and continued to write, "Repression is the culmination of all deprivations from which most women suffer. All women's concepts have been distorted, their feelings suppressed, even their feelings about normal human relations and their own bodies and biological needs and their humanity. This historic repression of women is what has pushed them from the domains of parity and participation to circles of deprivation." (p. 113)

These "circles of deprivation" sometimes map the worlds of both men and women, owing to the hypocrisy, blackmail, and exaggerations that have characterized Arab politics and colored the Arab method of dealing with defeats, crises, and setbacks.

The writer envisions an age in which women engage in politics and strategic thinking.

> To your right is Olga who is preparing for a PhD in Arabic literature, and to your left is Sariyya who is looking for strategic changes following Camp David and the true role of the Palestinian authority, while you are unleashing different psychological aspects of rebellion by women against class, type, and social and psychological motives . . . The three of you are participating in three different things. (p. 114)

Throughout the text, the author addresses social mores that aggravate social hypocrisy and encourage blackmail, and discusses the need to adopt new thinking in the social sphere in order to change reality: "Once you finish formulating new convictions, you will wear these over your fear, shyness, and old heritage. You will continue to prepare for a future that will transform you into a butterfly that will express her yearning for light" (p. 119).

Laylā 'Usayrān's novel, *Ḥiwār bilā Kalimāt fī al-Ghaybūba (A Dialogue Without Words in a Coma)* is unique in Arabic literature. It is 'Usayrān's autobiographical account of her seventy-five days in a coma. As she recovered, language was restored to her, with all its elegance and subtlety. She relies on her gift to draw a picture for her readers of a world the essence of which can only be portrayed by someone who has undergone such a traumatic experience, and to use her ordeal to enrich the human experience. The text leaves the soul suspended between life and death. The woman exists in an amorphous world, unable to reach a chair situated not more than one step away from her. In a self-pitying tone, she thinks to herself that "the longest distance between me and my self is the exact distance that separates me from the chair! Only one step" (p. 155). The author's own situation is a poignant metaphor for the crisis gripping her city of Beirut: both awaken to realize that their pain and suffering threaten to annihilate them.

'Usayrān is an experienced novelist with more than ten novels to her credit. (Her novel *Aṣāfīr al-Fajr [The Birds of Dawn]* was discussed earlier in this book.) Because few people emerge from a coma able to register the memories of their experience, 'Usayrān knew that by writing about it, she would open doors on a closed world. Her courage in retracing her deeply personal journey across precarious terrain is firm proof that the Arab woman novelist is fully in control of her potential, talent, and subject matter.

The Jordanian writer Fayrūz al-Tamīmī has also detected a growing maturity in Arab women writers. After winning third prize in a contest in al-Shāriqa, United Arab Emirates, for a novel she called *Naṣṣ al-Mar'a (Woman's Text)*, she commented:

> I was trying to write what I would call "a woman's text," enjoying penetrating small details and invading the neglected corners of each scene. I was trying to enter into the soul of the woman—the mother of the neglected—when I found that everything I had written was staring me in the face and telling me that this was a novel. After that, I was no longer able to spare any time or effort away from this work.[7]

The creativity of Arab women novelists manifests itself in their new approach both to language and to social and political issues. Their linguistic novelty reflects their French perspectives on social and political dilemmas. As al-Tamīmī tackles the very act of writing, Saḥar Khalīfa brings new insight to the Palestinian political struggle for independence and freedom.

As I have already stated, Saḥar Khalīfa's novel *Al-Mīrāth* is the first Arabic novel that addresses the situation of the Palestinians in the post-Oslo era. The novel *Maṭar Aswad, Maṭar Aḥmar (Black Rain, Red Rain)* (1993) by Iraqi writer Ibtisām 'Abd Allah is the first Arabic novel to describe the Gulf War. It was followed in 1996 by two other novels on the same subject: *'Iṭr al-Tuffāḥ (The Perfume of Apples)* by Irāda al-Jabbūrī, and *Al-'Ālam Nāqiṣan Wāḥid (The World Minus One)* by Maysalūn Hādī. There is also the novel *Al-Qahr (Agony)* by Suhayla Dāwūd, published in 1994, about events that took place in the Iran-Iraq War. These novels, like those Arab women wrote about the war in Lebanon, do not focus on the front line or on fighting elsewhere. Rather, they reflect social, political, and human relationships at a time when war had disastrous effects on every child, woman, and man; on every city and village; and on every human relationship, both overt and covert.

As far as the history of the novel in Arabic can be traced, it is certain that Arab women were pioneers in the field. Women established this genre in Arabic literature, weaving words into works of art, just as they used to weave silk into carpets. Arab women now enter the twenty-first century as leaders in the art of novel writing.

This literary genre, in fact, has matured along with women. Throughout the twentieth century, the work of Arab women novelists has reflected Arab social and political concerns, and they have given expression in their writings to all kinds of issues that matter in their societies. Therefore, to accuse Arab women of not being engaged in public concerns and of confining themselves to personal issues is unfair. One only has to read Arab women's writings to gain an insight into the history, the battles, and the future inclinations of the Arab nation. Moreover, many Arab women novelists are now achieving the high status within the Arab literary world that their writings merit.

This chapter has described the work of a new generation of Arab women novelists who are unafraid of entering into the secret and detailed life of women, and who are proud that the female experience constitutes part and parcel of the social and political matrix, as well as the backbone of their creativity and work.

List of Novelists

EVERY EFFORT HAS BEEN MADE to find biographical information on the novelists included in this volume. Such data was not available for some novelists, and they are not included in this appendix.

Āshūr, Raḍwā: Raḍwā Āshūr is an Egyptian writer and scholar born in Cairo in 1946. She graduated from the Faculty of Arts at Cairo University in 1967 and earned an MA in comparative literature from Cairo University in 1972 and a PhD in African American literature from the University of Massachusetts at Amherst in 1975.

Āshūr coedited a major four-volume work on Arab women writers (2005). The English translation—*Arab Women's Writings: A Critical Reference Guide, 1873–1999* (2008)—is an abridged edition of the Arabic original.

Āshūr has co-translated, supervised, and edited the Arabic translation of volume 9 of *The Cambridge History of Literary Criticism* (2006). She has also translated Mourid Barghouti's *Midnight and Other Poems* (2008).

In 2007 Āshūr was awarded the 2007 Constantine Cavafy Prize for Literature.

Āshūr is currently professor of English and comparative literature at 'Ayn Shams University, Cairo. She is the author of *Ḥajar Dāfi' (A Warm Stone)*, 1985; *Khadīja wa Tūnis (Khadīja and Tunis)*, 1989; *Maryama wa al-Raḥīl (Maryama and the Departure)*, 1994; and *Gharnāṭa (Granada)*, 1994.

'Aṭiyya, Farīda: Born in Tripoli, Lebanon, Aṭiyya, studied at the American School in Beirut, where she later became a teacher. Besides writing novels, she contributed to newspapers and magazines and translated works from English into Arabic.

'Aṭiyya's books include *Bahjat al-Mukhaddirāt fī Fawā'id 'Ilm al-Nabāt (The Joy of Drugs on the Benefits of Botany)*, 1893; *Al-Rawḍa al-Naḍīra fī Ayyām Bombay al-Akhīra (The Green Garden in Bombay's Final Days)*, 1899; and *Bayn 'Arshayn (Between Two Thrones)*, 1912.

al-Aṭrash, Laylā: A TV producer and news editor, Laylā al-Aṭrash has won numerous awards for her documentaries about prominent figures in Arabic letters. She writes a regular column for the Jordanian daily *Al-Dustour* and comments on literary topics for *Amman Magazine*, where she also serves on the editorial board. Al-Aṭrash holds degrees in law and Arabic literature and is a member of the High Council and Executive Committee of the Jordanian Ministry of Culture, in charge of the Family Library Program. Currently, she serves as president of PEN Jordan.

Al-Aṭrash is the author of *Imra'a li al-Fuṣāl al-Khamsa (A Woman for Five Seasons)*, 1988; *Wa Tushriqu Gharban (Dawning from the West)*, 1988; and *Yawm 'Ādī wa Qiṣaṣ Ukhrā (An Ordinary Day and Other Stories)*, 1992.

al-'Aṭṭār, Mājida: She is the author of *Fī al-Bad' Kāna al-Ḥubb (In the Beginning Was Love)*, 1978; and *Murāhiqa (The Adolescent)*, 1969.

Ba'albakī, Laylā: Born in 1936 to a conservative Shi'ite Muslim family in southern Lebanon, Laylā Ba'albakī is the daughter of the poet 'Alī al-Ḥājj Ba'albakī, who had worked for the French high commissioner. She studied at Saint Joseph University in Beirut. From 1957 to 1960 she was the secretary of the Lebanese Parliament. Then she worked as a journalist for many newspapers *(Al-Ḥawādith, Al-Dustūr, Al-Yawm, Al-Usbū' al-'Arabī)*. She published her rebellious novel *Anā Aḥyā (I Live)* in 1958, and the book caused an outcry, partly because it was considered so unusual and so risqué. When the Lebanese war erupted in 1975, she emigrated to London, where she ended her career in journalism and withdrew from cultural and journalistic society.

Ba'albakī is the author of *Anā Aḥyā (I Live)*, 1958; *Al-Āliha al-Mamsūkha (The Dwarf Gods)*, 1960; and *Safīnat Ḥanān ilā al-Qamar (A Spaceship of Tenderness to the Moon)*, 1964.

Badr, Liyāna: Liyāna Badr was born in 1950 in Jerusalem to a nationalist family and was raised in Jericho. She obtained a BA in philosophy and psychology from Arab University in Beirut but was not able to complete her MA after the Lebanese civil war broke out. She worked as a volunteer in various Palestinian women's organizations, and as an editor in the cultural department of *Al-Hurriyya* review. After the 1982 Palestinian exodus from Lebanon, she lived in Damascus, Tunis, and Amman and then returned to Palestine in 1994. She is married and has two children. In addition to her literary work, she also runs the cinema department at the Palestinian Ministry of Culture in Ramallah and was the editor of the ministry's periodical, *Dafater Thaqafiyya*.

Badr's published works include *Būṣila min Ajl 'Abbād al-Shams* (1979), published as *A Compass for the Sunflower* in 1989; and *'Ayn al-Mir'āt* (1991), published as *The Eye of the Mirror* in 1995.

Barakāt, Hudā: Born in Beirut in 1952, Barakāt graduated from Lebanese University, receiving a BA in French literature in 1974. She worked as a teacher before leaving for Paris to study for her PhD, but the civil war in Lebanon prevented her from completing her degree.

After going back home, she established the Shahrazad, a women's society, in 1988. She now lives in Paris and works as a journalist.

In the 1990s she published *Ḥajar al-Ḍaḥik* (1990), published as *The Stone of Laughter* in 1994; *Ḥārith al-Miyāh (The Tiller of Waters)*, 1998; and *Ahl al-Hawā (People of Passion)*, 1994.

al-Bāti', Fatḥiyya Maḥmūd: Born in Jaffa, Palestine, al-Bāti' started her creative career as a painter and then became known as a writer. Her books include *Widā' ma' al-Aṣīl (Farewell at Sunset)*, 1970; *Mudhakkarāt Zā'ifa (False Memoirs)*, 1975; and *Nabta fī al-Baydā' (A Plant in the Desert)*, 1981.

Bīṭar, Ḥayāt: She is the author of *Nihāyat wa 'Ibrat Bayrūt (The End and the Lesson of Beirut)*, 1964.

Dāghir, Katherine Ma'rūf: She is the author of *Ghaṣṣa fī al-Qalb (A Sigh in the Heart)*, 1963; and *Kifāḥ Imra'a (A Woman's Struggle)*, 1965.

Fawwāz, Zaynab (1846–1914): Born in the village of Tabnin in southern Lebanon, Fawwāz moved around quite a bit, living in Alexandria, Cairo, and Damascus. She was a beautiful, fascinating character who rose from being a maid in a learned house to a leading writer, historian, and poet. She divorced two husbands in the quest for her freedom and intellectual development and women's emancipation. She wrote the first novel in Arabic literature.

Fawwāz is the author of *Al-Hawā wa al-Wafā' (Love and Loyalty)* (1893), reissued in 1984; *Al-Durr al-Manthūr fī Ṭabaqāt Rabāt al-Khudūr (Scattered Pearls in Women's Quarters)*, 1894; *Ḥusn al-*

'Awāqib: Ghāda al-Zahra (Good Consequences: Ghāda the Radiant), 1899; and *Al-Malik Qūrūsh (King Qūrūsh)*, 1905. *Al-Rasā'il al-Zaynabiyya (Zaynab's Letters)* was published in 1906.

Hādī, Maysalūn: She is the author of *Al-'Ālam Nāqiṣān Wāḥid (The World Minus One)*, 1996; *Ashyā' Lam Taḥduth (Things That Have Not Happened)*, 1992 (short stories); and *Al-Ṭā'ir al-Sīḥrī wa al-Nuqāṭ al-Thalāth (The Magic Bird and the Three Points)*, 1995 (short stories).

Hāshim, Labība Nāṣīf: Born in Kifrshīmā, Lebanon, Hāshim moved with a few members of her family to Egypt, where she became a student of Shaikh Ibrahīm al-Yāzijī and later delivered lectures at Egypt University.

She published the first issues of *Fatāt al-Sharq (The Orient Girl)* magazine in 1906. She traveled to Chile and there published *Al-Sharq wa al-Gharb (East and West)* magazine in Santiago in 1923. Then she returned to Egypt, where she continued issuing *Fatāt al-Sharq* magazine until she died.

Hāshim's books include *Al-Tarbiya (Education)*, 1911.

al-Ḥūmānī, Balqīs: Born in Nabaṭiyya, Lebanon, al-Ḥāmānī studied nursing in London and worked as a nurse as well as a journalist.

She published *Al-Laḥn al-Khayyir (The Good Tune)* (short stories), 1961; *Ḥay al-Lājī' (Al-Laji District)*, 1969; *Sa Amurru 'alā al-Aḥzān (I Shall Pass by Sorrows)*, 1975; and *Al-Asirra al-Bayḍa' (The White Beds)*.

Idlibī, Ulfat Abū al-Khayr 'Umar Bāshā (1912–2007): Born into a traditional Damascene family, Idlibī was affected by the French occupation of her country under the French Mandate of 1919. She educated herself by reading books from the library of her uncle, author Kazem Daghestani. Idlibī later wrote and published stories about the Syrian resistance movement; the injustice of the French aggressor; and the people struggling for their lives, freedom, and independence in a country already exhausted by the tyranny of the Ottoman Empire.

Later she became a lecturer and wrote novels and essays on the social position of women in the Middle East; the pressure to which women are subjected; and the methods they use to cope with that pressure, such as living in a fantasy world.

Idlibī's books include *Dimashq yā Basmat al-Ḥuzn*, translated into English as *Ṣabriya: Damascus Bittersweet* in 1997; *Ḥikāyat Jaddī (My Grandfather's Story)* (a novel for young adults); and *Alf Layla wa Layla (A Thousand and One Nights)*. Arab Writers Union, Damascus, 1998.

Jabbūr, Munā: Born in Lebanon, Jabbūr became a teacher. She was deeply influenced by the writings of Laylā Ba'albakī. She committed suicide while still young.

Jabbūr is the author of *Fatāt Tāfiha (A Silly Girl)*, 1962; and *Al-Gurban wa al-Musūḥ al-Baydā' (The Ravens and the White Sackcloth)*, 1966.

Karam, 'Afīfa (1883–1924): Born in the village of 'Amshīt, Lebanon, Karam attended a convent school. After getting married, she emigrated with her husband to Louisiana. There she began publishing *Al-'Ālam al-Jadīd (The New World)* magazine in 1912, the first Arab woman's magazine published in the United States. She became an editor at *Al-Hudā*, a newspaper in New York, before taking time off to write novels that were the first to consider the relationship between East and West from a feminist perspective.

Karam's novel *Badī'a wa Fu'ād (Badī'a and Fu'ād)* was published in 1906. No publication information is available for the following novels: *Fāṭima al-Badawiyya (Fatima, the Bedwin Woman)*, *Ghāda 'Amshīt (The Pretty Woman of 'Amshīt)*, *Ibnat Nā'ib al-Malik (The Daughter of the Viceroy)*, *Malikat al-Yawm (Queen of Today)*, *Muḥammad 'Alī al-Kabīr*, and *Cleopatra*.

Khalīfa, Saḥar: Born in 1941, Khalīfa received her elementary and secondary education in Nablus, Palestine, and pursued higher studies at the English Department of Beerzeit University in Palestine. She earned an MA in English Literature and a PhD in women's studies from the University of Iowa. The most respected Arab woman novelist, she has been writing novels for the last thirty years.

Khalīfa's books include *Lam Na'ud Jawāriya Lakum (We Are No Longer Your Maids)*, 1974; *'Abbād al-Shams (The Sunflower)* and *Al-Ṣabbār (Wild Thorns)*, 1984; *Mudhakkarāt Imra'a Ghayr Wāqi'iyya (Memoirs of an Unrealistic Woman)*, 1986; *Bāb al-Sāḥa (The Door of the Square)*, 1990; and *Al-Mīrāth (The Inheritance)*, 1997.

Khūrī, Colette: Born in Damascus in 1936, Khūrī studied at a convent school and at the Layeek School in Damascus, Syria. She joined the Faculty of Law at St. Joseph University in Beirut. She studied French literature at a Syrian university. She started writing when she was fifteen and is one of the pioneers of women's writing in Syria.

Khūrī is the author of *Ayyām Ma'ahu (Days with Him)*, 1st ed. 1959; 5th ed., 1980; *Layla Wāḥida (One Night)*, 1960; *Kiyān (Entity)*, 1968; *Wa Marra Ṣayf (A Summer Has Gone)*, 1975; and *Ayyām Ma'a al-Ayyām (Days with Days)*, 1980.

Khūst, Nādiya: Born in Damascus in 1935, Khūst got her bachelor of philosophy from Damascus University and a PhD in Russian literature from the University of Moscow. She is a novelist and an activist in social, environmental, and archaeological issues. She published *Ḥubb fī Bilād al-Shām (Love in Greater Syria)* in 1995 and *A'āṣīr fī Bilād al-Shām (Hurricanes in Greater Syria)* in 1998.

Kīlanī, Qamar: Born in Damascus in 1928, Kīlanī earned a BA in Arabic literature from Damascus University. She is an educator and a journalist who devotes her time and energy to writing and teaching.

Kīlanī's books include *'Ālam bilā Ḥudūd (A World Without Borders)*, 1972; *Al-Dawwāma (The Whirlpool)*, 1983; and *Awrāq Musāfira (Woman Traveler's Papers)*, 1987.

Mamdūḥ, 'Āliya: Born in Iraq in 1944, Mamdūḥ is known in the Arab world as a woman of letters and a journalist.

She graduated from Al-Mūstanṣiriyya University in 1971. She lives in Paris and works in the fields of literature and journalism. Her published works include *Laylā wa al-Dhi'b (Layla and the Wolf)*, 1981; *Ḥabbāt al-Naftālīn (Mothballs; Naphthalene in the UK)*, 1986, which was translated into English in 1996; and *Al-Walā' (Fondness)*, 1995.

Muḥammad, Zaynab: She published a novel in 1927 entitled *Asrār Waṣīfa Miṣriyya (The Secrets of an Egyptian Mistress)*. In 1970, her play *Dustūr al-Ajniḥa (The Wings Constitution)* was published in Beirut.

al-Musālima, In'ām: Born in Dar'a, Syria, in 1937, al-Musālima studied dentistry at Damascus University and worked as a dentist in the Syrian countryside before returning to Damascus and working at the Department of Health. She started publishing her work in newspapers and magazines in the late 1950s and won the Story Award in Syria in 1958. Her published books include *Al-Ḥubb wa al-Waḥl (Love and Mud)*, 1962; and *Al-Kahf (The Cave)*, 1973.

Mustighānimī, Aḥlām: Born in Tunisia in 1953, Mustighānimī is an Algerian novelist and poet. She graduated from the Faculty of Letters at the University of Algeria and got a PhD in the social sciences from the Sorbonne. Her novels are widely read all over the Arab world. She received the 1998 Naguib Mahfouz Prize for best novel for *Fawḍā al-Hawāss (Confusion of the Senses)*. Her other books include *Al-Kitāba fī Laḥzati 'Uryin (Writing in a Moment of Nakedness)*, 1976; *Al-Mar'a fī al-Adab al-Jazā'irī al-Mu'āṣir (Women in Contemporary Algerian Literature)*, 1981; and *Dhākirat al-Jasad (Memory in the Flesh)*, 1993.

al-Nālūtī, 'Arūsiyya: Born in Jabra, Tunisia, in 1950, 'Arūsiyya al-Nālūtī received her elementary and secondary education in Tunis, and then continued her studies at the Faculty of Letters at the University of Tunisia, attaining an MA in Arabic in 1975.

She is the author of *Marātīj (Shackles)*, 1985; *Tamāss (Contact)*, 1995; and a critical study, *Tamaththulāt al-Jadd min Khilāl al-Riwāya al-Tūnisiyya (Representations of the Grandfather Throughout Tunisian Novels)*, 1993.

Na'na', Ḥamīda: Born in the city of Idlib, Syria, in 1946, Ḥamīda Na'na' is a novelist and poet. She has a BA in Arabic literature from Damascus University. She worked as a journalist and translator and then earned a PhD in literature. She now lives and works in Paris.

Her published works include *Anāshīd Imra'a lā Ta'rif al-Faraḥ (Songs of a Woman Who Doesn't Know What Joyfulness Is)*, 1970 (poetry); *Man Yajru' 'alā al-Shawq? (Who Dares to Yearn?)*, 1989; and *Al-Waṭan fī al-'Aynayn (The Homeland Is in the Eyes)*, 1989, published in English as *The Homeland* in 1995.

Naṣrallah, Emily: Born July 6, 1931, in Kfeir village in southern Lebanon, Naṣrallah started her formal education in the public elementary school in Kfeir. She completed her secondary education at Shoueifat National College, near Beirut, and went on to university at Beirut University College (now Lebanese American University) and the American University of Beirut, where she received a BA in education in 1958.

A novelist and journalist, she worked as an editor at *Ṣawt al-Mar'a (Woman's Voice)* magazine and then joined the editorial board of *Al-Ṣayyād (The Hunter)* magazine in 1955.

Her novel *Ṭuyūr Aylūl (Birds of September)* won the Book Friends Award in 1962, the Sa'īd 'Aql award, the Fayrūz magazine award, and the Jubrān Khalīl Jubrān Award given by al-Turāth al-'Arabī (the Arab Heritage Association) in Australia. She has also published *Shajarat al-Diflā (The Oleander Tree)*, 1968, 4th ed., 1981; *Al-Iqlā' 'Aks al-Zamān (Flight Against Time)*, 1981; *Nisā' Rā'idāt (Women Pioneers)*, 1986; *Al-Rāhīna (The Pawn)*, 1986.

Nuwaylātī, Hiyām (1932–1977): A poet, novelist, woman of letters, and researcher, Hiyām Nuwaylātī was born and died in Damascus.

She earned her BA in philosophy from Damascus University and was well known as a journalist. She is the author of *Al-Ghazālī: Ḥayātuh-'Aqīdatuh (Al-Ghazālī: His Life–His Faith)*, 1958; and *Fī al-Layl (At Night)*, 1959.

al-Saʻdāwī, Nawāl: Born in Kifr Tahla, Egypt, in 1931, Saʻdāwī is a novelist, psychiatrist, and writer who is well known both in Arab countries and in many other parts of the world. She earned a medical degree in 1955 and then studied public health at Columbia University in New York, where she got an MA in 1966. As a practicing physician, she expressed great interest in women's lives and became a leading feminist.

She is a prolific writer with more than forty books to her name, including *Al-Unthā Hiya al-Aṣl (The Female Is the Origin)*, 1974; *Al-Rajul wa al-Jins (The Male and Sex)*, 1977; *Mawt al-Rajul al-Waḥīd ʻalā al-Arḍ (The Death of the Only Man on Earth)*, 1985; and *Imraʼatān fī Imraʼa (Two Women in One)*, 1986.

Saʻīd, Hādiya: Born in Beirut in 1969, Saʻīd got an MA in arts from Arab University and worked as a journalist in Lebanon, Iraq, and Morocco. Her novel *Bustān al-Wudd (Black Orchard)* won the prize of Writer Magazine in 1996.

Two other books by Saʻīd, *Raḥīl al Ribāṭ (The Departure of the Band)* and *Nisāʼ Khārij al-Qafaṣ (Women Outside the Cage)*, were both published in 1989.

Sakākīnī, Widād (1913–1991): Born in Sayda, Lebanon, Widād Sakākīnī was a well-known novelist, short-story writer, and scholar. She graduated from the Islamic College in Beirut, worked as a teacher, and dedicated most of her time to writing. Sakākīnī died in Damascus.

She is the author of two biographies, *Mayy Ziyāda: Ḥayātuhā wa Aʻmāluhā (Mayy Ziyāda: Her Life and Work)*, 1969; and *Al-ʻĀshiqa al-Mutaṣawwifa: Ḥayāt wa Afkār Rābiʼa al-ʻAdawiyya*, 1955, published in English as *First Among Ṣūfīs: The Life and Thought of Rābiʼa al-ʻAdawiyya, the Woman Saint of Basra*.

Sakākīnī also published *Inṣāf al-Marʼa (Doing Women Justice)*, 1950, reissued in 1989; and the novel *Arwā bint al-Khuṭūb (Arwā, the Daughter of Upheavals)*, 1949, which is widely considered to be the first novel by a woman in Arabic, although this book disputes that claim.

Salāma, Hind: She is the author of *Al Nisāʼ wa al-Khamriyyāt in the Torah (Women and the Russet in the Torah)*, 1950; *Al-Ḥijāb al-Mahtūk (The Profaned Veil)*; *Al-Dumā al-Ḥayya (The Living Toys)*, 1968; *Zallat al-Jasad (Sins of the Body)*; *Samrāʼ al-Shāṭiʼ (The Brunette on the Beach)*, 1973.

al-Sammān, Ghāda: Born in Damascus in 1942, Ghāda al-Sammān studied English at Damascus University and taught English there before moving to Beirut, where she settled and flourished as a journalist and novelist. During the Lebanese civil war she moved to Paris, where she still lives. She is a prolific writer, publishing stories, essays, columns, and novels such as *'Aynāka Qadarī (Your Eyes Are My Destiny)*, 1962; *Beirut 75*, 1975; and *Laylat al-Milyār (The Night of the Billion)*, 1989.

al-Shaykh, Ḥanān: Born in Beirut in 1945, Ḥanān al-Shaykh studied in Cairo and then went to the American College for Women for a couple of years. She spent some time in the Persian Gulf, where her husband works. During the Lebanese civil war, she left for London, where she still lives.

She is the author of *Ḥikāyat Zahra,* 1980, published in English as *The Story of Zahra,* 1986; *Misk al-Gazāl,* 1992, published in English as *Women of Sand and Myrrh;* and *Barīd Beirut,* 1995, published in English as *Beirut Blues.*

'Umar, Zahra: She is the author of *al-Khurūj min Sosrowaka (The Exodus from Sosrowaka: The Epic of the Circassian Diaspora)*, 1995.

'Usayrān, Laylā (1934–2007): Writer, novelist, journalist, and combatant, Laylā 'Usayrān was born in Tyre in southern Lebanon in 1934. She did her preparatory and secondary schooling in Cairo and then graduated from the American University in Beirut in 1954 with a BA in political science.

'Usayrān worked as a journalist at *Dār al-Ṣayyād* and *Al-Siyāsa* newspapers in Lebanon. She was awarded the National Cedar Legion in Lebanon with the rank of Knight in 1996.

Her books include *Jisr al-Ḥajar (The Stone Bridge)*, 1982; *'Aṣāfīr al-Fajr (The Birds of Dawn)*, 1991; and *Ḥiwār bilā Kalimāt fī al-Ghaybūba (A Dialogue Without Words in a Coma)*, 1998.

al-Yāfī, Laylā: Al-Yāfī was born in Damascus. Her 1962 novel *Snows Under the Sun* won an award from the Ministry of Culture in Egypt for being the best first novel published by a new author of that year. She also wrote *Hamasāt Qalbī (Whispers of My Heart)* (prose poems); and *Al-Wāḥa (The Oasis)* (prose), 1982.

al-Zayyāt, Laṭīfa (1923–1996): Born in Cairo, al-Zayyāt received a PhD in English literature from the University of Cairo, later becoming the head of the English Department at the same university. She had a distinguished academic career, occupying many important positions, and was deeply involved in the political life of the country. She received the highest national award for literary achievement in 1996 for her work in politics, education, and academic life.

Her published works include *Al-Bāb al-Maftūḥ (The Open Door)*, 1960, reprinted in 2003; *Al-Rajul al-Ladhī lam Ya'rif Tuhmatahu (The Man Who Did Not Know of What He Was Accused)*, 1995; and *Min Ṣuwar al-Mar'a fī al-Riwāya wa al-Qiṣaṣ al-'Arabiyya (Images of Women in Arabic Novels and Short Stories)*, 1989.

Notes

1. Nina Bayn, "Melodramas of Beset Manhood," in *New Feminist Criticism*, ed. Elaine Showalter, p. 82.

2. Bayn, *Woman's Fiction*, p. 178.

3. "An Interview with al-Zayyāt," *New Shahrazād* 22 (Cyprus) (June 1990), p. 54.

4. Ibid.

5. Ibid.

6. Ibid.

7. Spender, *Man Made Language*, p. 53.

8. Ibid.

9. Woolf, "Women and Fiction," in *Granite and Rainbow: Essays by Virginia Woolf*, ed. Leonard Woolf, p. 76.

10. For example, Simone de Beauvoir in *The Second Sex* and Spender in *Man Made Language* note the neglect and marginalization of literature written by women.

11. See, for example, 'Alī Jawād al-Ṭāhir, *Muqaddima fī al-Naqd al-Adabī (Introduction to Literary Criticism)*; and al-'Ānī and Nājī, *Ash'ār al-Nisā' (The Poetry of Women)*; see Introduction to *The Poetry of Women* for quote.

12. His full name is Jamal al-Deen Abu al-Hassan Ali Bin al-Qadi al-Ashraf Youssef al-Qifti.

13. Ibn al-Nadīm and Yāqūt testify to having seen *Al-Shā'irāt al-Nisā' (Women Poets)*. *Nuzhat al-Julasā' fī Ash'ār al-Nisā' (A Journey of Companionship in Women's Poetry)* was one of the sources used and quoted by 'Abd al-Qādir bin 'Umar al-Baghdādī in his work *Khizanat al-Adab*. 'Abd al-Qādir died in 1682, which logically suggests that the book might still have been found in Egypt up to the seventeenth century.

14. See also al-Jawziyya, *Akhbār al-Nisā' (Women's News)*; Ṭayfūr, *Balāghāt al-Nisā' (Women's Eloquence)*; Muḥammad bin Dāwūd al-Aṣfahānī, *Al-Zarqā'*; al-Mawṣilī, ed., *Al-Rawḍa al-Fayḥā' fī Tawārīkh al-Nisā' (The Fragrant Garden in Women's History)*.

15. al-Jawziyya, *Akhbār al-Nisā' (Women's News)*, p. 60.

16. *Maqāma* (plural *maqāmāt*) is a compositional device based on a scale with a particular interval pattern and includes a set of "performance rules" indicating which notes should be emphasized and key melodic patterns. Performing *maqāmāt* through an instrumental *taqsīm*, a semi-improvised form in which the performer may modulate to several related *maqāmāt* before returning to the original *maqāma*, is a highly skilled art that relies on an intimate knowledge of the structure of the different *maqāmāt* and the relationships between them, something that can be learned only after many years of study and experience.

17. Jarīr's full name is Jarīr bin Atyah bin Huzefa al-Khatfi bin Baker al-Kalbi al-Yarbui bin al-Tamimi.

18. al-Ma'badī, ed., *Ādāb al-Nisā' fī al-Jāhiliyya wa al-Islām* (*Women's Literature in the Pre-Islamic and Islamic Periods*), pp. 13–14.

19. The French historian Gustav Lupon believes that Arabs in Andalusia may well have introduced the idea of women's literary salons to twelfth-century France. See also Emily Naṣrallah, *Nisā' Rā'idāt* (*Women Pioneers*), p. 111.

20. See note 12 above for Jarīr's full name; the second and third are as follows: Humam bin Ghalib al-Farazdaq; Kuthayyir bin Abdol Rahman bin Aswad bin Amir al-Khuzai'.

21. Khurāsānī, *Al-Mar'a wa al-Islām* (*Woman and Islam*), p. 175.

22. Naṣrallah, *Nisā' Rā'idāt* (*Women Pioneers*), p. 108.

23. Woolf, "Women and Fiction," p. 77.

24. Woolf, *A Room of One's Own*, pp. 30–32.

25. George Ṭarābīshī, "The Female of Nawāl al-Sa'dāwī and the Myth of Singularity," *Arab Studies* 12, no. 2 (1975), pp. 47–71.

26. Spender, *Man Made Language*, p. 87.

27. Spender, *Man Made Language*, p. 198.

28. Zaynab Fawwāz, *Ḥusn al-'Awāqib: Ghāda al-Zahra* (*Good Consequences: Ghāda the Radiant*), privately printed in Cairo, 1899; *Al-Malik Qūrūsh* (*King Qūrūsh*), privately printed in Cairo, 1905. The two novels in manuscript form are *Madārik al-Kamāl fī Tarājim al-Rijāl* (*Attempts at Perfection in Men's Writings*) (no date), and *Al-Durr al-Naḍīd fī Ma'āthir al-Malik al-Ḥamīd* (*Precious Jewels in the Works of a Decent King*) (no date). For a sample of Zaynab Fawwāz's writing, see Badran and cooke, eds., *Opening the Gates*, pp. 220–224.

29. Ibid., pp. 224.

30. See Fawwāz, *Al-Rasā'il al-Zaynabiyya* (*Zaynab's Letters*), pp. 31–32.

31. See, for example, *Anīs al-Jalīs*, edited and published by Alexandra Afernūh (Egypt, 1898); *Shajarat al-Durr*, edited and published by Sa'diyya 'Abd al-Din (Alexandria, 1901); *Al-Mar'a*, edited and published by Anīsa 'Aṭallah (Egypt, 1901); *Al-Sa'āda*, edited and published by Rūjīnā 'Awwād (Egypt, 1902); *Al-'Arūs*, edited and published by Mary 'Ajamī (Damascus, 1905); *Al-Khaḍir*, edited and published by 'Afīfa Ṣa'b (Lebanon, 1912); *Fatāt Lubnān*, edited and published by Salīma Abū Rashīd (Lebanon, 1914); and *Fatāt al-Nil*, edited and published by Sāra al-Mihāya (Cairo, 1913).

32. Hind Nawfal, *Al-Fatāt* 1, no. 1, November 20, 1892, p. 4.

33. Nawfal, *Al-Fatāt*, p. 4.

34. Showalter, *A Literature of Their Own*, p, 36.

Chapter Two: The Beginnings

1. See, for example, the thesis submitted by the Moroccan woman poet Malīka al-'Āṣimī, "The Popular Story in Morocco," 1987.

2. *Maqāma* is a story written in classical poetry, popular at the time when the Arabs used poetry to converse with each other; *ḥikāya* is a written story-telling form, more complex than a short story but not as comprehensive as a novel; *sīra* (which in Arabic can be either autobiography or biography) is an old Arabic literary genre and a common specialization among writers. These forms predate the appearance of the novel in Arabic literature. Unlike novel writing, which seems to have been adapted from the West, these three genres are intrinsic to Arabic literature in the early stages of its development.

3. Qāsim Amīn was an Egyptian writer who in the late nineteenth century published his call for women's liberation under the title *Tahriral Mar'a* (*Emancipating Women*), which appeared in a book published in Egypt in 1899. This book became the Bible of Arab women feminists.

4. Muḥyi al-Dīn Ṣubḥī, "A Conference on Arab Women's Creativity: The Masculinity of Political Objections—a Point of View," *Al-Safīr* newspaper, Beirut, September 26, 1992, p. 13.

5. The seven novels are *Ghādat 'Amshīt, Fāṭima al-Badawiyya, Malikat al-Yawm, Ibnat Nā'ib al-Malik, Nancy Styar, Muḥammad 'Alī al-Kabīr,* and *Cleopatra;* they are listed in *Nisā' min Bilādī,* by Nādiya al-Jurdī Nuwayhiḍ (al-Mu'assasa al-'Arabiyya li al-Dirāsāt wa al-Nashr, Beirut, 1986), p. 217. Besides *Badī'a wa Fu'ād,* I was able to locate only *Ghādat 'Amshīt.* I found both novels in the Library of Congress.

6. Servants who are close to sexual slaves.

7. 'Aṭiyya, *Bayn 'Arshayn (Between Two Thrones),* pp. 61–62.

8. Private conversation between the author and Muḥammad Dakrūb.

9. Published by Dār al-Saqi, London, no. 69, 1992.

10. *Al-Sharq al-Awsaṭ* newspaper, February 17, 1993.

Chapter Three: The Quest for Parity

1. Millett, *Sexual Politics,* p. 225.

2. Ibid., p. 232.

3. For an account of women's position in the Soviet Union from the 1930s to the 1960s, see ibid., pp. 222–249.

4. Laṭīfa al-Zayyāt, *Min Ṣuwar al-Mar'a fī al-Riwāya wa al-Qiṣaṣ al-'Arabiyya (Images of Women in Arabic Novels and Short Stories),* p. 77.

5. Millett, *Sexual Politics,* p. 222.

6. al-Khaṭīb, "Ḥawl al-Riwāya al-Nisā'iyya fī Sūriyya" (About Women's Novels in Syria), *Al-Ma'rifa* (1975), p. 86.

7. Ibid., pp. 130–131.

8. Ibid., p. 87.

9. Ibid., p. 132.

10. "Al-Adība Widād Sakākīnī Rā'idat al-Qiṣṣa al-Qaṣīra fī Sūriyya" (Widād Sakākīnī: The Pioneer of Short Story Writing in Syria), *Tishrīn* newspaper, Damascus, July 2, 1990.

11. Widād Sakākīnī, *Nuqāṭ 'alā al-Ḥurūf (Dots on Letters)*, in *Naqd wa Ta'līq (Criticism and Comment)*, a series of books on literary criticism (Dār al-Fikr al-'Arabī, Cairo, 1965), p. 57.

12. *La'nat al-Jasad (The Curse of the Body)* is the title of a novel by the Egyptian writer Ṣūfī 'Abd Allah (Beirut, al-Maktaba al-Tijāriyya, 1958).

13. The cover of *Fī al-Layl (At Night)* advertises a forthcoming work by Hiyām Nuwaylātī, *Ayyāmī (My Days)*, prose extracts, with an introduction by Ṭāha Ḥusayn. The fact that Ṭāha Ḥusayn introduced Nawaylātī's work indicates the literary status Nawaylātī enjoyed at the time.

14. When Arab women say or write something that they feel is controversial, or something they feel might incite an unpredictable reaction, they try to be less, rather than better, understood. Hence Nuwaylātī's resort to writing poetry.

15. My belief is that this novel was written in the 1950s. Either there was a long span between the date of writing it and the date of its publication, or the state of Palestinian society in the 1950s froze in the author's mind, only to be depicted two decades later. Her other novel, *Widā' ma' al-Aṣīl (Farewell at Sunset)* (1970), which is about the partition of Palestine in 1948, supports the latter view.

16. Al-Khaṭīb, "Ḥawl al-Riwāya al-Nisā'iyya fī Sūriyya" (About Women's Novels in Syria), part 3, pp. 77–88 and p. 83. See also George Ṭarābīshī, "Al-Ḥirmān fī al-Riwāya al-Nisā'iyya al-'Arabiyya" (Deprivation in Arab Women's Novels), *Al-Ādāb* (March 1963).

17. "Nūr" in Arabic means light. It is also used metaphorically to signify the dawning of a new day.

18. Private communication between the author and Evelyne Accad.

Chapter Four: The Emergence of the New Woman

1. In the Arab world during the late 1950s, national liberation movements gained prominence; it was a time of posing the most daring questions at all levels, particularly social and political questions.

2. The quotes come from an article in *Al-Ba'th* newspaper, Damascus, August 5, 1988; the author's name is not available.

3. Colette Khūrī's other four novels are *Layla Wāḥida (One Night)*; *Kiyān (Entity)*; *Wa Marra Ṣayf (A Summer Has Gone)*; and *Ayyām ma' al-Ayyām (Days with Days)*.

4. Hudā Sha'rāwī (1879–1947), who advocated equal opportunities for women, was a pioneer of the Egyptian feminist movement and participated in the national resistance against the British occupation of Egypt. She was elected vice president of the International Women's Association and formed and was president of the Pan-Arab Women's Union, founded in 1928.

5. Quoted in Laṭīfa al-Zayyāt, *Al-Bāb al-Maftūḥ (The Open Door)*, p. 364.

Chapter Five: Women and Nation

1. The first edition was published in 1960; the edition quoted from is 1970.

2. Farrāj, *Al-Ḥurriyya fī Adab al-Mar'a (Freedom in Woman's Literature)*, pp. 39–40.

3. In Arabic literature, the feminine is always weaker than the masculine, and if the two appear in different forms and a common form has to be found, the feminine always follows the masculine. Unlike English, the verb in Arabic is either masculine or feminine. If there are both masculine and feminine subjects, the verb would be masculine.

Chapter Six: Women's War Novels

1. See, for example, miriam cooke, *War's Other Voices*.

Chapter Eight: Masters of the Art

1. *A'ẓamiyyat* Baghdad is a place in Baghdad known for its folk stories. It is an important historical and religious place, recently highlighted for the many people killed in it every day.

2. Mamdūḥ, p. 146. The last sentence in this quotation is translated as "yet fortunate as well," although the Arabic means "unfortunate."

3. Mamdūḥ, p. 195. For some reason, this paragraph did not appear in the English translation, although I believe it to be a very important passage.

4. Constantine is a beautiful town, and one of the best-known historical sites in Algeria. It is also well known for its fierce battles against French occupation.

5. Bilād al-Shām comprised the countries that today are known as Syria, Palestine, Lebanon, and Jordan. In 1922, after World War I and under the terms of the Sykes-Picot pact, the borders of the current countries were drawn by Britain and France, which had reneged on their promises to the Arabs who had fought with them against the Ottoman Empire. Instead of granting the Arabs their independence, they reoccupied their land and tore their political identity (Bilād al-Shām) apart by creating the much smaller countries that exist today.

6. There is a saying in Arabic that someone has many skins. Here, however, all the skins are short and ugly because the people who wear them are weak and are unable to behave like real people who do important work or who deserve respect.

Chapter Nine: Recent Arab Women's Novels

1. Khalīfa, p. 24. This is an indirect reference to the so-called crime of honor, or the killing of women who are deemed by society to have been "rude." Here Khalīfa questions the criteria according to which women are judged.

2. Those who believe in the afterlife and in the value of martyrdom do not talk about a martyr being buried. Rather, they say that a martyr was groomed to his grave, to show that his death was a noble one.

3. Ishaq Rabin, the late Israeli prime minister, was known as the "bone breaker." After being arrested, Palestinians would have the bones in their hands broken, so that they could never throw stones at the occupying forces again. This brutality was shown on satellite TV channels.

4. That is not true, however, because so many Arab towns go back thousands of years. Damascus, for example, is known as the oldest inhabited city in the world.

5. "To weave" in Arabic also means to create beautifully.

6. Muḥammad Bū Diyāf is an Algerian political exile, and former fighter for the liberation of Algeria; Mustighānimī, p. 239.

7. Interview with Fayrūz al-Tamīmī in *Al-Dustūr* newspaper, March 18, 1999, p. 33.

Bibliography

'Abd Allah, Ibtisām. *Maṭar Aswad, Maṭar Aḥmar (Black Rain, Red Rain)*. Dār al-Mamoun, Baghdad, 1993.

'Abd Allah, Ṣūfī. *La'nat al-Jasad (The Curse of the Body)*. Al-Maktaba al-Tijāriyya, Beirut, 1958.

'Abd al-Dīn, Sa'diyya. *Shajarat al-Durr*. Alexandria, 1901.

Abouzeid, Leila. *'Ām al-Fīl. (The Year of the Elephant)*. Maṭ ba'at al-Ma'ārif al-Jadīda, Rabāṭ, 1983.

Abū Rashīd, Salīma. *Fatāt Lubnān (The Girl from Lebanon)*. Publisher and city unknown, Lebanon, 1914.

Accad, Evelyne. *L'excisée (The Excised)*. Three Continents Press, Washington, D.C., 1989.

———. *Veil of Shame: The Role of Women in the Contemporary Fiction of North Africa and the Arab World*. Naaman, Sherbrooke, Quebec, 1978.

Afernūh, Alexandra. *Anīs al-Jalīs (Kind Companion)*. Alexandria, 1898.

'Ajamī, Mary. A number of articles in *al-'Arūs* journal. Damascus, 1905.

Allen, Roger. *Al-Riwāya al-'Arabiyya: Muqaddima Tārikhiyya wa Naqdiyya (The Arabic Novel: A Historical and Critical Introduction)*. Al-Mu'assasa al-'Arabiyya li al-Dirāsāt wa al Nashr, Beirut, 1986.

al-'Ānī, Sāmī, and Hilāl Nājī, eds. *Ash'ār al-Nisā' (The Poetry of Women)*. Collected by Abī 'Ubayd Allāh Muḥammad bin 'Umrān al-Marzubānī. Dār al-Risāla, Baghdad, 1976.

al-Aṣfahānī, Abī al-Faraj, ed. *Al-Imā' al-Shawā'ir (Slave Women Poets)*. No information is available as to whether this book has been published.

al-Aṣfahānī, Muḥammad bin Dāwūd. *Al-Zarqā'*. Maktabat al-Manāra, 1985.

'Āshūr, Raḍwā. *Gharnāṭa (Granada)*. Dār al-Hilāl, Cairo, series vol. 544, 1994.

———. *Ḥajar Dāfī' (A Warm Stone)*. Dār al-Mustaqbal al-'Arabī, Cairo, 1985.

———. *Khadīja wa Tūnis (Khadīja and Tunis)*. Dār al-Hilāl Cairo, 1989.

———. *Maryama wa al-Raḥīl (Maryama and the Departure)*. Dār al-Hilāl, Cairo, series vol. 561, 1994.

———, ed. *Arab Women's Writings: A Critical Reference Guide, 1873–1999*. American University in Cairo Press, 2008.

'Aṭallah, Anīsa. *Al-Mara' (Entertainment)*. Publisher unknown, Cairo, 1901.

198   *Bibliography*

'Aṭiyya, Farīda. *Bahjat al-Mukhaddirāt fī Fawā'id 'Ilm al-Nabāt (The Joy of Drugs on the Benefits of Botany)*. Beirut, 1893.

———. *Bayn 'Arshayn (Between Two Thrones)*. Maktabat al-Najāḥ, Ṭarābuls al-Shām, Lebanon, 1912.

———. *Al-Rawḍa al-Naḍīra fī Ayyām Bombay al-Akhīra (The Green Garden in Bombay's Final Days)*. Translated from English into Arabic. Al-Hilāl Press, Cairo, 1899.

al-Aṭrash, Laylā. *Imra'a li al-Fuṣūl al-Khamsa (A Woman for Five Seasons)*. Al-Mu'assasa al-'Arabiyya li al-Dirāsāt wa al-Nashr (Arab Publishing Association), Beirut, 1988.

———. *Wa Tushriqu Gharban (Dawning from the West)*. Al-Mu'assasa al-'Arabiyya li al-Dirāsāt wa al-Nashr (Arab Publishing Association), Beirut, 1988.

———. *Yawm 'Ādī wa Qiṣaṣ Ukhrā (An Ordinary Day and Other Stories)*. Al-Mu'assasa al-'Arabiyya li al-Dirāsāt wa al-Nashr (Arab Publishing Association), Beirut, 1992.

al-'Aṭṭār, Mājida. *Fī al-Bad' Kāna al-Ḥubb (In the Beginning Was Love)*. Dār al-Rawā'i', Beirut, 1978.

———. *Murāhiqa (The Adolescent)*. Dār al-Rawā'i', Beirut, 1969.

'Awwād, Rūjīnā. *Al-Sa'āda*. Publisher unknown, Cairo, 1902.

Ba'albakī, Laylā. *Al-Āliha al-Mamsūkha (The Dwarf Gods)*. Al-Maktab al-Tijārī, Beirut, 1960.

———. *Anā Aḥyā (I Live)*. Al-Maktab al-Tijārī, Beirut, 1958.

———. *Safīnat Ḥanān ilā al-Qamar (A Spaceship of Tenderness to the Moon)*. Al-Maktab al-Tijārī, Beirut, 1964.

Badr, Liyāna. *'Ayn al-Mir'āt*. First published 1991; published as *The Eye of the Mirror* by Garnet Publishing, Reading, UK, 1995.

———. *Būṣila min Ajl 'Abbād al-Shams*. Dār Ibn Rushd, Beirut, 1979; published as *A Compass for the Sunflower* by the Woman's Press, London, 1989.

Badran, Margot, and miriam cooke, eds. *Opening the Gates: A Century of Arab Feminist Writing*. Indiana University Press, Bloomington, 1990.

al-Baghdadi, Abd al-Qadir bin Umar. *Khizanat al-Adab: (Treasure of Literature)*. Dār Sad, Beirut, 1986.

Bakr, Salwā. *Al-'Araba al-Dhahabiyya lā Taṣ'ad ilā al-Samā' (The Golden Chariot)*. Egypt, 1991, and Dār Sahar, Tunis, 2006.

———. *Al-Bashmūrī* [the name of an ethnic group in Egypt]. Riwāyāt al-Hilāl, Cairo, 1998.

Barakāt, Hudā. *Ahl al-Hawā (People of Passion)*. Dār al-Nahār, Beirut, 1994.

———. *Ḥajar al-Ḍaḥik*. First published by Riad El-Rayyes Books, London, 1990; translated by Sophie Bennett and published as *The Stone of Laughter* by Garnet Publishing, Reading, UK, 1994.

———. *Ḥārith al-Miyāh (The Tiller of Waters)*. Dār al-Nahār, Beirut, 1998.

Barakāt, Najwā. *Bāṣ al-Awādim (The Bus of Human Beings)*. Dār al-Ādāb, Beirut, 1996.

———. *Yā Salām (Oh, My God)*. Dār al-Ādāb, Beirut, 1999.

al-Bāti', Fatḥiyya Maḥmūd. *Mudhakkarāt Zā'ifa (False Memoirs)*. Al-Mu'assasa al-Waṭaniyya li al-Kitāb, Algiers, 1975.

———. *Nabta fī al-Baydā' (A Plant in the Desert)*, Algiers, 1981.

————. *Widā' ma' al-Aṣīl (Farewell at Sunset)*. Al-Sharika al-Waṭaniyya li al-Nashr wa al-Tawzī', Algiers, 1970.

Bayn, Nina. "Melodramas of Beset Manhood: How Theories of American Fiction Exclude Women Writers." In *New Feminist Criticism*, edited by Elaine Showalter. Pantheon, New York, 1985.

————. *Woman's Fiction: A Guide to Novels by and About Women in America, 1820–1870*. Cornell University Press, Ithaca, New York, 1978.

Bīṭar, Ḥayāt. *Nihāyat wa 'Ibrat Bayrūt (The End and the Lesson of Beirut)*. Beirut, 1964.

Boullata, Issa. *Critical Perspectives on Modern Arabic Literature*. Three Continents Press, Washington, D.C., 1980.

Boullata, Kamal. *Women of the Fertile Crescent: An Anthology of Modern Poetry by Arab Women*. Three Continents Press, Washington D.C., 1978.

cooke, miriam. *War's Other Voices: Women Writers on the Lebanese Civil War*. Cambridge University Press, Cambridge, 1988.

Dāghir, Katherine Ma'rūf. *Ghaṣṣa fī al-Qalb (A Sigh in the Heart)*. Dār al-Ḥayāt, Beirut, 1965.

————. *Kifāḥ Imra'a (A Woman's Struggle)*. Maktabat al-Ḥayāt, Beirut, 1965.

Dhurayl, 'Adnān bin. *Al-Riwāya al-Sūriyya: Dirāsa Nafsiyya (The Syrian Novel: A Psychological Study)*. Maṭba'at al-'Ulūm wa al-Ādāb, Damascus, 1973.

Farrāj, 'Afīf. *Al-Ḥurriyya fī Adab al-Mar'a (Freedom in Woman's Literature)*. Mu'assasat al-Abḥāth al-'Arabiyya, Beirut, 1980; and Dār Ibn Hānī, Damascus, 1986.

Fawwāz, Fawziyya. "Muqaddima" (Introduction) to *Ḥusn al-'Awāqib*. Al-Majlis al-Thaqāfī li Janūb Lubnān, Beirut, 1984.

Fawwāz, Zaynab. *Al-Durr al-Manthūr fī Ṭabaqāt Rabāt al-Khudūr (Scattered Pearls in Women's Quarters)*. Al-Maktaba al-Kubrā al-Amīriyya, Cairo, 1894.

————. *Al-Hawā wa al-Wafā' (Love and Loyalty)*. Al-Maṭba'a al-Hindiyya, Cairo, 1893; reissued by al-Majlis al-Thaqāfī li Janūb Lubnān, Beirut, 1984.

————. *Ḥusn al-'Awāqib: Ghāda al-Zahra (Good Consequences: Ghāda the Radiant)*. Al-Maṭba'a al-Hindiyya, Cairo, 1899; Al-Majlis al-Thaqāfī li Janūb Lubnān (Southern Lebanese Cultural Council), Beirut, 1984.

————. *Al-Malik Qūrūsh (King Qūrūsh)*. Privately printed in Cairo, 1905.

————. *Al-Rasā'il al-Zaynabiyya (Zaynab's Letters)*. Al-Maṭba'a al-Mutawassiṭiyya, Cairo, 1906.

al-Fayṣal, Samar Rūḥī. *Tajribat al-Riwāya al-Sūriyya (The Experience of the Syrian Novel)*. Ittiḥād al-Kuttāb al-'Arab, Damascus, 1985.

Ghurayyib, Ros. *Mayy Ziyāda, Her Prime and Decline: Her Life, Literature, and Art*. Nawfal Publications, Beirut, 1978.

Gilbert, Sandra M., and Susan Gubar. *The Madwoman in the Attic*. Yale University Press, New Haven, Conn., 1979.

Hādī, Maysalūn. *Al-'Ālam Nāqiṣān Wāḥid (The World Minus One)*. Mudīriyyat al-Shu'ūn al-Thaqāfiyya, Baghdad, 1996.

————. *Ashyā' Lam Taḥduth (Things That Have Not Happened)*. Cairo, 1992 (short stories).

————. *Al-Ṭā'ir al-Sīḥrī wa al-Nuqāt al-Thalāth (The Magic Bird and the Three Points)*. Amman, 1995 (short stories).

al-Ḥakīm, Tawfīq. *Al-Ribāṭ al-Muqaddas (The Holy Bond)*. Maktabat al-Ādāb, Cairo, n.d.

————. *'Uṣfūr min al-Sharq (A Bird from the East)*. Maṭba'a Lajnat al-Ta'lif wal Tarjama wal Nashre, Cairo, 1938.

al-Ḥasan, bin Muḥammad bin Ja'far bin Tāra, ed. *Al-Shā'irāt al-Nisā' (Women Poets)*. Collected by Ibn 'Abd Allah Muḥammad bin 'Umrān al-Marzubānī. Original publisher, place, and date unknown. New edition edited by Sāmī al-'Ānī and Hilāl Nājī, Dār al-Risāla, Baghdad, 1976.

Hāshim, Labība Nāṣif. *Mubaḥathāt fī al-Akhlāq (Discussions on Ethics)*.

————. *Qalb al-Rajul (Man's Heart)*. Cairo, 1974, and Dāl Al-Mada, Damascus, 2002.

————. *Al-Tarbiya (Education)*. Dār al-Ma'ārif, Cairo, 1911.

Haykal, Muḥammad Ḥusayn. *Zaynab*. Dār al-Ma'ārif, Cairo, 1914.

Haywood, John A. *Modern Arabic Literature, 1800–1970*. Lund Humphries, London, 1970.

al-Ḥūmānī, Balqīs. *Al-Asirra al-Bayḍa' (The White Beds)*.

————. *Ḥay al-Lājī' (Al-Laji District)*. Manshūrāt Hamad, Beirut, 1969.

————. *Al-Laḥn al-Khayyir (The Good Tune)*. Cairo, 1961 (short stories).

————. *Sa Amurru 'alā al-Aḥzān (I Shall Pass by Sorrows)*. Maktabat al-Ma'ārif, Beirut, 1975.

Ibn Qayyim al-Jawziyya. *Akhbār al-Nisā' (Women's News)*. Maktabat al-Taqaddum al-'Ilmiyya, Cairo, 1901.

Idlibī, Ulfat. *Dimashq yā Basmat al-Ḥuzn* (literally, *Damascus: The Smile of Sorrow*). Wizārat al-Thaqāfa, Damascus, 1980; and Dār Ṭalās, Damascus, 1989. Translated into English by Peter Clarke as *Sabriya: Damascus Bittersweet*. Interlink Books, New York, 1997.

————. *Ḥikāyat Jaddī (My Grandfather's Story)* (a young adult novel). Dār Talas, Damascus, 1998.

Idrīs, Yūsuf. *Al-'Ayb (Shame)*. Serialized in *Rose al-Yūsuf,* no. 102, edited by al-Kitāb al-Dhahabī; first published at the Reading for All Festival in 1995.

Jabbūr, Munā. *Fatāt Tāfiha (A Silly Girl)*. Maktabat Dār al-Ḥayāt, Beirut, 1962.

————. *Al-Gurban wa al-Musūḥ al-Bayḍā' (The Ravens and the White Sackcloth)*. Maktabat al-Ḥayāt, Beirut, 1966.

al-Jabbūrī, Irāda. *'Iṭr al-Tuffāḥ (The Perfume of Apples)*.

Jelloun, Tahar Ben. *Ibnat al-Rimāl (The Sand Child)*. Translated by Alan Sheridan. Harcourt Brace Jovanovich, New York, 1987.

Karam, 'Afīfa. *Badī'a wa Fu'ād (Badī'a and Fu'ād)*. Al-Hudā Press, New York, 1906.

————. *Cleopatra*. Publisher, place, and date unknown.

————. *Fāṭima al-Badawiyya (Fatima, the Bedwin Women)*. Al-Huda Press, New York, 1906.

————. *Ghādat 'Amshīt (The Pretty Woman of 'Amshīt)*. Al-Huda Press, New York, 1914.

————. *Ibnat Nā'ib al-Malik (The Daughter of the Viceroy)*. Publisher, place, and date unknown.

————. *Malikat al-Yawm (Queen of Today)*. Publisher, place, and date unknown.

————. *Muḥammad 'Alī al-Kabīr*. Publisher, place, and date unknown.

————. *Nancy Styar*. Publisher, place, and date unknown.

Kaylānī, Qamar. *Al-Dawwāma (The Whirl)*. Wizārat al-Thaqāfa, Damascus, 1983.

Khalīfa, Saḥar. *'Abbād al-Shams (The Sunflower)*. Dār al-Jalīl, Amman, 1984.

———. *Bāb al-Sāḥa (The Door of the Square)*. Dār al-Ādāb, Beirut, 1990.

———. *Lam Na'ud Jawāriya Lakum (We Are No Longer Your Maids)*. Iqra' Series, Dār al Ma'ārif, Cairo, 1974.

———. *Al-Mīrāth (The Inheritance)*. Dār al-Ādāb, Beirut, 1997.

———. *Mudhakkarāt Imra'a Ghayr Wāqi'iyya (Memoirs of an Unrealistic Woman)*. Dār al-Ādāb, Beirut, 1986.

———. *Al-Ṣabbār (Wild Thorns)*. Dār al-Jalīl, Amman, 1984.

al-Khaṭīb, Ḥusām. "Ḥawl al-Riwāya al-Nisā'iyya fī Sūriyya" (About Women's Novels in Syria), part 1. *Al-Ma'rifa* (Damascus), no. 166 (December 1975), pp. 79–94.

———. "Ḥawl al-Riwāya al-Nisā'iyya fī Sūriyya" (About Women's Novels in Syria), part 2. *Al-Ma'rifa* (Damascus), no. 168 (February 1976), pp. 47–59.

———. "Ḥawl al-Riwāya al-Nisā'iyya fī Sūriyya" (About Women's Novels in Syria), part 3. *Al-Ma'rifa* (Damascus), no. 169 (March 1976), pp. 77–88.

Khurāsānī, Ghāda. *Al-Mar'a a wa al-Islām (Woman and Islam)*. Publisher unknown, Beirut, date unknown.

Khūrī, Colette. *Ayyām Ma'a al-Ayyām (Days with Days)*. Al-Kitāb al-'Arabī, Damascus, 1980.

———. *Ayyām Ma'ahu (Days with Him)*. 1st ed., Dār al-Kutub, Beirut, 1959; 5th ed., Dār al-Anwār, Damascus, 1980.

———. *Kiyān (Entity)*. Dār al-Wathba, Damascus, 1968.

———. *Layla Wāḥida (One Night)*. Zuhayr Ba'albakī, Beirut, 1960.

———. *Wa Marra Ṣayf (A Summer Has Gone)*. Dār Ṭalās, Damascus, 1975.

Khūst, Nādiya. *A'āṣīr fī Bilād al-Shām (Hurricanes in Greater Syria)*. Arab Writers Union, Damascus, 1998.

———. *Ḥubb fī Bilād al-Shām (Love in Greater Syria)*. Arab Writers Union, Damascus, 1995.

Kīlanī, Qamar. *'Ālam bilā Ḥudūd (A World Without Borders)*. Ministry of Information, Department of Culture, Baghdad, 1972.

———. *Awrāq Musāfira (Woman Traveler's Papers)*. Dar al-Jalīl, Damascus, 1987.

———. *Al-Dawwāma (The Whirlpool)*. Ministry of Culture, Damascus, 1983.

al-Kuzbarī, Salmā al-Ḥaffār, ed. *Al-A'māl al-Kāmila li Mayy Ziyāda (The Complete Works of Mayy Ziyāda)*. Mu'assasat Nawfal, Beirut, 1982.

al-Ma'badī, Muḥammad bin Badr, ed. *Ādāb al-Nisā' fī al-Jāhiliyya wa al-Islām (Women's Literature in the Pre-Islamic and Islamic Periods)*. Maktabat al-Adab, Cairo, 1983.

Maḥfouẓ, Naguib. *Bidāya wa Nihāya (The Beginning and the End)*. Maktabat Miṣr, Cairo, 1956.

Maḥmūd, Fāṭima Mūsā. *Al-Riwāya al-'Arabiyya fī Miṣr, 1914–1970 (The Arabic Novel in Egypt, 1914–1970)*. Al-Hay'a al-Miṣriyya al-'Āmma li al-Kitāb, Cairo, 1975.

Mamdūḥ, 'Āliya. *Ḥabbat al-Naftālīn (Mothballs)*. Al-Hay' a al-Miṣriyya al-'Āmma li al-Kitāb, Cairo, 1986; translated by Peter Theroux as *Naphthalene* and published by Garnet Publishing, Reading, UK, 1996.

———. *Laylā wa al-Dhi'b (Layla and the Wolf)*. Iraq, 1981.

———. *Al-Walā' (Fondness)*. Dār al-Ādāb Beirut, 1995.

al-Māni', Samīra. *Ḥabl al-Surra (The Umbilical Cord)*. Al-Ightirāb al-Adabī, London, 1990.

Marrāsh, Francis. *Ghāyat al-Ḥaq (The Objective of Justice)*. Privately printed, Syria, 1865.

al-Mawṣilī, Yāsīn al-Khaṭīb al-'Amrī, ed. *Al-Rawḍa al-Fayḥā' fī Tawārīkh al-Nisā' (The Fragrant Garden in Women's History)*. Reissued by al-Dār al-'Ālamīyya, Beirut, 1987.

Mikhail, Mona. *Images of Arab Women: Fact and Fiction*. Three Continents Press, Washington, D.C., 1979.

Millett, Kate. *Sexual Politics*. Ballantine Books, New York, 1989.

al-Mufjī, Muḥammad bin Aḥmad bin 'Abd Allah, ed. *Ash'ār al-Jawārī (The Poetry of Maids)*. Publisher, place, and date unknown.

Muḥammad, Ḥarbiyya. *Jarīmat Rajul (A Man's Crime)*. University of Baghdad, Baghdad, 1953.

―――. *Man al-Jānī (Who Is the Culprit?)*. University of Baghdad, Baghdad, 1954.

Muḥammad, Zaynab. *Asrār Waṣīfa Miṣriyya (The Secrets of an Egyptian Mistress)*. Publisher unknown, Cairo, 1927.

―――. *Dustūr al-Ajniḥa (The Wings Constitution)*. Beirut, Scientific Research Publishing, 1970 (play).

al-Muhyā, Sāra. *Fatāt al-Nīl (The Girl of the Nile)*. Publisher unknown, Cairo, 1913.

Munīf, 'Abd al-Raḥmān. *Al Katib wal Mānfa (The Writer and Exile)*. Publisher unknown, Beirut, 1992.

al-Musālima, In'ām. *Al-Ḥubb wa al-Waḥl (Love and Mud)*. Dar al-Thaqāfa (Cultural House), Damascus, 1963.

―――. *Al-Kahf (The Cave)*. Dār al-Ajyāl, Damascus, 1973.

Mustighānimī, Aḥlām. *Dhākirat al-Jasad (Memory in the Flesh)*. Dār al-Ādāb, Beirut, 1993.

―――. *Fawḍā al-Ḥawāss (Confusion of the Senses)*. Dār al-Ādāb, Beirut, 1998.

―――. *Al-Kitāba fī Laḥzati 'Uryin (Writing of a Moment Nakedness)*. Dār al-Ādāb, Beirut, 1976.

―――. *Al-Mar'a fī al-Adab al-Jazā'irī al-Mu'āṣir (Women in Contemporary Algerian Literature)*. Algiers, 1981.

Nājī, Suzān. *Al-Mar'a fī al-Mir'āt: Dirāsa Naqdiyya li al-Riwāya al-Nisā'iyya fī Miṣr, 1888–1985 (Woman in the Mirror: A Critical Study of Women's Novels in Egypt, 1888–1985)*. Al-Ra'ī, Cairo, 1989.

al-Nālūtī, 'Arūsiyya. *Marātīj (Shackles)*. Dār Srās, Tunis, 1985.

―――. *Tamāss (Contact)*. Dar al-Janūb, Tunis, 1995.

―――. *Tamaththulāt al-Jadd min Khilāl al-Riwāya al-Tūnisiyya (Representations of the Grandfather Throughout Tunisian Novels)*. 1993.

Na'na', Ḥamīda. *Anāshīd Imra'a lā Ta'rif al-Faraḥ (Songs of a Woman Who Doesn't Know What Joyfulness Is)*. Dār al-Ajyāl, Damascus, 1970 (poetry).

―――. *Man Yajru' 'alā al-Shawq? (Who Dares to Yearn?)* Dār al-Ādāb, Beirut, 1989.

―――. *Al-Waṭan fī al-'Aynayn (The Homeland Is in the Eyes)*. Dār al Ādāb, Beirut, 1989. Translated into English by Martin Asser as *The Homeland* and published by Garnet Publishing, Reading, UK, 1995.

Naṣrallah, Emily. *Al-Iqlā' 'Aks al-Zamān (Flight Against Time)*. Dār Nawfal, Beirut, 1981.

————. *Nisā' Rā'idāt (Women Pioneers)*. Mu'assasat Dār Nawfal, Beirut, 1986.

————. *Al-Rahīna (The Pawn)*. Mu'assasat Dār Nawfal, Beirut, 3rd ed., 1986.

————. *Shajarat al-Diflā (The Oleander Tree)*. Mu'assasat Dār Nawfal, Beirut, 1968; 4th ed., Mu'assasat Nawfal, Beirut, 1981.

————. *Ṭuyūr Aylūl (Birds of September)*. Mu'assasat Dār Nawfal, Beirut, 1962.

Nuwayhiḍ, Nādiya al-Jurdī. *Cleopatra, Nisā' min Bilādī*. Al-Mu'assasa al-'Arabiyya li al-Dirāsāt wa al-Nashr, Beirut, 1986.

Nuwaylātī, Hiyām. *Fī al-Layl (At Night)*. Maṭabi' al-Ṣarkha, Damascus, 1959.

————. *Al-Ghazālī: Ḥayātuh–'Aqīdatuh (Al-Ghazalī: His Life–His Faith)*. New Printer, Damascus, 1958.

Olsen, Tillie. *Silences*. Laurel/Seymour Lawrence Books, New York, 1978.

al-Qāḍī, Īmān. *Al-Riwāya al-Nisā'iyya fī Bilād al-Shām, 1885–1950 (Women's Novels in Greater Syria, 1885–1950)*. Al-Ahālī, Damascus, 1992.

al-Sa''āfīn, Ibrāhīm. *Taṭawwur al-Riwāya al-Ḥadītha fī Bilād al-Shām, 1870–1967 (The Development of the Modern Novel in Greater Syria, 1870–1967)*. Dār al-Manāhil, Beirut, 1987, 2nd ed.

Ṣa'b, 'Afīfa. *Al-Khaḍir*. Publisher and city unknown, Lebanon, 1912.

al-Sa'dāwī, Nawāl. *Imra'atān fī Imra'a (Two Women in One)*. Dār al-Ādāb, Beirut, 1986.

————. *Mawt al-Rajul al-Waḥīd 'alā al-Arḍ (The Death of the Only Man on Earth)*. Dār al-Ādāb, Beirut, 1985.

————. *Muthakarat Tabiba (Memoirs of a Woman Doctor)*. Dār al-Maarif, Cairo, 1965.

————. *Al-Rajul wa al-Jins (The Male and Sex)*. Beirut, 1977.

————. *Al-Unthā Hiya al-Aṣl (The Female Is the Origin)*. Beirut, 1974.

al-Sa'īd, Amīna. *Al-Jāmiḥa (The Wild Woman)*. Iqra' Series no. 92. Dār al-Ma'ārif, Cairo, July 1950.

Sa'īd, Hādiya. *Bustān Aswad (Black Orchard)*. Al-Mu' assasa al-'Arabiyya li al-Dirāsāt wa al-Nashr, Beirut, 1996.

————. *Nisā' Khārij al-Nass (Women Outside the Text)*. Dār Matabi al-Mustakbal, Alexandria, Egypt, 1989.

————. *Raḥīl al Ribāṭ (The Departure of the Band)*. African-Arab Publication, Cairo, 1989.

Sakākīnī, Widād. *Arwā bint al-Khuṭūb (Arwā, the Daughter of Upheavals)*. Dār al-Fikr al-'Arabī, Cairo, 1949.

————. *Al-'Āshiqa al-Mutaṣawwifa: Ḥayāt wa Afkār Rābi'a al-'Adawiyya (The Mystic Lover)*, Dār Ṭalās, Damascus, 1989; also Dār al-Ma'ārif, Cairo, 1955. Translated by Nabīl Ṣafwat as *First Among Ṣūfīs: The Life and Thought of Rābi'a al-'Adawiyya, the Woman Saint of Basra* and published by Octagon Press, London, 1982. Introduction by Doris Lessing.

————. *Inṣāf al-Mar'a (Doing Women Justice)*. Cairo, 1950; reissued by Dār Ṭalās, Damascus, 1989.

————. *Mayy Ziyāda: Ḥayātuhā wa A'māluhā (Mayy Ziyāda: Her Life and Work)*. Dār al-Ma'ārif, Cairo, 1969.

————. *Nuqāṭ 'alā al-Ḥurūf (Dots on Letters)*. In *Naqd wa Ta'līq (Criticism and Comment)*, a series of books on literary criticism. Dār al-Fikr al-'Arabī, Cairo, 1965.

Salāma, Hind. *Al-Dumā al-Ḥayya (The Living Toys)*. Beirut, 1968.

————. *Al-Ḥijāb al-Mahtūk (The Profaned Veil)*. Dār al-Thaqāfa, Beirut, no date.

————. *Al Nisā' wa al-Khamriyyāt in the Torah (Women and the Russet in the Torah)*. 1950.

————. *Samrā' al-Shāṭi' (The Brunette on the Beach)*. Beirut, 1973.

————. *Zallat al-Jasad (Sins of the Body)*. Beirut.

Ṣāliḥ, Laylā M. *Adab al-Mar'a fī al-Khalīj (Women's Literature in Arabia and the Arabian Gulf*, vol. 1, *Saudi Arabia, Baḥrain, Qaṭar and the United Arab Emirates)*. Maṭābi' al-Yaqaẓa, Kuwait, 1982.

————. *Adab al-Mar'a fī al-Khalīj (Women's Literature in Arabia and the Arabian Gulf*, vol. 2, *Yemen and Oman)*. Zat al-Salasil, Kuwait, 1987.

————. *Adab al-Mar ?a fī al-Kuwait (Women's Literature in Kuwait)*, vol. 3. Dār Dhāt al-Salāsil, Kuwait, 1979.

Ṣāliḥ, al-Ṭayyib. *Mawsim al-Hijra ilā al-Shamāl (Season of Migration to the North)*. Dār al-'Awda, Beirut, 14th printing, 1987.

al-Sammān, Ghāda. *'Aynāka Qadarī (Your Eyes Are My Destiny)*. Dār al-Ādāb, Beirut, 1962.

————. *Beirut 75*. Dār al-Ṭalī'a, Beirut, 1975.

————. *Laylat al-Milyār (The Night of the Billion)*. Dār al-Ṭalī'a, Beirut, 1989.

al-Shaykh, Ḥanān. *Barīd Beirut (Beirut Post)*. Riwāyāt al-Hilāl, Cairo, 1992. Published in English as *Beirut Blues*.

————. *Ḥikāyat Zahra*. Dār al-Ādāb, Beirut, 1980. Published in English as *The Story of Zahra*. Quartet Books, London, 1986.

————. *Misk al-Gazāl (The Musk of the Gazelle)*. Dār al-Ādāb, Beirut, 1988. Published in English as *Women of Sand and Myrrh*. Women's Press, London, 1992.

Showalter, Elaine. *A Literature of Their Own: British Women Novelists from Brontë to Lessing*. Princeton University Press, Princeton, N.J., 1977.

Spender, Dale. *Man Made Language*. 2nd ed. Routledge and Kegan Paul, London, 1980.

Ṣubḥī, Muhyi al-Dīn. "Mu'tamar Ḥawl Ibdā' al-Nisā' al-'Arabiyyāt: Dhukūrat al-I'tirāḍāt al-Siyāsiyya: Wujhat Naẓar" (A Conference on Arab Women's Creativity: The Masculinity of Political Objections: A Point of View), *Al-Safīr* (Beirut), September 26, 1992.

Sulaymān, Nabīl. *Al-Riwāya al-Sūriyya: 1967–1977 (The Syrian Novel: 1967–1977)*. Wizārat al-Tarbiya, Damascus, 1982.

————. *Wa'ī al-Dhāt wa al-'Ālam: Dirāsāt fī al-Riwāya al-'Arabiyya (Consciousness of the Self and the World: Studies in the Arabic Novel)*. Dār al-Ḥiwār, Latakya, 1985.

al-Suyūṭi, 'Abd al-Raḥmān bin Abī Bakr Jalāl al-Dīn. *Nuzhat al-Julasā' fī Ash'ār al-Nisā' (A Journey of Companionship in Women's Poetry)*. Dār al-Kitāb al-Jadīda, Beirut, 1978; Maktabat al-Qur'ān, Cairo, 1986; Maktabat Usāma, Aleppo, 1995.

al-Ṭaḥḥāwī, Mīrāl. *Al-Bādhinjāna al-Zarqā' (The Blue Eggplant)*. Dār al-Sharqiyyāt, Cairo, 1998.

al-Ṭāhir, 'Alī Jawād. *Muqaddima fī al-Naqd al-Adabī (Introduction to Literary Criticism)*. Al-Mu'assasa al-'Arabiyya li al-Dirāsāt wa al Nashr, Beirut, 1979.

al-Tamīnī, Fayrūz. *Naṣṣ al-Mar'a (Woman's Text)*. Amman, Jordan, 1998.

Ṭarābīshī, George. "The Female of Nawāl al-Saʿdāwī and the Myth of Singularity." *Arab Studies* 12, no. 2 (1975).

———. "Al-Ḥirmān fī al-Riwāya al-Nisāʾiyya al-ʿArabiyya" (Deprivation in Arab Women's Novels). *Al-Ādāb* (March 1963).

———. *Woman Against Her Sex: A Critique of Nawal El-Saadawi*. Saqi Books, London, 1988.

Ṭayfūr, Ibn. *Balāghāt al-Nisāʾ (Women's Eloquence)*. Reissued by Dār al-Nahḍa al-Ḥadītha, Beirut, 1972.

Ṭūqān, Fadwā. *Al-Riḥla al-Aṣʿab (The Most Difficult Journey)*. Dār al-Shurūq, Amman, 1993.

ʿUmar, Zahra. *Al-Khurūj min Sosrowaka (The Exodus from Sosrowaka: The Epic of the Circassian Diaspora)*. Dār al-Azmina, Amman, 1995.

ʿUsayrān, Laylā. *ʿAṣāfīr al-Fajr (The Birds of Dawn)*. Sharikat al-Maṭbūʿāt li al-Tawzīʿ wa al-Nashr, Beirut, 1991.

———. *Ḥiwār bilā Kalimāt fī al-Ghaybūba (A Dialogue Without Words in a Coma)*. Markaz al-Ahrām li al-Tarjama wa al-Nashr, Cairo, 1998.

———. *Jisr al-Ḥajar (The Stone Bridge)*. Dār al-ʿAwda, Beirut, 1982.

al-ʿUthmān, Laylā. *Al-Marʾa wa al-Qiṭṭa (The Woman and the Cat)*. Al-Muʾassasa al-ʿArabiyya li al-Dirāsāt wa al-Nashr, Beirut, 1985.

Walker, Alice. *The Color Purple*. Washington Square Press, Washington, D.C., 1982.

Woolf, Virginia. *A Room of One's Own*. Harcourt Brace Jovanovich, New York, 1929.

———. "Women and Fiction." In *Granite and Rainbow: Essays by Virginia Woolf*, edited by Leonard Woolf. Harcourt, Brace and Company, New York, 1954.

al-Yāfī, Laylā. *Hamasāt Qalbī (Whispers of My Heart)* (prose poems).

———. *Thulūj Taḥt al-Shams (Snows Under the Sun)*. Dār al-Fikr al-ʿArabī, Cairo, 1962.

———. *Al-Wāḥa (The Oasis)*. Arab Writers Union, Damascus, 1982.

al-Zayyāt, Laṭīfa. *Al-Bāb al-Maftūḥ (The Open Door)*. Al-Hayʾa al-Miṣriyya al-ʿĀmma li al-Kitāb, Cairo, 1960; reprint, 2003.

———. *Al-Rajul al-Ladhī lam Yaʿrif Tuhmatahu (The Man Who Did Not Know of What He Was Accused)*. Dār Sharkiyyan, Cairo, 1995.

———. "An Interview with al-Zayyāt." *New Shahrazād* 22 (Cyprus) (June 1990).

———. *Min Ṣuwar al-Marʾa fī al-Riwāya wa al-Qiṣaṣ al-ʿArabiyya (Images of Women in Arabic Novels and Short Stories)*. Dār al-Thaqāfa al-Jadīda, Cairo, 1989.

Zeidan, Joseph T. *Arab Women Novelists: The Formative Years and Beyond*. State University of New York Press, New York, 1995.

Ziyāda, Mayy. *Warda al-Yāzijī*. Cairo, 1924.

———. *ʿĀʾisha al-Taymūriyya, 1840–1902*. Cairo, 1925.

Zuhayr, Suʿād. *Iʿtirāfāt Imraʾa Mustarjila (Confessions of a Masculine Woman)*. Serialized in *Rose al-Yūsuf*, Cairo, 1961.

Index

Teachers, harassment from, 47–48, 85
A Thousand and One Nights, 19, 173
Thulūj Taht al-Shams (*Snows Under
the Sun*; al-Yāfī), 81–83
The Tiller of Waters (*Ḥārith al-Miyāh*;
Barakāt), 171–173
Translations of Arab women's novels,
117
Treachery/betrayal, 113; assumption
that all women are potential adulteresses, 30, 40, 42–43, 49–51;
betrayal of friends and family
members in Iraq, 149, 150, 151;
betrayal of self, 89, 94; difference
perceived as treachery, 105; and
need for broader sense of honor
related to the nation, 87, 91. *See
also* Adultery/infidelity
Tunisian writers. *See* al-Nālūtī,
'Arūsiyya
Ṭuyūr Aylūl (*Birds of September*;
Naṣrallah), 92–94

Um Jundub, 6–7
'Umar, Zahra, 189; *Al-Khurūj min
Sosrowaka* (*The Exodus from
Sosrowaka: The Epic of the
Circassian Diaspora*), 154
The Umbilical Cord (*Ḥabl al-Surra*;
al-Māni), 148–151
United States, 37, 55
'Usayrān, Laylā, 189; *'Aṣāfīr al-Fajr*
(*The Birds of Dawn*), 102–104;
compared to Kīlanī, 107; *Ḥiwār
bilā Kalimāt fī al-Ghaybūba* (*A
Dialogue Without Words in a
Coma*), 177–178
al-'Uthmān, Laylā: *Al-Mar'a wa al-
Qiṭṭa* (*The Woman and the Cat*),
154–156

Village life, 92, 109–110, 131–135,
163
Virginity, 99, 123, 134, 163, 171. *See
also* Honor

Wa Tushriqu Gharban (*Dawning from
the West*; al-Aṭrash), 108–111
Walker, Alice, 43
War: Arab myths about revolution,

147; connection between the political and the personal, 151; contrast
between war generation and following generations, 145–147; distortions of psychology, values, and
morality, 130, 170–171; in early
poetic works, 4; and ideology, 129;
and the imperative for survival,
128–129; and martyrdom as a commodity, 128; painting as outlet,
107–108; people's vested interest
in, 112–113, 128; and refusal to
learn from history, 173; and
wartime relationships, 123–125.
See also Revolution/resistance
movements; Six Day War (1967);
Suez War (1956); War literature;
specific countries
War literature, 95–115; *Adab al-
Naksa* (*Literature of the Setback*),
96; al-Aṭrash's portrayal of the
lives of ordinary people throughout
the wars and upheavals of the mid-
twentieth century, 108–111; Badr's
account of the moral, psychological, and physical violence of war,
114–115; (Hudā) Barakāt's exploration of civil war in the context of
the history of Beirut, 171–173;
(Hudā) Barakāt's portrayal of
Lebanese civil war's effects on
ordinary people, 125–131; (Najwā)
Barakāt's depiction of psychological effects of war in Beirut,
170–171; portrayal of women's
actions in times of crisis, al-Bāti',
108; differences between men's
and women's writings, 95–96, 115;
Hādī's *Al-'Ālam Nāqiṣan Wāhid*
(*The World Minus One*), 151–153;
Idlibī's portrayal of Damascus in
the 1920s and 1930s, 97–102;
Kīlanī's portrayal of moral awakening following Six Day War,
105–108; Mustighānimī's portrayal
of Algerian revolution and its aftermath, 144–148; al-Sammān's
exploration of the causes of the
Lebanese civil war, 111–114; al-
Shaykh's portrayal of women's

About the Book

SPANNING MORE THAN a century, this systematic study brings to the forefront a dazzling array of novels by Arab women writers.

Bouthaina Shaaban's analysis ranges from the work of Zaynab Fawwāz, published at the end of the nineteenth century, to that of Saḥar Khalīfa, and Najwā Barakāt, published at the cusp of the twenty-first. The novels discussed reflect not only specifically Arab concerns, but also those that are universally relevant to women. Perhaps most notably, Shaaban makes it abundantly clear that Arab women were pioneers in the creation of the Arab novel—though until now they have been little known—and that the development of this literary genre occurred very much in tandem with the changing role of women in Arab countries.

Bouthaina Shaaban is author of *Both Right- and Left-Handed: Arab Women Talk About Their Lives*. She has been professor of English literature at Damascus University since 1985 and also served for five years as vice president of Syria's Arab Writers Union. Dr. Shaaban was recently honored by Ziad Hamzeh's film *Woman*, which is based on her work and life and was awarded the Golden Palm for the best film at the 2008 Beverly Hills Film Festival.